A Barnabas Life-style

Donald A. Atkinson

A BARNABAS Life-style

Discovering the joy of unselfish living

BROADMAN PRESS
Nashville, Tennessee

© Copyright 1987 • Broadman Press

All rights reserved

4257-28

ISBN: 0-8054-5728-3

Dewey Decimal Classification: 225.92

Subject Headings: BARNABAS // CHRISTIAN LIFE

Library of Congress Catalog Card Number: 87-9309

Printed in the United States of America

Scripture quotations are from the *Good News Bible,* the Bible in Today's English Version. Old Testament: Copyright © American Bible Society 1976; New Testament: Copyright © American Bible Society 1966, 1971, 1976. Used by permission. Quotations marked (NIV) are from HOLY BIBLE *New International Version,* copyright © 1978, New York Bible Society. Used by permission.

Library of Congress Cataloging-in-Publication Data

Atkinson, Donald A., 1935-
  A Barnabas life-style.

  1. Barnabas, Apostle, Saint. I. Title.
BS2452.B28A94   1987   226'.60924   87-9309
ISBN 0-8054-5728-3

Foreword

When I first met Don Atkinson he was pastor of the Fern Creek Baptist Church in Louisville, Kentucky. As a pastor Don was a very effective communicator. His people loved him not so much, however, for his capable preaching, but for his genuine interest, concern, and involvement in their lives. He communicated well from the pulpit; he communicated well in a one-on-one relationship.

Years later when I was an editor of adult curriculum materials for the Church Training Department of the Baptist Sunday School Board, I remembered Don's ability as a communicator and invited him to write for me. Through his expertise as a writer he conveyed not only knowledge, but something of his feelings about the worth of humans. He affirmed the wondrous potential of God's greatest creation.

For about ten years we developed an effective editor-writer relationship. A friendship was solidified by the interchange of Christian love. A Christian brotherhood grew on the basis of commitment to common ideals.

In 1984 Don became a coworker in the Church Training Department. He continued to show his appreciation for human potential especially related to the discipling of fellow Christians. His gifts—of communicating well and his genuine interest in the needs of others—have endeared him to many.

A Barnabas Life-style has been in his heart and mind for a long time. It is as much a book about Don's concept of friendship, loyalty, and love as it is about Barnabas, the friend and colaborer of Paul. As you read about Barnabas, something deep within the soul of Don Atkinson will be revealed to you. The book will inform you, but more than this it will inspire you to affirm those who are God's wondrous creations.

MIC MORROW

Preface

We hear a lot about "life-style" these days, but what is a life-style? Without resorting to a dictionary definition, maybe the best way to understand what life-style means is to turn the words around. A life-style is plainly a style of life, a way of living.

There are many different life-styles. A recent television series celebrates the life-styles of very wealthy and famous people, a manner of living that most of us will never know. By contrast, many people have a very simple life-style. I have always been fascinated by the Amish people. They have been able to maintain a life-style that is largely unaffected by the world around them.

This book is about life-style, a special life-style. It is about a way of living exemplified by Barnabas, a New Testament personality. Not much is known about the life of Barnabas, but what we do know about him speaks eloquently. He was a man whose life-style was focused on caring about people.

We live in a world where self-centered living is too

often the norm. In our drive toward achievement and self-realization we have sometimes allowed ourselves to imagine that we can live solely for ourselves. Barnabas points us in a different direction. His caring life-style serves as an inspiration to us to discover joy in unselfish living. The word *discover* is used deliberately. It is a discovery indeed to find that we are happiest and most fulfilled when we let ourselves care deeply about other people.

These pages are not merely a tribute to Barnabas and his way of living. They are also intended to be a kind of thank-you to the many people who have been Barnabas to me. There are far too many for me to name them all. Most of them know who they are. I hope they also know that they make my life worth living.

Contents

1
What's in a Name?   "Barnabas"

"What are you, some kind of klutz?" Everyone laughed when Jim asked the question—everyone except me. I was a participant in a pastoral ministry conference. The group had been dealing with some pretty heavy content throughout the day. The final session was supposed to help the participants understand the concept of teamwork in ministry.

As a demonstration of ways ministers can work together, our conference leader involved us in a game often played by children. We were divided into teams of five, and each team was given a collection of variously shaped blocks of wood. Each team member, in turn, would stack a block on top of the last block laid down. This was to be done as quickly as possible. The team able to stack their blocks first would be the winner. If a team member knocked the stack over at any point in the process, the team had to start over.

Those who know me best are aware that my hands are unsteady; and if I am the least bit nervous, they tremble.

I felt panic rising within me as the game began that night. I felt I would be the one to knock the blocks over. The more I thought about it, the more my hands trembled. I did fairly well the first time around. On the second round I made the stack wobble. The third time around I knocked it down, and we had to start over again. After I knocked the blocks over the third time, my hands were trembling, and my brow was covered with a cold sweat.

At this point, Jim, one of my unfortunate team members, made his "klutz" remark. I wanted to run. I felt embarrassment and anger. I felt like a failure and a laughingstock. My name for the moment—"klutz"—devastated me.

Names have power. Our name comes to represent all that we are. Even nicknames are often descriptive. Names such as "Slim," "Shorty," "Red," and "Tex" conjure up mental pictures that tend to describe the people to whom they are attached. Endearing names, such as "Mom," "Dad," and "Sweetheart," suggest sentimental images of those who mean the most to us. Names like "Boss," "Officer," "General," and "Judge" are given to persons who are authority figures to us.

A person's name was serious business in biblical days. Names were chosen carefully and worn proudly. A person's name was more than just a "handle." A name stood for all that made the person who wore it special and unique.

The Old Testament tells of a woman who grieved for years because she could not have a child. Finally, the woman, whose name was Hannah, became pregnant. When her son was born, she named him Samuel. She explained the choice of Samuel as the name for her child like this: "I asked the Lord for him" (1 Sam. 1:20). The name Samuel means "name of God." How it is used in reference to Hannah's baby can best be understood to mean "asked of God." The naming of Samuel was no light matter for Hannah. She accepted the fact that the little boy belonged to God. His name was a self-fulfilling prophecy. Few men have been greater in their time than Samuel.

One of the best examples of how seriously a name was taken by Bible people relates to John the Baptist. John's parents waited long years for their baby to be conceived and born. When the baby was born, the neighbors and friends suggested that it would be appropriate to give him his father's name, Zacharias. Elizabeth would have nothing to do with that idea. She responded: "No, his name is to be John." This did not seem right to the friends and kinfolks. After all, a man as old as Zacharias deserved to have his son bear his name. So they appealed the matter to Zacharias, who was unable to speak at the time. Old Zacharias asked for a writing pad and wrote the message: "His name is John" (Luke 1:63). The name *John* is a derivative of Jehohanan. It means "gift of God." The name described John's destiny. It predicted the kind of life he would live.

When Mary was given the startling news she would bear a child, she was given specific instructions about his name. She would name Him Jesus (Luke 1:31). No other name would do. There were plenty of good Jewish names available for boys in those days; but His name had to be Jesus. The name *Jesus,* like *Joshua* in the Old Testament, means deliverer or Savior. He must be named Jesus because: "He will save his people from their sins" (Matt 1:21).

The name, *Jesus,* still has great power. I can remember hearing my mother sing as she did her housework, "The name of Jesus is so sweet, I love its music to repeat." A more modern gospel song proclaims: "There's just something about that name." Christians are told that salvation comes when we call upon His name (Rom. 10:13). We are also instructed to gather in His name (Matt. 18:20) and to pray in His name (Matt. 28:19). When a crippled man was healed outside the Temple in Jerusalem, Peter refused to take the credit. He insisted: "It was the power of His name that gave strength to this lame man (Acts 3:16).

All of this emphasis on the name of Jesus is not some kind of religious magic. It simply means that the name *Jesus* represents all that Jesus is. His name is synonomous with His person. His name is who He is; so when we believe on, pray to, worship, or witness in the name of Jesus, we confess all He is and all He has done. That is how important a name is in biblical thought.

Today a name may be chosen for a person without thought as to its meaning. Many young couples spend a lot of time picking out a name for their soon-to-be-born baby. They may even purchase a book of names to provide them with ideas concerning a name for this new human being. Often a baby is given a family name; but more often, babies are named according to some fad or trend of the day. This is why you will find so many boys and girls in one community, church, or school with the name Jeffrey, Michael, Jennifer, Amy, or whatever was in style when the children were born.

In many cases, little thought was given to the meaning of the name. Even in these circumstances the name by which a person is known takes on significance. The name comes to stand for the person. It tends to describe the individual in a way that no other name could. To test this for yourself, try to imagine your child, or someone close to you, with some other name. For example, think about your very best friend—say his name is Tom. Can you imagine calling him anything other than Tom? It just wouldn't fit.

Some characters in the Bible were given new and descriptive names. Jacob was renamed *Israel* which means "perseverer with God" (Gen. 32:28). Jesus gave Simon a new name. He called him *Cephas* (Peter). The name *Peter* means rock. The giving of this new name was like a prophecy of what Simon would become. Simon was often tempestuous and unpredictable. He was anything but a rock. Could it be that by calling Simon by that new name Jesus called out of him a potential for greatness no one else could have recognized?

The name by which we refer to a person not only describes that person, but it also may actually serve as a positive or negative influence in that person's life. For this reason, we must be careful by what name we call a person. A child who is called "stupid," "dumb," "ugly," or "clumsy" may find it difficult to think of himself or herself otherwise.

I once heard of a father who would become irritated with his young son and say things to the boy that he really didn't mean. Once in anger, he said: "You're bad. You'll probably be in prison by the time you're eighteen." The boy grew to responsible manhood without ever going to prison. Yet, the name *bad* and the dire prophecy concerning the boy's future followed him and caused him pain and uncertainty as he journeyed toward manhood.

The truth that a name has meaning and power is clearly seen in a biblical character who is best known as Barnabas. Actually Barnabas was not his name. His name was Joseph, and we first meet him in Acts 4. There is not much background material on Joseph. Acts 4:36 states he was a Levite from Cyprus. From this we realize he was from a Jewish priestly family. That is all we really know about him.

A number of interesting legends have developed around Barnabas (Joseph). One has it that Barnabas was a personal disciple of Jesus, and perhaps one of the seventy workers sent out by Jesus (Luke 10:1). Another legend claims Barnabas was a missionary to Cyprus; still another goes that he was a martyr who gave his life for Christ in Salamis in AD 61. One of the most persistent legends concerning Barnabas is that he is the author of the

Epistle to the Hebrews. None of these legends are supported by biblical evidence. In fact, we know nothing at all about Barnabas prior to his first mention in Acts. We know nothing at all about his later years or his death.

The setting in which we first meet Barnabas is the sharing fellowship of the early church in Jerusalem. According to Acts, the love among those believers was so deep that it motivated them to share everything they owned with one another. They were determined that no one should have an unmet need, even if it meant selling their houses and property so those needs could be met. The writer of Acts says: "And so it was that Joseph, a Levite born in Cyprus, whom the apostles called Barnabas (which means One who Encourages) sold a field he owned, brought the money, and turned it over to the apostles" (Acts 4:36-37).

His name was Joseph, but his fellow Christians gave him a new name. They called him Barnabas. What does the name *Barnabas* mean, and why did the believers decide to give the name to Joseph? The writer of Acts tells us the meaning of the name. It means "one who encourages." We need only examine the passages in the New Testament that refer to Barnabas to understand why they gave Joseph this name. In every incident recorded concerning Barnabas, he is seen to be an encourager and a helper to others. It is no wonder this man was given a new name, a name that described his caring and concerned approach of relating to other people.

The word used in Acts to interpret the name *Barnabas*

—encourager—is a special one. It comes from a Greek word *parakleseos.* A form of the same word is used in John 14:16. In this verse Jesus referred to the promised Holy Spirit as the *parakletos.* In this context the word means Helper or Comforter. The Holy Spirit is the Helper or Comforter who is given by God to every believer, but God also has some flesh-and-blood human encouragers. These people, like Barnabas, are given a special task. They love and lift. They look for the best in other people. They affirm others. They make life easier for other people because they care deeply and genuinely. They give people a special gift—the gift of encouragement.

Notice that Joseph did not give himself the name *Barnabas.* He did not proclaim himself to be the Encourager. The name was given to him by others. They called him Barnabas—Encourager—because he had already gained the reputation of being that kind of person. Future events would serve to affirm and call out the qualities his fellow Christians had already seen in him.

Names given to us by those who work with us, worship with us, socialize with us, or live with us are probably more descriptive than are names we would use to describe ourselves. What people call us might not become a name everyone will know. Others might not give us an actual name like the Christians gave to Barnabas. They are more likely to use words to describe us. These words become "names" because they describe the way other people see us.

For example, we might say of a person: "He is just plain

lazy." The word *lazy* becomes a descriptive name. We might say of someone else: "She is conceited," or of someone else, "He is the most arrogant person I've ever known." We might even become so exasperated with a person that we say: "She is just impossible." On the other hand, we may say of someone: "She is the most generous person I've ever known." Or we may ask: "Isn't he the kindest person you ever met?" Best of all, we may say of someone: "She is truly a loving person." All of these words: *lazy, conceited, arrogant, impossible, generous, kind, loving* are really descriptive names which relate how we feel about other people.

The Cardinals of the University of Louisville won the NCAA basketball championship in 1986. The hero of the championship game with Duke University was a giant-sized freshman named Purvis Ellison. Senior players are expected to be the stars in championship games, but this eighteen-year-old was the man of the hour for Louisville. He scored twenty-five points, had numerous rebounds, and was selected MVP in the Final Four tournament— quite an accomplishment for a freshman. Ellison has a special name given to him by fellow players, media, and fans. They call him "Never Nervous Purvis." The name describes the way the young superstar plays his game, with total calmness and confidence. "Never Nervous" earned his name anew that night in Dallas when his team won the national championship. He made it look easy!

No doubt you know people you could give a special name. Perhaps it would be a physically descriptive name, a humorous name, or even a behind-the-back negative name (like referring to the boss as "Old Tightwad"). With only a little thought, you can also give special names to some Barnabas-like persons in your life. These names will describe endearing qualities such as *generosity, integrity,* or *kindness.* Can you think of some examples?

I am blessed to have several Barnabas-like people in my life. For example, I have a good friend and working associate whose friendship I have valued for many years. This person has many admirable qualities, but if I had to give him a descriptive name, it would be something like "Care-giver." This man spends much of his time taking care of others. He is so sensitive to those of us who work with him that he seems to sense when one of us is carrying a heavy load. Then, he does whatever he can to lighten the load for us. He looks after those he loves (and that is almost everyone). His friends realize that they can count on his caring.

To one who is a dear and treasured friend I would give the name "Loyal." She has a beautiful quality of faithfulness I can depend upon. I believe she would stand by me if everyone else in the world turned away. I believe she would come to my side if ever I needed her, no matter the cost.

I met a remarkably brave woman at Glorieta Baptist Conference Center; I'll call her Sherrie (not her real name). Sherrie was a participant in a conference I was leading. The group was doing some sharing one morning when Sherrie told us she had cancer. She said that in her struggle with the illness there was a friend whose caring had "made the difference between life and death." I was intrigued by this comment, and I sought a time when I could learn more about the friend who had made the difference. The next afternoon, over a cup of coffee, Sherrie told her story to me.

Three years earlier Sherrie had been diagnosed as having cancer. Since that time, she has spent a considerable time in the hospital. She has had extensive surgery and several rounds of therapy. The prognosis is not at all good. She was told some time ago that, barring a miracle or a medical breakthrough, she will not live for long. This has been devastating to Sherrie. She is a wife, the mother of three children, and an active member of her church and community. Sherrie is only twenty-nine years old. She has much to live for.

Sherrie told me that it has been terribly difficult for her to accept the fact that she has a terminal illness. She has often found herself anxious and depressed. She has sometimes felt that she had no one to turn to. She has not sensed that she could share her inner pain with her family. In her viewpoint, she believed it was unfair to add to the problems they are having with her illness by sharing her own depression and fears with them.

Sherrie began to pray for someone with whom she could talk. Immediately, she thought of a woman in her church who was known to be caring and who always seemed to be helping someone. Since Sherrie heard that this woman had helped many people through difficult times, she assumed the woman would be the answer to her prayers. Time passed and, even though Sherrie prayed for this woman to notice and hear her silent cry for help, it didn't happen. She confided in me that she did everything in her power to put herself in the woman's path. Incredibly, this caring, sensitive woman never noticed.

One night Sherrie had attended a meeting at the church. She was feeling so depressed she only half listened to the speaker, then hurried out. She didn't want to talk with a soul. Just as she reached her car, a man she hardly knew called to her and rushed over to speak with her. Sherrie wondered what he could want. Up to that moment, he was only a nice man with whom she had attended church activities. She was amazed when he said: "Sherrie, I watched you tonight. I sense that you need a friend. I just want you to know that I will listen if you ever want to talk." Sherrie thanked him politely, got in her car, and drove away with no intention of sharing her pain with this stranger.

More time passed, and still Sherrie's prayer was apparently not answered. Still she needed, and prayed for, a special friend, someone with whom she could really talk. The man at the church—we'll call him Jack—wasn't pushy, but he continued to express concern for Sherrie. Several times he repeated his offer to help. Finally, it dawned on Sherrie that Jack was the answer to her prayers. God had answered; she simply hadn't realized it.

Sherrie's eyes misted as she told me about Jack. He was the friend who had "made the difference between life and death" to her. Over a period of months, he did so many things. He listened to Sherrie. He befriended her family. He shared special passages from the Bible with her. He organized a prayer vigil when she was critically ill in the hospital. He drove many miles to the hospital where Sherrie was treated. He did everything a person could do to express love, concern, and friendship.

Sherrie talked about one particular time when Jack went the extra mile with her. She was ill and depressed, and she didn't want to live. She didn't want to see anyone or talk to anyone about her despair, not even Jack. She decided to hide herself away.

Somehow Jack found her. She became angry and frustrated when she saw him. She demanded that Jack leave her alone, but Jack wouldn't hear of it. He explained he had found her so he could listen and help. Then, the pent-up anger, hurt, and frustration exploded inside Sherrie. She burst into tears, charged toward Jack, and began to beat his chest with her fists. Jack didn't move. Finally, when Sherrie had spent her anger, she collapsed in a sobbing heap at his feet. After a moment of silence, Jack began quietly to pray for her at this desperate time of need. Sherrie's tears explained to me how deeply this kind of caring had touched her. She said: "I know I hurt him. If I didn't hurt him physically, I know I hurt him emotionally, but he just stood there, took it, and prayed for me." No wonder she called him "the friend who made the difference between life and death."

Most of us will never face circumstances as dramatic as

Sherrie's. Yet, all of us have people who make the difference in our lives. Barnabas was the kind of person who made the difference for many people. That's why they gave him a new name, from Joseph to Barnabas—the encourager.

Do you see the point? Everyone is known for something. In that sense, everyone is given a name by others. People looked at Joseph, saw his practice of encouraging and helping others, and gave him a name—Barnabas.

No doubt you could give a name to almost everyone you know, a name describing that person's way of living and relating to others. Have you made your list of names yet? Are they positive names or negative? Now let me ask you to consider something else. If those who know you—work with you, go to church with you, live with you, love you—gave you a descriptive name, what would that name be?

2
Generosity Was His Middle Name

Joe has always been high on my favorite-person list. He has many admirable qualities. He is successful in his profession, winsome in his personality, and sparkling with friendliness and warmth. One of his best qualities is generosity. Joe gives to others with obvious enjoyment. Because he has earned more money than most people, he is able to give, but there is more to it than that. Generosity is such a part of him that, even if he were poor, he would still be a giver.

A few years ago when I was involved in the expensive process of going to graduate school, I served on the staff of the church where Joe was a member. I am certain that my wardrobe in those days reflected the fact that I was a student with very little money to spend on clothes. One day I received a call from the best men's clothing store in town. I was told to come in and choose a suit that had been paid for by a friend. At first, I thought there had been a mistake, but I finally was convinced I really was the person he intended to call.

Later that day I visited the store and, with the help of a salesman, made my choice. I tried to talk the salesman into telling the name of my benefactor. He was sworn to secrecy. I couldn't even get a hint.

I immediately thought of Joe. I suspected it was the kind of thing he would do, but I was not certain. I wore my new suit to church on Sunday. When I met Joe in a corridor of the building, he looked me up and down, and then remarked, with a twinkle in his eye: "Hey, that looks pretty nice, but tell me, since you are wearing this suit now, what is your old dog using for a bed?" With that, he walked away laughing. He never mentioned the suit again. Joe enjoyed giving. He did it because of who he was.

It will probably come as no surprise that Joseph, the man renamed Barnabas by his friends, was a generous man. As a matter of fact, the introduction to Barnabas in the Book of Acts is through an act of generosity.

Apparently, most of the believers in Jerusalem were poor. They came from the rank and file of hardworking fishermen, sheepherders, farmers, street vendors, and slaves. Many needs existed among them. For example, women who were abandoned or whose husbands had died were often destitute. These women, and others with dire needs, had no place to turn for help.

These early believers felt a deep responsibility for one another. Those who had resources shared with those who had none or little. Luke, the writer of Acts, describes the situation in these words: "The group of believers was one in mind and heart. No one said that any of his belongings was his own, but they all shared with one another everything they had" (Acts 4:32). The happy result of this spirit of sharing is described in Acts 4:34: "There was no one in the group who was in need."

The sharing went beyond the giving of available money or goods. Some even went so far as to sell houses and properties and give the money to the apostles to be used to meet the needs of others in the church. Barnabas was one who demonstrated this kind of generosity. We are informed that Barnabas "sold a field he owned, brought the money, and turned it over to the apostles" (Acts 4:37).

We do not know how much money was involved nor do we have any information concerning the exact circumstances of the gift. The fact that Luke chose Barnabas as an example of the sharing that characterized the early church seems to indicate that the Barnabas's gift was unusually generous and noteworthy.

The generosity of Barnabas can serve as a model for those of us who want to live a life of giving. Several important qualities characterize the giving of Barnabas. These same qualities always are present in the giving style of a truly generous person. For one thing, Barnabas was a willing giver. No demand was placed upon any of the Christians in Jerusalem to give. When a man named Ananias and his wife, Sapphira, sold their property and pretended to give all the money to the apostles, while actually holding part of it back, they were sharply rebuked by Peter. Peter's words are reported by Luke:

"Before you sold the property, it belonged to you; and after you sold it, the money was yours" (Acts 5:4). There was no need for Ananias to pretend. He was not required to give the money. The same could be said for the giving of Barnabas. He was not required or expected to sell his property and give the money to meet needs in the church. He did it because he wanted to give. His was a willing gift.

Another fact about the giving of Barnabas is that it was sacrificial. There is no reason to believe Barnabas was a wealthy man. His gift of money probably involved a great sacrifice on his part. At the very least, Barnabas could have used the money for personal needs or enjoyment.

Most of us do not give sacrificially. We tend to give out of our abundance and never really miss what we give. It requires a truly generous person to give when the giving requires sacrifice.

A visit to an older friend who was a patient in the hospital taught me a valuable lesson concerning sacrificial giving. She lived on a very limited income and her style of living was very simple. She sometimes had a difficult time just making ends meet. After we talked for a while, I said good-bye and started toward the door. She called me back to her bedside and said: "I almost forgot to ask you to do a favor for me. I won't be able to attend church Sunday. Will you take this for me?" With that, she handed her church offering envelope to me. Her giving represented sacrifice.

The generosity of Barnabas also was unpretentious. The contrast between Barnabas and Ananias and Sap-

phira seems intentionally drawn by Luke. Chapter 5 of
Acts spoke of Ananias and Sapphira selling some of their
property. The couple then agreed to give part of the
money from the sale of the property, and to keep the rest,
while publicly pretending to give it all. It takes only a
little reading between the lines to understand the motive
behind their actions. They wanted praise and recognition
for being generous. So they played their deceitful little
game. They pretended to give it all, as Barnabas had done.
In reality, they kept back part of the money. The reason
for the stern judgment pronounced upon them was their
deceit. Peter said to Ananias: "You have not lied to men—
you have lied to God!" (Acts 5:4). They lied in order to
appear generous. They wanted praise for their giving.

Many times people do good things for the wrong reasons. It is good to give, but if the reason for giving is to
be seen and praised, it becomes no more than an ego trip.
This kind of giving is tainted and self-serving.

The membership of a rural church was made up mainly
of the members of two influential families. The families
had become rivals across the years. This rivalry extended
to every area of their lives. They competed in their farm-
ing, in politics, in the activities of their children, and in
the church.

Both families were fairly well-off financially. Often,
one of the families would give something special to the
church. Perhaps it would be new hymnals, church pews,
furnishings, or some other costly item. The giving family
would always expect public recognition for the gift.

Sometimes the gift would have a memorial plate attached to honor some departed member of the family. When one family would make such a gift, it was usually followed by a gift from the other family. That family would then expect the same kind of recognition given the rival family. Over a period of time, the church acquired many useful items. Some felt the gifts were tainted by a pretentious desire to be noticed and praised.

When Jesus spoke about the giving of the hypocrites, He said: "They do it so that people will praise them" (Matt. 6:2). His message is clear. Pretentious giving for the sake of praise and glory to the giver has no reward beyond the empty notice and praise of others.

Barnabas's generosity was real. Other people did notice and praise him; but this was a by-product. Barnabas gave willingly, sacrificially, and unpretentiously.

The giving of Barnabas had no strings attached. There is no evidence in the Book of Acts that Barnabas tried to use his giving as a way to gain leverage or to obligate those to whom he gave. Sometimes the cost of a gift is too great, not so much for the giver as for the recipient.

Did you ever try to trap a bird in a box? When I was a boy, I sometimes tried to make a trap for birds by using a cardboard box, a stick, and a long piece of string. I would tie the string to the stick and use the stick to prop up one end of the box. On the ground under the box, I would put some bread crumbs to lure the bird. When the bird trap was set, I hid behind a tree or a bush, holding the string in my hand. The idea was to wait for an unsuspecting bird to hop into the box to get the crumbs. Then (so the plan went), I would pull the string, drop the box, and trap the bird inside. The birds always outwitted me. They wouldn't come near my trap. I did a lot of planning, trap setting, and hiding behind trees. I never trapped a bird!

Some people use my bird-trapping philosophy in their giving. Their gift has strings attached. When the gift is taken, the trap is sprung, and the one who receives the gift is trapped in a box of obligation.

Have you ever heard anyone say, "How could she do me that way after all I've done for her?" The idea behind this sentiment is that giving obligates the person who receives the gift. There is also the commonly heard bit of worldly wisdom that goes: "I scratch your back, and you scratch mine." Translated into simple language this means: "If I give you something, or if I do anything for you, you owe me."

This phony kind of giving is done at every level of relationship. Husbands and wives do this to each other. Parents can be guilty of giving to their children with strings attached to the gift. ("I've sacrificed so much for you, and this is the thanks I get!") Business relationships and friendships are too often spoiled by this kind of giving. Some even try to obligate God by their giving. Have you ever heard a preacher or teacher come very close to promising their hearers that if they give, God is obligated to prosper them?

Giving does have extra-special rewards. Nothing feels better than giving. Giving brings tremendous satisfaction and happiness to the one who gives, as well as to the one who receives. This is what Jesus meant when He said: "There is more happiness in giving than in receiving" (Acts 20:35). Givers are always prosperous, but often their riches are not measured in dollars or possessions.

What about your giving? Is it free and genuine? Or does it have strings attached? Giving with strings attached is calculated selfishness. It is devoid of any joy. People are better off without our gift if that gift obligates them. Some of us would do well to practice a very simple exercise. We could give to someone when there is no expectation or even possibility of return. Giving unselfishly, and even anonymously, is good medicine for the spirit. We can make the choice to release our gifts once we give them. When we give the gift, it is no longer ours, and it places no obligation upon the one who receives it. How the recipient responds is entirely up to that person. Jesus put the whole matter in perspective when He instructed His disciples: "You have received without paying, so give without being paid" (Matt. 10:8).

The example of Barnabas calls us to a life-style of generosity. Barnabas gave out of the context of who he was and how he felt about others. He was an encourager —so named by those who knew him best. It was part of his encouraging nature to be generous. If we are to be encouragers, we too will develop a life-style of generosity.

This life-style will involve far more than giving money to the church. This is important, but it is only the beginning. It will involve our recognition that God has given us all things. It especially will involve a recognition that, in Christ, God has given Himself to us. This will affect the way we feel about others. Out of our relationship to a giving, loving God, we will come to recognize our own worth and the value of other people. God considered persons worthy of the gift of His Son. People have value, beyond money. Their value as persons makes our giving appropriate.

Another factor in developing a Barnabas-like life-style of generosity is recognizing that all of us have a profound responsibility for other people. Barnabas must have recognized that truth. The needs of persons in the church stirred him to action. He felt a sense of responsibility for other people.

There is a sense in which the lonely, destitute man who walks the city streets is my brother. In a profound way, the child half a world away, who is starving, is my child. No one of us can meet the myriad of needs that can be found all around us, but neither can we turn our heads as if those needs do not exist. The generous person must give and do whatever is possible. This grows out of a sense of love and responsibility for other people.

Finally, a giving life-style must flow out of a positive attitude toward oneself. The giver must feel he is a person of value and worth, with something worth sharing. Such a person is not arrogant but recognizes that he has received much. This person knows the meaning of grace—God's love in action. He or she can receive good gifts from

God or from others without shame, embarrassment, or false humility. This person recognizes that every gift is an affirmation of love to be received with thanksgiving. Out of the context of self-esteem, such a person can give to others. Giving is a way to affirm others, as we have been affirmed. Generosity becomes a way of life, a natural way to relate to others. The size or monetary value of the gift is beside the point.

Sam was a man of limited means. He lived alone in a low-rent apartment. He did not own an automobile. He walked the streets of the city, doing any menial work that could provide a few dollars for necessities. Sam was a member of our church. He held no position of leadership. He was just a quiet man who attended the services of the church regularly.

Even though Sam had little money, he was a Barnabas to me. He was always encouraging, appreciative, and affirming when we met. He demonstrated his generosity in a special way that always touched me deeply. Each year on the Sunday nearest Christmas day, he would wait at church to see me after everyone was gone. He would give me a small package wrapped in Christmas paper and say, "Merry Christmas." The package always contained a white pocket handkerchief. The gift was small but probably represented genuine sacrifice on his part. More importantly, the gift revealed a generous spirit that was beautiful to behold.

You can give your way to riches. This is no empty promise that you will become wealthy if you give. Many, like my friend Sam, give and yet remain poor. The riches gained by generosity are far more important and lasting. They are the riches of investing in the lives and happiness of others. These are riches beyond the reach of money.

3
Looking for the Best— and Finding It

Have you ever been asked to vouch for someone or to give someone a recommendation? I once heard of a man who was asked to give a recommendation for someone who had applied for a job. He didn't really feel confident about recommending him, but he didn't want to damage his chances of getting the job. He solved his dilemma in a novel way. His response was: "When you have known John as long as I've known him, you will feel about him exactly as I feel about him." I wonder whether John got the job.

I recently needed to cash a check in a city I was visiting. When I walked into a surburban office of the bank and made my request, the response of the teller was less than enthusiastic. When I mentioned that the vice-president of the downtown office was a personal friend of mine and suggested that she call him for authorization, the situation changed. Within minutes I was able to cash my check. It was a case of having the right person vouch for me.

All of us have been in a situation where we have needed

someone to speak a good word for us. It is great to have
friends who are willing to do that.

A far more serious need is to have someone to believe
in us, to see the best in us. Often this requires looking
beyond the obvious and seeing the possible. People who
look for the best in others, and find it, are special people.
Such people refuse to take the cynical, short view of people. Somehow, they are able to see in others what many
people miss. Many times their confidence in people gives
that extra push which makes the difference between success and failure.

Mrs. McKee was that kind of encourager for me. She
happened in my life exactly when I needed someone to
believe in me. Mrs. McKee was my eighth-grade homeroom teacher. For several years before that time, I had
been losing interest in my schoolwork. I did barely
enough to make a passing grade, and I believe I was headed toward becoming a dropout. Even worse, my attitude
toward school was beginning to affect the rest of my life.

What did Mrs. McKee do? That is difficult to pinpoint.
It was more her attitude toward me than anything else.
She found ways to let me know she believed in me. She
did this by affirming the good she saw in me. She involved
me in class projects and activities. Soon my grades
showed remarkable improvement. It began to matter to
me that I did my work well. Besides, I would have done
anything to keep from disappointing Mrs. McKee.

To this day, I mark my year in Mrs. McKee's homeroom
as a turning point in my life. I completed high school,

college, and graduate school. I was never the top student in my class, but after Mrs. McKee, my studies were always important to me. She made me believe that I have worth. She turned my life around by looking for the best in me.

Barnabas, the man who was given his special name because he was an encourager, was a person who looked for the best in other people. He probably did this over and over, but the best example we have in the Bible revolves around the conversion and early ministry of Saul of Tarsus, better known to us as Paul the apostle.

Saul was an avowed enemy of Jesus and His followers. He was a brilliant, well-trained Pharisee. No doubt, he saw the new Jesus movement as a heresy and a threat to everything he had been taught and to all he stood for.

Saul was not a man to do things in a halfhearted manner. He was not only opposed to Christ, he was militant in his opposition. He poured all his energy and enthusiasm into the task of eradicating the followers of Jesus and wiping this new faith off the face of the earth. When Stephen was stoned because of his bold preaching about Jesus, Saul was present and in full agreement with Stephen's murder (see Acts 7:54 to 8:1).

We would be mistaken if we thought of Saul only as an evil murderer. He was sincere in the belief that those who were preaching about Jesus had to be stopped. His zeal was mistaken, but it was sincere. We do not know how many people Saul had arrested and killed. There must have been many. The Book of Acts tells us: "Saul kept up his violent threats of murder against the followers of the Lord" (Acts 9:1). He was so dedicated to hunting down believers in Jesus that he got letters of introduction from the high priest in Jerusalem to the synagogues in Damascus to facilitate arresting followers of Jesus and bringing them to Jerusalem. No doubt, many of these men and women would have to die for their faith.

What happened to Saul en route to Damascus has become legendary. When we want to refer to a dramatic conversion experience, we often call it a "Damascus-road experience." The ninth chapter of Acts records the details of Saul's experience. Suffice it to say here that the angry, determined, and haughty Saul had his life turned all the way around. Saul came out of the experience having to be led into the town by the hand because he was blind. This man who hated Christians with a passion now had to go to the house of a man named Judas and accept the ministry of a believer named Ananias (see Acts 9:8-19). Saul, the enemy of Jesus, had met his Master. He would never be the same.

Saul wasted no time in getting started promoting the gospel of Jesus with as much energy as he had opposed it. According to the Book of Acts, he was preaching within a matter of days in the synagogues of Damascus (see Acts 9:20). Saul's bold preaching about Jesus created such a stir in Damascus that a plot to kill Saul was made. Fortunately, the plan was discovered and foiled when friends of Saul put him in a basket and let him down through an opening in the city wall.

Bible students find it difficult to determine exactly what happened next in the life of Saul. The Book of Acts records a visit to Jerusalem immediately after it tells of Saul's escape from Damascus. When we read the apostle's own account in Galatians, we find that Paul wrote of going from Damascus to Arabia and then back to Damascus. He further wrote that three years passed before he went to Jerusalem (see Gal. 1:15-18). While it is impossible to be dogmatic about the exact sequence of events in those early days of Saul's life as a follower of Jesus, my opinion is that Saul made the visit to Jerusalem described in Acts 9:26-30 soon after his conversion. I believe the Jerusalem visit described in Galatians was an official visit. Galatians 1:18 relates that Saul went to Jerusalem to "obtain information from Peter." Paul probably wanted to question Peter about the life and ministry of Jesus, which Peter knew so well.

The visit Saul made to Jerusalem was near enough to the time of Saul's dramatic conversion that most of the Jerusalem Christians were not aware that the persecutor had become a follower of Jesus. As a matter of fact, when Saul tried to visit the disciples in Jerusalem, he was met with rejection.

We are told: "But they would not believe that he was a disciple, and they were all afraid of him" (Acts 9:26). Before we are too harsh in our judgment of those frightened believers, we should ask ourselves what we would have done in their circumstances. Some of them probably had relatives and friends who had been arrested and perhaps killed due to the fanatical zeal of Saul. It is not difficult to understand why those believers were afraid of Saul. They might have believed that his claim to be a disciple was only a cruel hoax, designed to create more suffering for them. No doubt, this rejection was deeply hurtful to Saul. Anyone whose motives have ever been misunderstood can sense a little of his pain.

This is where Barnabas—the encourager—stepped in. How did Barnabas know about Saul's conversion? How could he be certain of Saul's sincerity? We have no answers to these questions. The record of what Barnabas did is written in Acts 9. "Then Barnabas came to his help and took him to the apostles. He explained to them how Saul had seen the Lord on the road and that the Lord had spoken to him. He also told them how boldly Saul had preached in the name of Jesus in Damascus" (v. 27). The disciples in Jerusalem accepted Saul as a brother on the word of Barnabas. Apparently "The Encourager" was so loved and respected that his judgment concerning Saul was accepted without question.

Pause and think for a moment about this incident from the early Christian experience of Saul. Saul was destined to become the mightiest champion for Jesus Christ in all of history. He would soon be known as Paul. He would evangelize all over the world. He would write timeless letters that would become part of our New Testament. Back of all the accomplishments of this great apostle lies the magnificent ability of Barnabas to look for the best. Barnabas could have been cynical about Saul. He could have taken a wait-and-see attitude toward him, but that was not the character of Barnabas. He believed that Jesus had changed Saul and that Saul was sincere to the very heart. Because Barnabas looked for and saw the best in Saul, the arms of the believers in Jerusalem were opened. Saul was received as a brother.

Who taught Barnabas to look for the best in other people? Some might answer that Barnabas was just naturally that type of person. I believe there is more to it than that. Remember, everything we know about Barnabas teaches us that he was a sincere, from-the-heart follower of Jesus. Barnabas might have been a kind and gentle person by nature, but that was reinforced by what he learned from his Master—Jesus—concerning how to look at people.

Have you ever thought about the stark contrast between how Jesus viewed people and how the Pharisees saw them? The Pharisees and Sadducees were the religious elite of their day. They spoke the "right" words and did the "right deeds," as required by their legalistic religion; but when it came to people, they were cynical. They saw good in very few people. Most people were outcasts, Gentiles, or "sinners" to them. Jesus, on the other hand, seemed always to be looking for worth and value in others.

Some well-known incidents in the life of Jesus point up the contrast for us. For example, Jesus called a man named Matthew to follow Him. Matthew was a tax collector for the hated Romans. To the religious leaders of the day, that was about as low as a person could go. Matthew invited Jesus to eat at his house along with a group of his friends. These friends are called "tax collectors and other outcasts" (Matt. 9:10). They were a rather motley crew by Pharisaic standards. The Pharisees asked the disciples: "Why does your teacher eat with such people?" (v. 11). Jesus responded by telling them that it is sick people who need a doctor. Life had been awfully cruel to some of these outcasts. Jesus saw them more as patients who had the potential of being healed than as bad people who needed to be shunned. With the right medicine or treatment, a sick person can be healthy again. It's all in how you look at people.

Then, there is the much-loved story of Zacchaeus. This little man was a chief tax collector, and he was hated by the people. When Jesus called Zacchaeus down from the tree he had climbed to see Jesus over the crowd, it created quite a stir. Zacchaeus was ready to follow Jesus, even prepared to give half of his money to the poor. He was also willing to make things right toward those he had cheated. Jesus invited Himself to be Zacchaeus's house guest for the day.

The people, probably urged on by the Pharisees, were indignant. They complained: "This man has gone as a guest to the home of a sinner!" (Luke 19:7). Jesus had a vastly different view of Zacchaeus. He rejoiced that salvation had come to him. Then, He said a really remarkable thing: "For this man, also, is a descendant of Abraham" (v. 9). Do you see the contrast? When the cynics looked at Zacchaeus, they saw only "a sinner." They found nothing worth saving in him. When Jesus looked at him, He saw something entirely different. He saw a "son of Abraham." Abraham was the greatest man of the Old Testament.

On another occasion, the religious leaders repeated their most frequent criticism of Jesus. "This man welcomes outcasts and even eats with them" (Luke 15:2). Jesus responded by telling them three masterful parables, all found in Luke 15. He told of a lost sheep and a shepherd who would not give up until he found the sheep and put it to safety on his shoulders. He told of a woman who lost a silver coin and valued it so much she would not stop looking until it was found. Finally, He told of a rebellious son who broke his father's heart when he went away. So anxious was the father for the son's return that he watched for him, ran to meet him, and restored him to a position of honor in his home.

Each of these stories ended with joy. The shepherd was ready to celebrate when he found his sheep. The woman was overjoyed when she found her coin. The father was ready for a feast when his son came home. The lesson is obvious. God feels like that about people. He values them. He forgives them. He rejoices in their well-being. Do you see the difference? The Pharisees saw "outcasts" and "sinners." Jesus looked at people and saw worth and value.

The deep cynicism of the religious leaders concerning people even colored their thinking about Jesus. On one occasion Jesus had demonstrated His power over the demoniac by setting a man free who was possessed by demons. The judgment of the Pharisees was: "It is the chief of the demons who gives him the power to drive out demons" (Matt. 9:34). How sad! In their self-righteous prejudice, they couldn't even see the good in Jesus.

Jesus had tremendous appeal to people. On the other hand, it is my impression that most people kept their distance from the Pharisees. The reason was, I believe, that people sensed Jesus was looking for the best in them. They knew from His words, His touch, and the expression in His eyes that He valued them. He viewed what they were and what they could be. In Jesus, Barnabas found the example he needed concerning how to look at people and recognize their value. He is also our example.

In a world too often characterized by cynicism and mistrust, there is a profound need for people who are able to look for the best in others. Barnabas certainly had that ability. He recognized in Saul of Tarsus what others did not look deeply enough to see. Barnabas was really demonstrating a Jesus-like attitude toward Saul. He had learned well from the example of his Master.

What of us? How do we look at people? Are we able to look for the best? Or do we have a critical, cynical attitude toward others? How can we develop and cultivate looking for the best? Let us examine some of the necessary ingredients of this kind of life-style that majors on seeing the best in others.

First, if we are going to look for the best in others, we

are going to have to walk away from our prejudices and preconceived ideas about people. As long as we place people in categories, we will have a difficult time finding good in some of them.

When the ministry of Jesus was in its early days, He gathered the group of men who would be His friends and co-workers. One of those early disciples was Philip. When Philip decided to accept Jesus' invitation and follow Him, he was so excited that he contacted a man named Nathanael and exclaimed: "We have found the one whom Moses wrote about in the book of the Law and whom the prophets also wrote about. He is Jesus, son of Joseph, from Nazareth" (John 1:45). Nathanael's cynical response was: "Can anything good come from Nazareth?" (v. 46a). Nathanael was from Cana, about eight miles from Nazareth. Nazareth had a bad reputation. It was a trade center, and it attracted some very undesirable people. Apparently, Nathanael had been taught that people from Nazareth were low class. Nothing good could come from Nazareth, certainly not the promised Messiah.

Before we are too harsh in our judgment of Nathanael, we need to take a close look at our own attitudes toward certain groups of people. It will not be possible for us to see any good in another person if our prejudice has so blinded us that we have already made up our minds about them.

Santa Fe, New Mexico, is located in an area rich in history. Among other things, Santa Fe and the surrounding areas are home to large numbers of American Indians.

These people were living in the Southwest long before the white man came. There is a monument in the center of the plaza in Santa Fe to commemorate those who died in wars with the Indians who inhabited the area. The words carved on the marker used to read: "To the heroes who have fallen in the various battles with *savage* Indians in the territory of New Mexico."

Can you understand how offensive this was to the Indian population of the area? How would you react if your ancestors had been driven off the land that was theirs and called "savages" because they fought for what belonged to them? The monument reads a little differently now. The word *savage* has literally been chiseled off the stone. With that word gone the monument now reads: "To the heroes who have fallen in the various battles with Indians in the territory of New Mexico." Hopefully, we are learning that a person who happens to be an Indian is a person with feelings, dignity, needs, and the ability to make a contribution—not a *savage.*

Our prejudices can be sexist, as well as racial. Statements such as, "She's just a woman," or "That's the way all men are," are examples of this kind of thinking. I once knew of a church whose building committee had both male and female members. When the committee met for the first time, one of the men suggested that the men on the committee would deal with things such as site preparation, architects, building contractors, and fund raising. He ventured the opinion that the women on the committee would be able to deal with such things as color schemes, furnishings, and flower beds. The incredible truth about this story is that two of the women on the committee had graduate degrees and were professionals. By the way, the church eventually chose one of these women to chair the committee.

My childhood years were prior to the successes of the Civil Rights movement. I grew up in a part of the country where racial prejudice was an accepted part of the culture. I heard nothing in the home where I grew up, the school where I learned, or the church where I worshiped to challenge these racist ideas. I was appalled and ashamed when I began to think about my prejudice. I am thankful to God for the unrest I felt about it.

As a teenager, I began to look at people in a different way. I came to understand that there is no place in the gospel of Jesus Christ for any notion that one race of people, or either sex, was inferior. I saw many examples of people whose skin was a different color from mine or who spoke with a different accent going to the top in their chosen fields. I began to learn that competence and worth are not related to race or sex. It began to dawn on me that people can grow and achieve when they are treated with dignity and respect.

Recently, I visited the Taos Pueblo in New Mexico with a coworker. We walked from shop to shop examining the pottery, jewelry, and fresh-baked Indian bread. We paused for a while in one little house. An Indian woman and her nine-year-old son were our hosts. The very personable and well-educated young mother talked with us about Indian culture and religious beliefs. While we were there, we looked at various pieces of pottery the family offered for sale. Among the items for sale was a flat rock with an animal painted on one side. The nine-year-old boy told us he had painted that rock. After a few moments, we walked out of the little house and made our way to the next shop.

As we walked along, my coworker said: "I think I'll go back and buy that little boy's rock. I want to encourage him." A few moments later, we went back to find the little Indian boy and his mother still there with their souvenirs for sale. When my coworker told the boy she had returned to purchase his rock, a smile came to his face. Then, she asked him to sign his full name on the other side of the rock so she would be certain to remember him. It was a special joy to watch that boy sign his name and proudly hand it to its new owner. This incident may seem ordinary and trivial to some people, but it is never ordinary or trivial to affirm a person. It is special to look at the work of a person's hands, to sense the feelings of his heart, and to say: "What you have done is good." My friend did a Barnabas-like deed that day. She looked for the best—and found it. I doubt if the boy will ever forget it.

Go back with me for a moment to Nathanael's cynical and prejudicial statement about nothing good coming from Nazareth. Have you ever been guilty of that kind of thinking? Have you put people in categories without really giving them a chance? Have you looked down on persons because they were of a different race or culture? Have you acted condescendingly to someone because she was a woman? Have you expressed mistrust to someone because he was a man?

Philip did not argue with Nathanael about his jaundiced view of anyone from Nazareth. Instead, he simply said: "Come and see" (John 1:46*b*). It didn't take Nathanael long to change his mind. Soon, he was exclaiming: "You are the Son of God. You are the King of Israel" (v. 49).

"Come and see" is still good advice. Take time to look at someone. You'll be surprised at what you see.

Another quality we must cultivate if we are ever able to see the best in others is a firm belief that people can change. Unless we believe that change is possible, it will be impossible for us to see the best in some people.

Barnabas believed that Saul had changed, even though he knew all about Saul's recent past. He knew full well that Saul had been angry and fierce in his battle against Jesus and His people. He also was aware that his fellow believers had every reason to be afraid of Saul. But Barnabas believed that Saul had been changed by his encounter with Jesus. Now, Saul was a different person, ready to serve Jesus and wanting to be a part of His people. In this context Barnabas looked for and saw the best in Saul.

Jesus also believed that people could change. He took time to care for a lot of unlikely people. Many of these people had been written off by the religious "establishment." He cared for and redeemed an assortment of tax collectors, merchants, fishermen, and women who had no status in society. I am convinced that Jesus cared for these people because they were human persons with feelings and a need to be loved. But I sense there is more to it than that. I believe Jesus looked at these people as they were and saw what they had the potential to become. He believed that people could grow and change. That is why He was able to look for the best in people.

I have often thought about the twelve men Jesus chose to be His closest followers. They were a pretty unpromising group. Some were rough and smelly fishermen; some had quick tempers. One was a tax collector. Not one of them was in the good graces of the religious establishment.

Suppose Jesus had appointed you to serve on a "disciple committee" to choose His followers. Would you have voted for any of the men He chose? Why did Jesus pick these men? I am persuaded that He saw qualities in these men of which no one was aware. Jesus knew these men could change and become all He intended them to be.

The possibility of change is uniquely human. Change is often difficult, but it is always possible by the grace of God. This fact, the fact that with God's forgiveness and help people can change, should cause us to look for the best in people.

While leading a conference at the Glorieta Baptist Conference Center, I met an interesting man who reaffirmed my belief that people can change. His name is Tino, a

Hispanic American. Tino is a big man. When he came into my conference, I noticed that he was very muscular and that his arms were covered with tattoos. He quickly got my attention. I soon noticed that this big man had a very gentle and cooperative spirit. He seemed eager to learn and willing to do whatever was asked of him in the conference. As a part of the conference, the participants were sharing things about themselves. Some spoke of their hometowns, others of their hobbies, and some of their business or work. When Tino spoke, he had quite a story to share. Tino reported that he first got into trouble when he was eleven years old. Since then, he had spent most of his time in prison. As a matter of fact, Tino said that his jail and prison time totaled twenty-nine years. Along the way, Tino developed a heavy drug habit. He had ingested, smoked, and injected a lot of drugs into his body over the years. When Tino's sister talked with him about a God who loved him and would help him with his problems, it sounded like nothing more than empty talk to him. Life had held so many disappointments for Tino that he just couldn't believe anyone could love him, especially God.

One day several years ago Tino stuck a dirty needle into his vein. The result was a massive infection that almost claimed his life. While he was in the hospital, near death, Tino became ready to listen to his sister and others who cared about him. He asked for God's forgiveness and help. Tino did not die. More importantly, Tino began to live. Now, he told us he is eager to learn all he can because he has dedicated his life to helping prisoners understand that

God loves them, and that with His help, change is possible.

The most important factor of all, if we are to look for the best in people, is love. Love compels us to look for the best. I have always been impressed by something in Mark's account of the rich young ruler. This story is recorded by three of the Gospel writers. Each writer gives us a little bit more information about this young man who almost followed Jesus. Mark tells us: "Jesus looked straight at him with love" (Mark 10:21). This, to me, is remarkable. Jesus looked at him through the filter of love. I'm certain that He understood the man's weakness, his love of possessions. Still, He saw him through eyes of love. Even more remarkable is the fact that He sees each one of us the same way—through the eyes of love. That is why He seemed always to look for the best in people. He loved them, and when you love someone, you see things that others absolutely cannot see.

Have you ever heard someone say, concerning a loving couple: "I just don't see what she sees in him"? Then, someone will reply: "Well, you know what they say. Love is blind!" When I hear people say this kind of thing, I want to cry out: "No—you just don't understand! Love is not blind! Only love has eyes to really see." When you love someone, you see so much in them, things that nobody else can see.

Looking at people through eyes of love is easy if we feel warm toward them and emotionally involved with them. It is even easier when that person is returning our feelings of love. But what about people to whom we don't feel close? What of those with whom we don't have a meaningful relationship? How do we look at those people in love and see the best in them? It is foolish and false to claim that we experience the same emotional attachment to everyone. We do not, and we should not. There are special people in our lives for whom the words "I love you" are used in a special way. But we *can* love everyone. We can *choose* to love them. The word used for the way God loves people is the Greek word *agape.* This is more a life of intention than of emotion. It is a deliberate love. We may be "in love" only a few times in our lives. We may feel a powerful attachment to our mates, parents, children, and friends, but we can choose to love others. We can look at them through eyes of love and see the best in them, even if our involvement with them is casual and brief.

Someone will ask: "Suppose I look at people with love and try to see the best in them, and then they fail me or even take advantage of me?" I would answer by admitting that this can and does happen. The person who decides to act lovingly and to think the best of other people is vulnerable. Such a person can be let down, disappointed, and even deeply hurt. But what is the alternative? Do we want to play God by deciding in advance that a person is worthless, faithless, and without possibility of good? I would far rather err on the side of love and take my chances, than to live in cynicism about people.

One of my favorite stories is the story of Don Quixote.

Don Quixote, a slightly deranged old nobleman, imagined himself to be a gallant knight. Don Quixote set out to right all wrongs and ended up doing unusual things like battling a windmill which he imagined to be a monster enemy. The story is humorous in many places, but it is also profoundly moving. The old, would-be knight affected the lives of many people with his idealism and gallantry. As you read the story, you wonder if the old man was not saner than most of us.

To me, the most moving part of the story revolves around a lowly scullery maid in the inn that Don Quixote and his faithful squire, Sancho Panza, visited. Don Quixote imagined that the inn was a castle and that Dulcinea, the kitchen maid, was the pure and beautiful Princess Aldonza. Actually, Dulcinea was a crude and abused servant who was used by many of the inn's customers. Don Quixote would not accept what Dulcinea believed about herself.

He held to the belief that his Lady Aldonza was the one for whom he had searched all his life. He longed for the time when he could prove himself worthy of her hand. The laughter at a deranged old man dies out when you begin to see that his love and idealism changed the way Dulcinea saw herself. In fact, by the end of the story, she becomes Aldonza in her own mind. She began to think of herself the way Don Quixote saw her—a worthy and beautiful princess. She was transformed because Don Quixote believed in her and looked for the best in her.

In the real world, this still works. People tend to believe

in themselves if others believe in them. They are inclined to rise to the expectations of those who look for the best in them—and find what they are looking for.

Barnabas looked for the best . . . and found it!

4
Willing to Follow

I am fascinated by the personalized license plates I see everywhere. Most states now permit auto owners to custom design their license plates—for a fee. People put many things on their license plates. Some put their names; others, their hobbies or professions. Many put the name of their favorite football or baseball team.

Recently, I saw a car with a plate that must have expressed the philosophy of its owner. The message on the car tag proclaimed ME-B-4-U. This self-centered slogan expresses the way many people feel about life. It is the old idea that says "look out for number one" and "take care of your own interests and let the other fellow do the same."

The Christian life-style, as demonstrated by Barnabas, looks at life differently. A study of events in the life of the early church will help us to understand. The early church was experiencing what might be called growing pains. In the initial excitement generated by the believers in Jerusalem, one thought seems never to have surfaced—

namely that persons other than Jews could be believers in
Jesus.

Oh, there were a few indicators here and there. For
example, Stephen was stoned to death because he angered
the Jewish leaders. His eloquent speech in Acts 7 strongly
points to the truth that God has purposes that cannot be
contained in a Temple in Jerusalem or related to only one
race of people. Then, Philip the evangelist took a giant
step forward when he ventured to preach Christ in a
Samaritan city. His encounter with an Ethiopian official
on a desert road was yet another bold step. This Ethiopian
is the first Gentile whose conversion to Jesus is recorded
in Scripture. Even this man had some connection with
Jewish belief. Remember, he had been to Jerusalem to
worship when he met Philip. He was also reading Old
Testament Scripture when Philip climbed aboard his
chariot (see Acts 8:26-40).

Then, there was the dramatic vision experienced by
Peter that persuaded him to go to the home of Cornelius,
a Roman military leader in Caesarea. When the gospel
was proclaimed in this Gentile home, Cornelius and others believed the message. When Peter saw the clear evidence of the Spirit's work, he asked those with him: "Can
anyone, then stop them from being baptized with water?"
(Acts 10:47). A milestone had been reached because Peter
had entered a Gentile household and had preached the
gospel on Gentile turf.

Peter learned a valuable lesson. When he was called to
account for entering a Gentile house and associating with

Gentiles (against Jewish law and custom), he defended his actions. He related the way God had dealt with him in the vision (see Acts 11:1-18). This led to a major break-through. The Christian leaders in Jerusalem concluded: "God has even granted the Gentiles repentance unto life" (Acts 11:18, NIV).

But what had been hinted at, and timidly done before, came to full, blazing light in Antioch. Believers in Jesus arrived in Antioch in the wake of the persecution that followed the death of Stephen. At first, they gave the message about Jesus only to the Jews; but then, some of them "went to Antioch and proclaimed the message to Gentiles also, telling them the Good News about the Lord Jesus" (Acts 11:20). A large number of people believed the message. The first church without racial or cultural barriers was born. The Jesus movement would never be the same, and the church would not be a sect including only a few. It would be a mighty fellowship with a place for everyone. Significantly, it was in Antioch, where Jewish and Gentile believers became one, that the name "Christian" was first used to describe followers of Jesus Christ (see Acts 11:26).

When the news about Antioch reached Jerusalem, the leaders of the church there decided to send Barnabas to investigate the situation. True to his nature, Barnabas quickly recognized that God was at work in Antioch. His reaction was one of gladness, and he "urged them all to be faithful and true to the Lord with all their hearts" (Acts 11:23).

What happened next is one of the most important events to take place in all of Christian history. We are told: "Then Barnabas went to Tarsus to look for Saul. When he found him, he took him to Antioch" (Acts 11: 25-26). What was Saul doing when Barnabas found him in Tarsus? He was probably faithfully preaching Christ, but he was in obscurity, out of the mainstream of the advance of the gospel. What Barnabas did was to bring Saul to Antioch and put him on the cutting edge of the worldwide expansion of the gospel. We can only marvel at the insight Barnabas displayed in bringing Saul, because it was from Antioch that Saul launched his missionary career. In point of fact, Barnabas's keen insight and encouragement helped give us the great apostle Paul, the mightiest Christian of history.

Barnabas and Saul worked together in Antioch for a year. Their ministry was highly successful, reaching large numbers of people (see Acts 11:26). These two spiritual giants taught the people well. Not only did the church grow in numbers, it also grew in its scope of concern for ministry. For example, when news of a famine in Jerusalem came to the Christians in Antioch, they responded by sending much-needed relief. Barnabas and Saul took the generous gifts to Jerusalem. Antioch was truly a caring, outreaching fellowship.

What could be more appropriate than for such a caring church to become the launching pad for a worldwide spread of the gospel? That is exactly what happened. Chapter 13 of Acts records the story of Barnabas and Saul being sent out by the church at Antioch to carry the message of Jesus to other provinces and cities. The rest is history. Saul, soon to be better known as Paul, made three major missionary journeys. His mighty intellect, preaching, and church-planting ability were poured into the missionary task. Paul and his fellow workers evangelized much of the Roman world in the next several years. Along the way, Paul wrote numerous letters that have become a major part of the Christian's Bible.

When Barnabas and Saul worked together in Antioch and when they left Antioch to preach in other cities, Barnabas was clearly the leader of the team. Remember, Barnabas was one of the most respected leaders among all the believers. This had been true from the earliest days of the church in Jerusalem. Barnabas, as you recall, was so loved by his fellow Christians that they had given him the name Barnabas, "one who encourages."

On the other hand, Saul had an infamous past, so far as the believers were concerned. He had actually helped put Christians to death. Had it not been for Barnabas's willingness to believe in him, Saul's ministry might never have had a chance for success.

It is not surprising, then, that *every* reference to the two men prior to Acts 13:42 puts the name of Barnabas first. Always, it is "Barnabas and Saul." Barnabas was the tried, true, and respected leader. Saul was subordinate to him, a newer believer who had not yet fully proven himself. Then, something happened. Saul, now known as Paul, became the obvious leader of the team. The Scriptures are subtle about this. There is no passage or verse that explains exactly how or when the change took place; but the mantle of leadership and prominence passed from Barnabas to Paul. As you read the Book of Acts beginning in chapter 13, you will note that Paul is out front. He is preaching the sermons, dealing with the critics, and leading the way. Then in Acts 13:42 when the two missionaries are mentioned by name, the order is "Paul and Barnabas." Three other later references refer to the men as "Barnabas and Saul" (Acts 14:14; 15:12,25). But a new order of leadership is seen. As the work of the two men progressed, it is clearly Paul the leader and Barnabas the follower.

How do you imagine Barnabas felt when it became obvious to him he was no longer the leader? Remember, he was a human being with feelings. It is never easy to watch someone slip past us on their way to the top. Sometimes, it is hard to be a gracious follower when you are accustomed to being out front. Did Barnabas have to deal with some feelings of wounded pride and deflated ego? Probably so, but if he did, he didn't let it show. More importantly, he didn't let it interfere with the work he and Paul shared. I think it is highly possible that Barnabas had to get alone for a while to sort out his feelings about losing the reins of leadership. If that is true, he did not dwell on it or waste much time fretting about it. You see, Barnabas was a big, big man in spirit. He was not the kind of person who would nurse wounded pride or ego. All along his role had been that of an encourager. He wasn't about to turn petty now. If someone had to play second fiddle, he would play it with grace and class.

Thus, we can identify yet another characteristic of a Barnabas life-style. Barnabas and those who would seek to follow his gentle path demonstrate a willingness to let others move out front. Such people are willing to come in second, if necessary. Their concern is for the cause they represent, and if that means letting someone else lead the way, they are willing. The Barnabas-type person is always calling out someone else's gifts and potential. Sometimes this may mean stepping aside while that person takes command. If that is the case, the Barnabas person will not permit petty, hurt feelings to spoil things for everyone.

Barnabas is not the only person in the Bible who was willing to accept second place. Think, for example, of Jonathan in the Old Testament. As the son of King Saul, Jonathan was the apparent heir to his father's throne. Jonathan was a bright, sensitive young man. He probably could have ruled well as king of Israel. But God had given special gifts to a young shepherd boy named David. This man, David, was destined to become the greatest king of Israel and one of the most important men of history. Jonathan could have been petulant and jealous like his father, Saul. He decided instead to love David as his dearest friend and to support his rise to prominence in Israel.

And what of John the Baptist? Few people have ever had the power to move people as John could. His unusual appearance and life-style made him an overnight sensation. When he started preaching out by the Jordan, just about everyone crowded the riverbanks to see and hear him. Although his message was harsh and unrelenting, he made numerous converts. Placed alongside John, the religious leaders of that time looked pale and pathetic. Nobody with John's star quality had been seen among the Jews for generations. As he thundered forth his message and baptized multitudes, his name became a household word. If ever there was an unlikely candidate for playing second fiddle, it was John the Baptist.

Then one day while John was at the height of his popularity, a young man appeared at the Jordan River. His appearance was not as bizarre as John's and when He spoke it was with more gentleness and love than judgment. John the Baptist stopped his sermon and pointed dramatically to the stranger. "There is the Lamb of God," he said, "who takes away the sin of the world." (John 1:29). Things were never the same for John the Baptist after that day. More and more, it became clear that the stranger—Jesus was His name—would step out in front and lead the way. John had commanded the attention of thousands, but Jesus would turn history upside down. Even death would not stop Him. He would face death and become the Living Lord of the universe.

I don't believe that John the Baptist had the slightest problem with second billing. His own words about Jesus put it best: "He must become more important while I become less important" (John 3:30).

It takes a magnificent person to step aside and let someone else have the limelight; but it is done every day by people in all walks of life. For example, in the world of sports, how often has a good steady quarterback who has played well for his team had to step aside and make room for a rookie or an underclassman who is better than good? It takes a real man to sit on the bench while a new, young superstar runs the team.

Or what of the worker who is nearing retirement? This person, who has been right in the thick of the battle for the company, now finds that he is being left out of the decision-making process. To make matters worse, he may be witnessing the hiring and training of the person who will replace him. This younger person seems to have fresh ideas and energy. The soon-to-be retired person watches his sun go down while someone else's star rises.

Then, there are people like secretaries and nurses who do the detailed work that makes the big things happen. A secretary might work endless hours on a report or a project. There are numerous telephone calls to make. There are many letters to write. The arrangements for travel and meeting places have to be made. The report has to be typed letter perfect. Copies have to be made and readied for the meeting. When the project is finished, everyone tells the boss what a terrific job *he* did. There is not much credit or praise for the secretary. After all, all she did was to play second fiddle—and do most of the work!

And what about nurses? The brilliant surgeon is praised, honored, and handsomely paid. He drives to the hospital in his expensive sports car. The nurse bathes the patients, empties the bed-pans, listens to all the complaints, and is paid a nominal salary. She comes to work in a well-used economy car.

Or what of editors? Do you know what editors do? They take a good book and make it even better. They take poorly written books and work on them until they are worth reading. They do all the little technical things that authors depend on them to do. They also play second fiddle. Have you ever seen the editor of a book signing autographs at an autograph party?

It is especially hard to accept second place when you know you deserve the credit someone else receives. There really are not very many bona fide superstars. Most of us know we are in the back-up crew or the supporting cast. I feel certain Barnabas recognized that Paul was someone with special gifts. He would have been the last person to resent Paul's greatness. But what of those times when it just doesn't seem right? What about times when the boss takes your idea, makes it his own, and gets a bonus for it? What about those times when your sales efforts earn your supervisor a trip to Jamaica? What about the times when a bone-rattling block makes it possible for the superstar to cross the goal line? The next day's paper, of course, only mentions the star's brilliant running. What about a hardworking staff and scores of volunteer workers who do the tough work while the minister is lauded for the outstanding job he is doing in *his* church? Let's face it!

Taking second place is not only difficult, sometimes it is downright unfair.

We could go on endlessly giving examples of situations in which people have to accept second place in life. Sometimes, as in the case of Barnabas and John the Baptist, it is necessary, right, and part of God's plan that we step out of the spotlight and let someone else lead the way. At other times, it is forced upon us by circumstances that do not seem fair. The real question is: How do we cope with playing second fiddle in life's band? Permit me now to suggest some answers to that question.

The first answer I would offer is to feel so good about yourself that you don't always have to be number one. This is the logical place to begin because people who must always be praised, noticed, and catered to display a problem with their self-image. Everyone likes to win, but if I always have to win I am proclaiming loud and clear that I really don't feel very good about myself. If my self-esteem is predicated upon being out front, winning all the time, I am riding for a fall. For one thing, sooner or later, someone is going to come along who can beat me. Every record set today will be broken on some tomorrow.

Recently, an ardent baseball fan told me he was in the stands when the great Stan Musial set the record for the most career hits. According to this fan, the record was set in a game between Musial's Saint Louis Cardinals and the Cincinnati Reds. A young player just beginning his major league career was playing second base for the Reds that day. His name was Pete Rose. Years later Pete Rose would break the record Musial set that day. And that, my friend, is the way life goes. Someone will run faster, jump higher, sing better, and sell bigger tomorrow or the day after than anyone who can do those things today. Someone will be more talented, better looking, too, and certainly many will be younger because the only alternative to getting older is not getting older (dying). So you see, always having to be number one is a futile, empty, losing game.

Barnabas, I believe, was happy with who he was. He had earned the respect of his fellow Christians. He did this not so much by winning but by loving and encouraging others. He didn't need to "beat" Paul in some foolish game.

My work requires me to spend considerable time in airports and on airplanes. I have observed something that fascinates me concerning air travel. Passengers are treated with friendliness and respect on board airplanes. But they are often treated with disrespect and rudeness in air terminals. As a matter of fact, I think air terminals in large cities are about the most unfriendly places I know. I especially have problems with this at the security gates. The people who work at these gates have a difficult and important job. I am certain they grow tired of having to deal with thousands of travelers every day.

Not too long ago, I was on my way to a boarding gate at the Orlando International Airport. I was trying to manage two bags and make it through security to reach my flight. I thought I was moving along at a reasonable pace, but apparently the security officer didn't see it that way.

She scowled at me as I walked through the metal detector. "Move quickly, please!" she barked. I smiled at her but got only a frown in return.

Now I will admit that I am sometimes overly sensitive to this kind of treatment. I don't have to be pampered, but I do want to be treated with a measure of kindness and respect. I honestly try to be courteous and considerate to people who work with the public. I expect that kind of treatment in return. When someone treats me rudely, I feel devalued as a person. Part of me wanted to turn to that security officer and say: "Look lady, I'm moving as fast as I can. I paid $400 for a ticket to board that airplane. I don't need you to make me feel like a slow, clumsy oaf." Of course, I didn't do that. She probably had enough problems that day. Besides, why should I let someone who is rude and unfriendly make me feel badly about myself? I know I have value and worth, and there are people who love me. I know I don't deserve to be herded like an animal through an airport security gate. So I shook off the hurt to my pride and went on with my business.

This is a simple, everyday illustration of an important principle. The principle is this: "If I like myself, I don't have to prove anything to anybody if I know I am OK with God and happy with myself."

The second suggestion I would offer to cope with being in second place is to be committed to a cause that is bigger than your personal concerns. I am not suggesting the kind of self-effacement that denies all concern with one's own best interests. There is a threadbare kind of false humility that says: "I am not

important. I am a nobody. What I want doesn't matter."
I have two problems with this kind of humility. First, I
don't believe it is biblical. After all, Jesus taught us to love
our neighbor *as* ourselves, not instead of ourselves. The
right kind of self-love is *not* condemned in the Bible. In
fact, it is essential for healthy living. Secondly, I am trou-
bled by the "I am nothing" and "What I want doesn't
matter" ideas because I seriously doubt if very many people really feel that way. It is natural and right to love
yourself and to want happiness and fulfillment in your
life. Some exaggerated confessions of unworthiness may
actually grow out of pride. Do some people want to be
known and praised for their humility?

Having mentioned this, though, it is still valid to say we
all need something bigger than ourselves to live for. I
believe Barnabas is a good example of this quality. Everything we know about Barnabas indicates he was totally
committed to Jesus Christ. I'm certain he had some ambi-
tions of his own. He certainly achieved immense respect
and affection among his fellow Christians. But above all,
he wanted the gospel to be spread. He wanted Jesus Christ
to be known. This was his passion and cause. I believe it
mattered more to him than his pride or ambition. When
Paul moved out front and became the leader, Barnabas
could have engaged Paul in a power struggle. Perhaps he
could have won the battle for prominence. He had earned
the loyalty of the Christian leaders in Jerusalem. They
would have favored him in any struggle with Paul. But
Barnabas was more concerned with the overall war than

any personal battle with Paul. Both he and Paul were fighting hard to spread the gospel. Paul had special leadership gifts that Barnabas did not have. He was prepared by training, background, temperament, and calling to become the mightiest champion for Jesus Christ in history. Deep down inside the heart of Barnabas what really mattered was the cause of Christ. This is why Barnabas moved aside with grace when Paul became the leader and he became the follower. Barnabas lived for a cause bigger than himself.

Recently, I read about a man who decided to start publishing a magazine. The idea for the magazine grew out of the man's interest in historical matters he felt were not being given attention. At first, the project was small, and the operation was relatively simple. The man invested a good bit of his own time and money in the magazine. For awhile, running the magazine was pretty much a one-man project. Then, other people began to take notice. Soon the magazine had a surprisingly large circulation and a lot of advertisers.

At this point, the man had to make some hard decisions. He found himself in the magazine business over his head. As the business grew, there was more and more need for expertise and sound management. So, the man fired himself! He became a chairman of the board and remained an adviser for the magazine but turned the operation over to experts in the field of publishing. The success of the magazine was more important to him than running the whole show.

If we have a cause we have given our lives to, it will matter less that we get the credit and more that the job gets done. This will be true whether our cause is a business venture, an athletic team, a political crusade, or the spread of the gospel.

There are superstars in every field. For example, in the political world there are men and women who just seem to be born with charisma and power to move others to action. I remember trying so hard not to like John F. Kennedy for ideological reasons that were important to me at the time. I did not want him to be elected president of the United States. But in spite of myself, I found my emotions resonating with him. He spoke of a "new frontier." He seemed to have young Americans at heart, and he held out hope for minorities. He promised the conquest of space. He proposed a "Peace Corps," probably his most notable accomplishment. When he was elected, I found myself glad. When he died on the streets of Dallas, it broke my heart.

No matter how you felt about the late President Kennedy, there is no denying his tremendous attractiveness and appeal. As I have read more and more about Kennedy, I have learned that while he was out front leading the way there were hundreds and thousands who worked hard to plan and carry out his program. Many gave time, money, and energy to create and sustain his movement. Most of these people never got their names in the paper for what they did, but without them it would have been impossible. He was the leader. For personal and ideological reasons all these people worked in the background.

I am amazed when I read about "taxi squads" in pro football and their equivalent in college football. Do you know what these people do? They go out to the practice field each day before a big game. They run the plays of the upcoming opponent so the main team can learn how to defend against them. These players are not quite good enough to be on the varsity team. You never read their names on the sports page in the newspaper, yet, their work—playing second fiddle—gets the team ready. Their cause is the team's victory. Others receive the credit, but they help make it happen.

Do you see the point? If you are really committed to a cause, it is easier to be gracious about someone else leading out in accomplishing the cause's goals.

Finally, and I think most important of all, it is easier to accept being put in second place if you are a "people builder." Everything we know about Barnabas points to the fact that he was such a person. Barnabas had been Paul's strong supporter from the time of the apostle's conversion. He watched his progress and sent for him to come to Antioch. I believe he realized all along that Paul was destined for greatness. Furthermore, I believe he deliberately groomed Paul for leadership and he got a lot of satisfaction out of watching Paul's star rise. He did the same thing with John Mark. As we have already seen, Barnabas seemed able to see the best in people and to help them achieve it. He was, indeed, a "people builder."

One of my early mentors was Dr. John Milford. Dr. Milford, for many years pastor of the First Baptist Church in Huntsville, Alabama, was a unique man. He was a man of astute leadership, yet he had the common touch with people. He was witty, straightforward, and, at times, a bit blunt. After his retirement from the pastorate, Dr. Milford gave of himself to teach young ministers and older ministers who had not had the opportunity to go to a seminary. His teaching was practical and solidly biblical.

Dr. Milford made it a practice to visit the churches where his students preached. He was in my own little rural church several times. It was a delight to watch him beam with pride when one of "his boys" did a good job. He knew he had a part, and he took pride in any success we enjoyed. Dr. Milford was a "people builder."

Being a "people builder" is good for the soul. If we can learn to feel genuine joy when someone begins to move out front and excel, it will save us from pettiness, bitterness, and jealousy. If we can work behind the scenes and stand on the sidelines to cheer while others garner the applause, it will demonstrate we are big people indeed.

There aren't too many Paul's in the world. Apostles, scholars, best-selling writers, All-American quarterbacks, million-dollar salespersons, Academy-Award actresses, beauty queens, and superstar pastors are few and far between. The neat fact is: there is no limit to the number of Barnabas-like people. Anyone who feels good enough about herself/himself and others to stand and applaud while others lead can be a Barnabas. I'll let you in on a secret; it is the Barnabas-like people who really make things work. Great is their reward in heaven—even if no one here notices.

Once I heard the author of a book introduced to a gathering of people. The author was lavishly praised for his work. I was standing beside the editor of the book. I knew he had rewritten large parts of the book to make it acceptable and useful. I turned to him and asked, "How does it make you feel not even to be mentioned while that guy gets the credit?" His answer was quiet but to the point: "I don't mind," he replied, "as long as I know that the one who really matters knows the truth." Barnabas, himself, couldn't have expressed it better.

5
The Man Who Gave Second Chances

Curt was one of the most promising young leaders in our church. He was the teacher of a Youth Sunday School class. He worked with the boys' basketball team. He served on several important church committees. Recently, he had been selected by the congregation to serve as a deacon. Everyone liked Curt and admired his leadership style.

Then some things began to come apart in Curt's personal life. As it too often happens in church families, people began to whisper and come to their own conclusions concerning Curt. He was hurt by his circumstances and by the lack of understanding some of his fellow church members were demonstrating.

One morning Curt called me at my office. He asked me to have lunch with him. Curt's mind was more on talking than eating. He picked over his food and told me about some of his struggles. As he talked, his eyes misted with pain. Curt's voice quivered as he reached into his coat pocket and took out a long white envelope. "I know the deacons are meeting tonight," he said, "This is my resignation. I don't want to create any problems for the other fellows. I want you to have this read in the meeting tonight." I started to protest, but Curt stopped me in mid-sentence. "This is best for everyone," he went on, "please take it for me." With that our lunch came to an end.

That night at the deacons' meeting, I gave Curt's resignation to the chairman. When he read it, everyone sat in a stunned silence that seemed to last forever.

Finally, the silence was broken by Sam. He had been a member and active worker in the church for many years. Every eye was on him as he stood to speak. "Fellows," he began, "we've just heard Curt's resignation read to us. I think we all know that Curt is going through some hard times." Sam paused for a moment and put his hand to his face to wipe away a tear. Then he continued: "Some of you are young men. I've lived long enough to know that everyone makes mistakes, and everyone has to struggle. If it hadn't been for people believing in me across the years, only God knows where I would be today. Curt is a fine young man. He needs our confidence and encouragement. Mister Chairman, I move that we just send Curt's resignation back to him and offer our prayers and help. Let's not turn our backs on him now." With that, Sam sat down. A vote wasn't necessary. Sam's compassion had moved everyone.

In time, Curt solved his problems. He stayed in the church. The last I heard, he was still a deacon and was actively involved in many areas of his church's ministry.

Curt's story is very much like a much older story, the story of John Mark that is found in the New Testament. Caught up in that story were two of the greatest men of the early church, Paul and Barnabas. But let us start at the beginning.

We meet John Mark for the first time in the context of high drama. Herod Agrippa decided to persecute Christians. This ruthless tyrant went so far as to have John's brother James put to death. When he became aware that this pleased some of the Jewish leaders, he decided to take another bold and evil step. He arrested Simon Peter and put him under heavy guard. A public trial was planned. The real plan, no doubt, was to put Peter to death.

With James dead and Peter in jail, the Christian community was shaken. The Christians had no power to fight, but they had a greater power, the power of prayer. Acts 12:5 says, "The people of the church were praying earnestly to God for him" (Peter).

What happened next defies explanation. The night before Peter was to be tried, he was released from prison by an "angel of the Lord" (v. 7). Peter was amazed. After he was led out the gates and into the street, it dawned on Peter that this was no dream. He exclaimed: "Now I know that it is really true! The Lord sent his angel to rescue me from Herod's power" (v. 11).

Peter was eager to share the good news of his deliverance with his Christian friends. They were gathered at the home of a woman named Mary. Evidently, this was a regular gathering place for believers in Jesus. Peter knew exactly where to find them.

Who was this Mary? Several women with that name appear on the pages of the New Testament. We know very little about this Mary since this is the first mention of her in the Bible. She must have been a widow since her husband is never mentioned. Evidently, she was a very prominent member of the church. When Peter knocked at the door of her house, Rhoda, a servant girl, answered the door (v. 13). This probably indicates Mary was wealthy. She was generous with her home. It was a meeting place for believers in Jesus. In fact, many feel that Jesus and His disciples observed the Last Supper in Mary's home. Of course, there is no biblical proof of this. Oh yes, there is one more important fact about Mary. She had a son whose name was John Mark (v. 12). Since he is mentioned in this passage, he must already have been a well-known follower of Jesus.

John Mark was a young man with a destiny. As you already know, he would be used by God to write a very important account of the life of Jesus. We call it the Gospel of Mark. Many believe that Mark's Gospel grew out of his close association with Peter. The great apostle and the young man had such a bond between them that Peter referred to him as "my son Mark" (1 Pet. 5:13). This probably means that Peter had won him to faith in Christ or at least had been his spiritual mentor or "father." Of course, we also know that John Mark had an association with the apostle Paul. We'll look at that in more detail later.

Mark had an extra special connection with Barnabas. Not only was he under the spiritual influence of Barnabas, he was also related to him. Colossians 4:10 tells us they were cousins.

Several conjectures and legends have made the rounds concerning John Mark. Some have taught he was a pioneer for Christ in Egypt. Others have written that he died a martyr's death. The most intriguing idea about Mark relates to a mysterious passage in the Gospel he wrote. The passage, Mark 14:51-52, relates to an incident that happened just after Jesus was arrested in the Garden of Gethsemane. The verses read: "A certain young man dressed only in a linen cloth, was following Jesus. They tried to arrest him, but he ran away naked, leaving the cloth behind." Mark did not identify the young man. Many believe that this experience happened to young John Mark himself. The theory is that Jesus and His disciples had observed the Last Supper in Mary's house and that Mark followed Jesus and the disciples to the garden, probably hiding and watching while the important events of that night unfolded. Of course, this cannot be proven from Scripture.

John Mark must have been an impressive young believer. When Paul and Barnabas finished their task of delivering money that had been collected in Antioch for the needy in Jerusalem, they returned to Antioch. They brought young Mark back to Antioch with them. The fact that Mark was related to Barnabas might have influenced the decision to invite him to Antioch, but obviously Mark showed promise for ministry. Otherwise, Paul would not have agreed to bring him along (see Acts 12:25).

When Paul and Barnabas were sent out from the church in Antioch on a missionary venture, John Mark accompanied them (Acts 13:5). The stage was set for one of the most interesting and dramatic stories in the Bible.

The mission undertaken by Paul, Barnabas, and John Mark was one of those events we refer to as turning points in history. It marked the first time that a church had actually sent missionaries to preach the gospel of Jesus Christ. The Christians in Antioch had already blazed a new trail. They had openly proclaimed the gospel without regard to race or religious background. Now, under the direction of the Holy Spirit, they sent Paul, Barnabas, and Mark to tell the good news in other cities. We should not miss the significance of this event. The church would never be the same again. Even today men and women are sent to all parts of the world as missionaries. They go with the blessing and support of churches to share Christ and minister in His name. It all began in Antioch.

Paul, Barnabas, and their young helper John Mark set out on what Bible students have called Paul's first missionary journey. They went to Seleucia and then to the island of Cyprus. At Salamis, they preached in the Jewish synagogue. Then in Paphos, they encountered Elymas, a magician who opposed their preaching. Paul confronted him and pronounced judgment upon him (vv. 4-12). From Paphos, they sailed to Perga in Pamphylia. It was in Perga that "John Mark left them and went back to Jerusalem" (v. 13). Paul and Barnabas continued the mission.

Why did John Mark leave Paul and Barnabas and return home? Did something happen in Perga that created bad feelings between Paul and Mark? Did Mark resent the fact that Paul had become the leader of the mission instead of his cousin, Barnabas? Was Mark, a Jerusalem Jew, unable to accept working among Gentiles? Was there a personality conflict between Paul and Mark that caused Mark to quit? Did young Mark get homesick and decide to give up? (That has happened to more than a few young men and women.) Why did Mark leave?

There are no final answers to those questions. We are never told *why* John Mark went home, only that he did. Whatever the reason, Paul considered Mark a deserter (see Acts 15:38). The parting must have been angry and unpleasant.

Barnabas and Paul finished the journey. When they returned to Antioch, they gathered the church and reported the success of the mission (Acts 14:27-28).

Sometime later Paul approached Barnabas about another trip. "Let us go back and visit the brothers in every town where we preached the word of the Lord," he said. "Let us find out how they are getting along" (Acts 15:36). Barnabas thought this was a good idea, but he also thought it would be good to take John Mark once again. Paul would have nothing to do with this suggestion. In the words of verse 38: "But Paul did not think it was right to take him, because he had not stayed with them to the end of their mission, but had turned back and left them in Pamphylia."

What followed is tinged with sadness. These two friends, partners, confidants, and brothers in Christ had a "sharp argument" over the matter (v. 39). Barnabas was a reconciler and peacemaker, but, in this instance, he didn't cave in to the powerful, determined, persuasive apostle. He stood his ground. Mark would be given another chance or Barnabas would not go with Paul. So the two giants separated. Paul found a new partner, Silas. Barnabas took Mark and returned to Cyprus (see vv. 39-40).

Who was right and who was wrong in this dispute? It depends on how you look at it. Paul certainly felt he was right. I believe Paul was a very intense and totally committed man. It must have been unthinkable to him that John Mark would have deserted the mission. To Paul, nothing was as important as making Christ known. Paul demonstrated over and over again that he was willing to suffer, go to jail, even die for the cause. It must have been difficult for him to recover from Mark's quitting. Then, when Barnabas wanted to give Mark another chance, Paul just couldn't see it. I feel certain Paul was perfectly sincere and honest in this. I doubt he was trying to be hard or unrelenting. He simply felt that the work was more important than anything or anyone in the world.

Barnabas must have taken a different view of things.

He, too, was deeply committed to spreading the gospel, but he was a people builder. Remember, he had been given the name Barnabas by others because he was known as an encourager. Every time we meet him in the pages of the Bible, he is believing in someone, encouraging someone, helping someone to realize his best potential. Barnabas just could not and would not give up on John Mark. While it was true that John Mark was a relative of Barnabas, I think there was more to it than that. I believe he knew John Mark needed to go back to the very scene of his failure and to make good. I feel he saw tremendous good in the young man, and he just couldn't let him go.

Time proved that Barnabas was right about Mark. We are not sure about all that Mark did after Barnabas gave him a second chance. We do know he became a close associate of the apostle Peter and that he was used by God to write a book in the Bible, the Gospel of Mark. And there is another fact that is quite remarkable. Paul, the man who refused to give Mark a second chance, later put a high value on him. Years later when Paul wrote his letter to Philemon, he referred to Mark as a "fellow worker" (Philem. 24). When he wrote to the Colossians from prison in Rome, he said Mark was with him. Then he gave instructions to the Colossians to "welcome Mark if he comes your way" (Col. 4:10). Near the end of his long and fruitful ministry, he wrote to Timothy "get Mark and bring him with you because he can help me in the work" (2 Tim. 4:11).

Time proved that Barnabas was right to give Mark another chance. I believe that time also proved that Paul was wrong. What would have happened to Mark if Barnabas had not given him a chance? Perhaps he would have become so discouraged he would have been lost to the cause of Christ.

Not giving up on people and being willing to give them a second chance when they failed was in keeping with how Barnabas felt about people, but this manner of treating people is more than Barnabas-like—it is Christlike!

Jesus was constantly picking up people who had stumbled and setting them on their feet again. One example is how Jesus treated Peter when he failed so miserably. Do you remember Peter's story? Peter was sure he would never fail Jesus. Just before Jesus was arrested and killed, He predicted His disciples would run away and leave Him when the testing time came (see Matt. 26:31). Peter spoke quickly: "I will never leave you," he vowed, "even though all the rest do!" (v. 33). Then when Jesus prophesied that Peter would deny Him three times, Peter was strong and quick in rebuttal. He said: "I will never say that, even if I have to die with you!" (v. 35).

Peter meant well. He was very sure of himself, certain that he was much too strong to fail. Other lesser men might fold under pressure and deny Jesus, but Peter— never! But the next several hours were like a nightmare. Jesus was arrested, and it became clear there was no escaping the cross. Peter was confused, hurt, afraid, and angry. Outside the high priest's house in the courtyard,

he waited to see what would happen to Jesus. When
servants of the high priest and others tried to identify him
as one of Jesus' followers, Peter shamefully denied even
knowing Jesus. He denied Jesus three times. When the
crowing of a rooster reminded Peter of what he had done,
he was devastated. He "wept bitterly," a miserable failure
(v. 75).

The horrible, hopeless despair of crucifixion gave way
to the joyous celebration of resurrection. Jesus was alive!
His amazed friends found it hard to believe what their
ears heard and what their eyes saw, but finally they realized the wonderful truth—He had conquered death.
Guess who was among the celebrants on that resurrection
morning? If you guessed Peter, you are correct. John's
Gospel records that when Mary Magdalene found the
heavy stone rolled away from Jesus' tomb she ran to tell
Peter and another disciple. The two men ran to the tomb
and found it empty. Peter went into the tomb to investigate the mystery of Jesus' disappearance. Soon he would
understand that Jesus had risen from the grave (see John
20:1-10).

Later Jesus questioned Peter about his love for Him.
"You know that I love you," Peter repeated three times.
"Take care of my sheep," Jesus charged. Peter's love
would be demonstrated in service. Peter had been given
another chance, in spite of his shameful failure (see John
21:15-19).

Peter became the leader of the earliest church. His courage on the day of Pentecost and before the council is well

known. No more denying for Peter! When beaten and commanded not to preach about Jesus anymore, Peter and other apostles rejoiced that they were able to suffer for the sake of Jesus (see Acts 5:41). He had become a brave and fearless leader.

What if Jesus had not given Peter another chance? What if he had given up on Peter? His name would have been forgotten, or if remembered at all, Peter would only be thought of as a coward and a denier of the Lord.

So you see, when Barnabas refused to give up on John Mark and instead gave him another chance, he was doing a Jesus-like deed. He was treating John Mark the way Jesus treated Peter and so many other people.

Many times in my life I have needed to have people believe in me, refuse to give up on me, and give me another chance. I shudder to think of where I would be today if some Barnabas-like people had not done this for me.

Sometimes we tend to forget our own need for understanding and forgiveness when we are dealing with other people. I have often wondered why Paul couldn't remember his own past when he was unwilling to give Mark another chance. Remember, Paul's past was stained with a fanatical hatred of followers of Jesus. No doubt, many had died or languished in jail because of his mistaken zeal. Then when he became a believer, the Christians in Jerusalem were unwilling to believe he was a changed man. They were afraid of him. When they heard the name Saul of Tarsus, all they could think of was an angry fanatic who was trying to wipe them off the face of the earth. If it had not been for Barnabas who was willing to believe in Saul and give him another chance, Saul might never have been accepted as a brother by the believers (see Acts 9:26-28). Yes, Paul should have remembered his own past need for another chance when he refused to give Mark an opportunity to make good. But before we are too hard on Paul, what about our own attitude? Are we sometimes unforgiving and unrelenting toward other people while forgetting that others had to forgive us and give us another chance?

Where would you be today if all along the way people had not cared enough about you to believe in you, forgive you, and express confidence in you? The need for a second chance never ends. All of us are human and subject to mistakes and failure. Somewhere down the road of life all of us will need someone to forgive us and believe in us again. It is really a never-ending process because we are imperfect people living in an imperfect world. We often speak of getting a second chance. It would be more accurate to say that all of us need a lifetime of "second chances."

I have a friend who used to have the most rigid, judgmental, and unforgiving attitude toward others of anyone I have ever known. When we would talk about some things that had happened to destroy the unity of his church, his eyes would flash with anger, and his words would become harsh. He especially blamed a former pastor for what had happened. It never took him very long to tell me what he thought of that man. He angrily questioned the man's Christian commitment and integrity. He had no use for him and saw no good in him. One day I became exasperated with his tirade against the former pastor and told him that he was the most inflexible and unforgiving person I had ever known. Remarkably, we remained friends, but I always felt that he would turn on me and give up on me if I ever failed in his eyes.

My critical friend moved away, and we lost contact for a while. I heard from friends that he had suffered some reverses in his own life. He made some choices I'm certain he felt were necessary and right. Many of his "friends" did not understand and spoke critically of him. I tried to defend his right to make decisions about his own life, and I tried to remain his friend. I could not help, however, remembering how unwilling he had been to see any good in the former pastor whom he disliked so much.

Believing in people and being willing to give them a second chance is really living by the principle of grace. Grace has been defined in various ways; but what it really comes down to is this: Grace is receiving what we need, even if we don't deserve it. Grace is the way God treats each of us. He doesn't wait until we are deserving to extend His love and forgiveness to us. He gives us what we need freely just because He loves us.

Isn't it strange that we ask for God's forgiveness and help over and over again but tend to mark people off our list if they stumble? We become judgmental and legalistic instead of giving grace to others. Once Peter came to Jesus with a question, "Lord, if my brother keeps on sinning against me how many times do I have to forgive him? Seven times?" (Matt. 18:21). Peter's question betrays a legalistic attitude toward people. When is enough enough? His question had to do, specifically, with the matter of forgiving someone who was sinning against him, but it has broader implications. At what point do you quit forgiving, stop caring, and just give up on someone?

Jesus' answer was: "No, not seven times . . . but seventy times seven" (v. 22). His answer was not intended to establish a more generous legalism—forgive 490 times as opposed to 7 times. The idea is unlimited forgiveness. Jesus just didn't give up on people.

The problem with having a legalistic attitude toward people is it fails to take into account the fact that all of us need unlimited forgiveness. We also need others to believe in us enough to give us another opportunity when we fail. In other words, we need grace.

Jesus illustrated the incongruity of wanting grace for ourselves and being legalistic toward others by telling Peter a powerful story. He told of a man who owed his king millions of dollars. The debtor begged the king not to sell him as a slave and take all he had to satisfy the debt. The king felt sorry for him and wiped the debt off the books.

Then, the man who had been forgiven such a huge debt hunted down a fellow who owed him only a few dollars. He demanded payment—and got really rough with him when he could not pay. When the debtor begged for time to pay the small debt, the ungrateful man had him thrown into jail. Jesus brought the parable to a powerful conclusion. When the king heard what this ungrateful servant had done, he called him in: "You worthless slave!" he said. "I forgave you the whole amount you owed me, just because you asked me to. You should have had mercy on your fellow servant, just as I had mercy on you" (vv. 32-33). That is the principle of grace. Those who are forgiven should be willing to forgive.

I have experienced so much forgiveness from God and from others who love me. Across many miles and years, I have had people to believe in me and encourage me. More than a few times, I have been given the second chance I needed so much. My life has been filled with grace from God and from His people. I know it is not right for me to give up easily on people or mark them off my list. If I did that, I would violate the principle of grace.

A final word remains to be said about the matter of not giving up on someone and giving someone another opportunity when he has failed. That word is *redemption*. The word *redemption* has the idea of buying something back again. A gold watch that has been pawned in order to secure money can be redeemed or bought back again. A bond that has matured can be redeemed, bought back from the buyer with interest. In the Christian faith, redemption is a powerful concept. We have been redeemed or bought back by God. The price of our redemption was nothing less than the blood of Christ (see 1 Pet. 1:18-19).

In a beautiful sense of the word, Barnabas redeemed

Mark. He bought him back from failure, frustration, and wasted opportunity. Mark probably felt pretty bad about quitting on Paul and Barnabas. He must have gone through some long days and sleepless nights questioning his courage and his commitment to the gospel. I don't believe quitting did very much for his self-esteem. He may have felt like a failure, and he probably didn't think he deserved another chance.

That is where Barnabas stepped into the picture. He believed Mark had too much to offer for him to be lost to the cause of Christ. I don't believe he took Mark's failure lightly. It was serious business. He had broken trust with Paul and Barnabas, and he had quit on them, but Barnabas would not accept Mark's failure as final. He saw goodness and potential in the young man that was bigger than his failure. So he redeemed him, in the sense that he bought him back to usefulness and dignity. He knew Mark had failed, but he refused to think of him as a failure. He would take him on another journey and give him the opportunity to succeed the next time.

What if Mark failed again? Suppose Paul was right about him. Suppose somewhere at some strategic time, he quit and headed for home again. Barnabas was willing to take that risk. He believed in Mark and was confident that Mark would not fail, but there are no ironclad guarantees when you are dealing with people. Love is a risky business. It is not for the faint of heart. When you love someone and refuse to give up on that person, there is a price to be paid and a risk to be taken.

For example, even though Barnabas was proven right by Mark's later accomplishments, he paid a rather high price for giving him a second chance. It meant a face-to-face confrontation with his friend Paul. It meant stepping out of the mainstream of the ongoing missionary expansion. Paul took Silas and went on a second journey. The remainder of Acts is filled with thrilling stories from the ministry of the great apostle. Barnabas took Mark, and we don't hear very much about him after that.

In this time when prominence is so important to many in the religious world, Barnabas made a career choice that wasn't very wise. He chose to act redemptively toward one young man who needed someone to believe in him. He risked himself and his ministry to love redemptively. Yes, the price was steep, but redemption is always costly. It cost Jesus His blood. If you and I are going to love people, believe in them, and lift them, there will be a price to pay because, in a sense, love always involves going to the cross.

Well, there you have it! Barnabas being true to his name, "the encourager." Years before he had given Paul to the Christian world by looking for the best and believing in him. In this instance he gave us Mark by refusing to reject him and by granting him a second chance. We need more of Barnabas's kind these days. May his tribe increase.

The 1929 Rose Bowl game between Georgia Tech and the University of California provided the setting for a dramatic story. In the first half of that hotly contested bowl game, a California player, Roy Riegels picked up a loose ball that had been fumbled by Georgia Tech and started running with it. The only problem was that he became confused and ran the wrong way—right toward the California goal line. The crowd buzzed as Riegels's own teammates chased after him, trying to keep him from scoring a touchdown for Georgia Tech. Finally, after chasing him for sixty-five yards, one of Riegels's teammates tackled him just before he crossed the wrong goal line. A few downs later, when California attempted to punt out of their own end zone, they were unable to get the kick away. Georgia Tech scored a safety. Those points were the ultimate margin of victory.

The first half ended, and as the teams left the field, many fans were wondering what California's Coach Clarence "Nibbs" Price would do about Roy Riegels in the second half. In the dressing room, Roy Riegels wrapped a blanket around his shoulders, sat down in a corner, put his face in his hands, and cried a strong man's tears.

The coach said nothing to Riegels about his costly, embarrassing mistake, but when it was time for the team to take the field for the second half of play, Coach Price announced: "Men, the same team that played the first half will start the second."

The players started out of the dressing room to go to the playing field, but Roy Riegels did not budge. The coach called to him again. Still, Riegels did not move. Then Coach Price came over to him and said: "Roy, didn't you hear me? The same team that played the first half will start the second."

When Roy Riegels looked up, his cheeks were wet with tears. "Coach," he said, "I can't do it to save my life. I've ruined you. I've ruined the University of California, and I've ruined myself. I couldn't face that crowd in that stadium to save my life."

Then, Coach Price did a magnificent, redemptive thing. He reached out and put his hand on Riegels's shoulder and said to him, "Roy, get up and go on back; the game is only half over." Roy Riegels did go back. He played his heart out in that second half.[*]

A lot of us have fumbled the ball, run the wrong way, and even crossed the wrong goal line in our lives. What we need is a Barnabas to believe in us and to remind us that the game is not over. We also can do that for others. Because as long as there is life left to live, the game isn't over for anybody.

[*]From Haddon Robinson, "The Gospel of the Second Chance," *Christian Medical Society Journal,* Winter (1978). Used by permission from *Christian Medical Society Journal.*

6

A Call for Barnabas People

Washington, D.C., our nation's capital, is one of my favorite places. I am certainly not an expert on the city, but each time I return I try to see something I haven't seen before. I know I'll never make enough trips to Washington to see everything I want to see.

There are two points of historic interest in Washington I'll want to see again and again. One is the stately Lincoln Memorial. Many people share with me the opinion that Abraham Lincoln was our greatest President and perhaps the greatest American of all time. When I visit his Memorial, I think of his immense love for this nation, his wisdom and compassion in those difficult Civil War days, and his untimely death by the bullet of an assassin.

His statue is seated inside the huge Memorial. Above his head are written these words:

IN THIS TEMPLE,

AS IN THE HEARTS OF THE PEOPLE FOR WHOM

HE SAVED THE UNION, THE MEMORY OF

ABRAHAM LINCOLN IS ENSHRINED FOREVER.

The second place I plan to visit as many times as possible relates to more recent history. It is the impressive monument to those who died in the Vietnam War. Thousands of names are engraved on the curved wall that rises to its highest point in the center. Hundreds of thousands of people visit the memorial each year. They are able to locate the names of friends, family members, and loved ones who died in that war in books that look like huge city telephone directories. Beside each name is the information telling where that person's name is engraved on the wall. Loved ones can look up the name in the book, then go to the wall to find it there. It is a moving experience to watch people stand before that wall, reach out a hand to touch a name engraved there, and perhaps bow their heads in silent grief. All along the base of the wall are flowers left by family and loved ones to honor those who died in that tragic war.

All across the country in big city cemeteries and rustic country churchyards, one can find memorials and epitaphs. These are not well known like the national monuments in the nation's capital; but to families and friends, they have great significance. I am not much enamored with graveyards, so I don't spend a lot of time walking around in them. But sometimes I do read the words on someone's monument and wonder about the person the words honor. On some stones the words are very simple: perhaps just "Mother," "Father," or "Beloved Daughter." Sometimes the words describe the departed one: such as "Friend to All" or "Faithful Christian." Sometimes the words express the love of those left behind: perhaps "We'll Never Forget You" or "We'll Meet in Heaven."

A few months ago, I was passing through Crewe, Virginia. My traveling partner asked if I would like to visit the burial place of Lottie Moon. Lottie Moon was the pioneering Baptist missionary who gave her life to the people of China in sacrifice and love. I have heard the story of Lottie Moon all my life. Millions of dollars have been given to missions in her honor. I told my friend I would like to stop for a while and visit her grave. Her monument is starkly simple, as is fitting for her sacrificial life-style. I was moved by the inscription:

> LOTTIE MOON 1840-1912.
> FORTY YEARS A MISSIONARY
> OF THE SOUTHERN BAPTIST CONVENTION.
> FAITHFUL UNTO DEATH.

Barnabas lived centuries ago. We have no idea how he died, and, of course, we don't know where he is buried. No memorial or marker identifies his resting place for us. There is no place we can visit to bow our heads and give thanks for him.

Yet, I would propose a simple memorial I believe well describes Barnabas. If I could, I would carve it in stone somewhere for everyone to see and remember. It would read simply: BARNABAS WHO FOLLOWED CHRIST AND FOUND JOY IN UNSELFISH LIVING.

While we don't have such a monument for Barnabas, we do have a statement in the Book of Acts that pretty well sums up who and what he was. This statement is found in chapter 11 of Acts. Its setting is the church in Antioch where the gospel was being preached and people, even Gentiles, were believing the message. When the Christian leaders in Jerusalem heard about this, they sent the highly respected Barnabas to investigate. Barnabas arrived in Antioch and saw what was happening in the church. In this context we find the following revealing statement about Barnabas: "When he arrived and saw how God had blessed the people, he was glad and urged them all to be faithful and true to the Lord with all their hearts. Barnabas was a good man, full of the Holy Spirit and faith, and many people were brought to the Lord" (Acts 11:23-24). There you have it! In capsule form, that passage aptly describes this follower of Jesus, who discovered there is joy in unselfish living.

Although there is no way to improve on this beautiful description of Barnabas, I would like for us to look briefly at some of the truths it tells us about him. First of all, the very fact that the Christian leaders in Jerusalem sent him to investigate the situation in Antioch tells us a great deal about Barnabas. Remember, something totally new was happening there. The gospel was being preached openly and regularly to Gentiles. That was not easy for some of the Jewish believers to accept. Some of them were not yet free of their prejudice against the Gentiles. They honestly believed the gospel was mainly intended for the Jews. The fact that they sent Barnabas indicates how much they trusted him and depended on him. They knew Barnabas would deal with the situation in Antioch with fairness, wisdom, and love. That in itself speaks volumes about Barnabas.

Then, too, I am impressed with the attitude of Barnabas when he arrived in Antioch and observed firsthand what was going on there. We are told he was glad. There is evidence to support the conclusion that Barnabas spent a lot of time being "glad." Almost about every time he's mentioned, he is doing something good for someone. People like that are generally "glad" people. Barnabas was optimistic, upbeat, and positive. His fellow Christians would not have given him the name Barnabas—if he had not been a joyful, happy person. Religion is a grim and gloomy business to many people, but not to Barnabas; he was "glad."

We shouldn't be at all surprised at what Barnabas did in Antioch after he saw what was happening there. He "urged them all to be faithful and true to the Lord with all their hearts" (Acts 11:23). There he was again doing what he did so well, encouraging other people. I'm certain that his urging was positive, winsome, and persuasive. These people had found the Lord—or, more accurately, had been found by God's love. Now Barnabas, who knew Jesus so well and loved Him so much, encouraged these new believers to put their whole hearts into being Christians. For a living example of what it meant to do that, they had only to look at Barnabas, who was now urging them on.

After Luke, the writer of Acts, related the reaction of Barnabas to the excitement in Antioch, he seems to interrupt his story for a kind of parentheses. Before going on with what happened in Antioch, Luke wrote these words: "Barnabas was a good man, full of the Holy Spirit and faith" (Acts 11:24). Luke did not write exactly like that about anyone else in the Book of Acts. He was very impressed with Barnabas.

The three things he wrote about Barnabas are most revealing. *First, he wrote that Barnabas was a good man.* When we say that about a person, we generally mean more than the idea that a person is morally good. All of us know people who are legalistically "good"—that is, they don't do things that are normally considered "bad." But this is a negative means of measuring goodness. A person can live by high moral standards and yet be cold, selfish, and uncaring. When we say of someone, "She is a good person," or, "He is a good man," we mean more than this. We mean the person we refer to is "good" positively as well as negatively. Almost always when we call someone "good," we are referring to the way they treat other people.

I have known many "good" people. They were not self-righteous, legalistic, or "goody-goody." They were "good" because they were kind, forgiving, loving, and unselfish. My thoughts go to a quiet man—I'll call him

Bill. Bill was a deacon in his church, but he was not really a leader. He usually didn't have very much to say in the church. He didn't sing, teach, or make speeches. He even seemed timid about praying in public, and his prayer was always simple and brief. I feel certain he had high moral standards, but he didn't make a big deal of it. He was not a self-righteous man. Yet, everyone would agree Bill was a "good" man. In his quiet way, Bill really cared about people. He was always doing something kind for someone. Much of what he did went unnoticed because Bill didn't talk about it. When Bill died, a big empty space was left in the lives of all who knew him.

Barnabas was a "good" man in the best sense of that word. His goodness needed no blaring trumpet to proclaim it. His caring life spoke for itself.

Luke also wrote that Barnabas was "full of the Holy Spirit." I don't believe this was intended to mean Barnabas had some kind of ecstatic, emotional experience that set him apart from ordinary people. Some today might claim fullness of the Spirit as evidence they are part of the Christian elite or have experienced something that most of us have not experienced. Not so with Barnabas. He was no elitist nor did he claim special experiences. When we read that Barnabas was filled with the Spirit we are meant to understand that God's power was the source of Barnabas's ministry. Barnabas would probably have been a gentle, caring person even if he had not been a Christian, but his caring was far deeper and much more effective because he knew Christ. There was a spiritual dimension to his life. The living power of the Holy Spirit filled Barnabas with love that was beyond his human capacities. Barnabas did not merely care. He cared as a Christian who was filled with God's power.

Finally, this tribute to Barnabas in Acts 11 speaks of his faith. The faith of Barnabas shines through everything we know about him. It was a dynamic, permeating faith, a faith that meant far more than just believing a set of doctrines or using the right theological words.

First and foremost, Barnabas had a living, vibrant faith in God as revealed in Jesus Christ. Barnabas was, first of all, a believer. He not only believed in Jesus as his Savior and Lord, he also believed that God was at work in his church and in his world. That is why he sold his property and gave the money to the apostles to meet needs in the church. That is why he became joyfully involved in the pioneering work of the church in Antioch. Remember, he was glad when he came to Antioch and saw the barriers of prejudice fall as the gospel was proclaimed to the Gentiles. Barnabas had faith that God was at work in powerful and dynamic ways.

I believe Barnabas also had a healthy faith in himself. There was not a trace of arrogance or false pride in Barnabas, but he was a confident man. Think back to all the passages we have examined that relate to Barnabas. Do you recall any time when he was hesitant, faltering, or uncertain? The answer is no. Barnabas was decisive, willing to make decisions, even go out on a limb and take risks. In fact, Barnabas put himself and his future on the line when he stood up for Saul, and then later for John Mark.

When I was a teenager, I was part of a high school program that was presented to a business club in my hometown. After the program, an elderly man sought me out and introduced himself. When I heard his name, I recognized he was one of the wealthiest men in our town. He said he would like to share his life philosophy with me. I was flattered, and I listened carefully to hear what he would say. His words were simple: "The way to have a happy life is to have faith in God and faith in yourself." It sounded almost too simple to me at the time. But the more I've thought about it, the more I've realized that his simple words were filled with wisdom. Faith in God is the foundation upon which everything must be built. To believe that God lives, that He cares, and that He will forgive me and help me is the most important aspect of faith. Then, to believe in myself and to be willing to trust my own judgment is essential. If I let myself become immobilized by fear and self-doubt, I am defeated before I can begin.

I believe, however, that Barnabas's faith teaches us yet another element of dynamic believing. Barnabas believed in God; he believed in himself; and he also believed in other people. Over and over again Barnabas gave people that extra incentive to succeed by believing in them. He believed in Saul. He believed in John Mark. He believed in the Christians in Antioch. These are the ones we know about. Since he was called "Encourager" by others, I'm certain he believed in countless other people whose names we'll never know.

Did anyone ever let Barnabas down or betray his trust? Was he ever taken advantage of by anyone? We do not know for certain. My guess is that he had some disappointments along the way. If so, Barnabas did not let himself become cynical and unwilling to believe in people.

The Book of Hebrews says, "No one can please God without faith" (Heb. 11:6). The rest of chapter 11 illustrates the kind of faith that pleases God. It tells of people like Noah, Abraham, Moses, and Rahab who put themselves on the line, took risks, and gave all they had. That is the kind of faith Barnabas demonstrated. His was a living faith.

I am certain it will not surprise you when I admit that Barnabas is my favorite biblical character. Why? Well, I've thought a good bit about that question. I know that Barnabas is not one of the "superstars" of the New Testament. He played a significant role in the unfolding drama of the Book of Acts, but not a starring role. He would not be considered one of the great preachers of that time. We know of no church he founded. Some believe that Barnabas authored the material we refer to as the Book of Hebrews, but that is conjectural. Hebrews doesn't bear his name; as a matter of fact, no book in our Bible is known to have been written by him. We know less about Barnabas than about several other Bible personalities. After chapter 15 of Acts, he is mentioned only a few times. Apparently he did not play a leading role in the ongoing mission of Paul after the first missionary journey. Why then do so many Christians today, and I count myself among them, consider him to be a giant among the people of the Bible and a worthy example to follow?

My answer to that question is threefold. First, Barnabas demonstrated the very best in Christlike living. His generous spirit, his willingness to give, his deep kind of caring, and his redemptive attitude toward people remind me of Jesus.

I have met a few people like Barnabas who impress me in that way. I had a professor in college who was kind, caring, affirming, and willing to go the extra mile to help a student. I used to sit in his classroom and talk with him on campus and think to myself: *If Jesus were on this campus, I believe he would be a lot like that man.* More than anything else, it was just that professor's attitude toward students—his genuine concern for them—that caused me to feel that way. Barnabas was that kind of man. He reminds me of our Lord.

Second, Barnabas stands tall in my life because I believe this kind of person is so desperately needed in all areas of life today. For one thing, Barnabas did not seem interested in controlling anyone or anything. Some people seem to be controllers by their very natures. Such people have to have it all their way. People like this are in every business office, every club, every social circle, and behind the doors of many homes. I once was told by a teenage girl that her father was such a controller that the whole family had to "pass inspection" when he came home at night. Everyone had to be dressed for dinner to meet his approval. The family was not allowed to sit down for the evening meal until he got home, no matter how late he was. His plate was served; his every wish was granted at the table. Then when dinner was over, he would go to his easy chair while his wife fetched his slippers for him. The television was tuned to whatever he wanted to watch, and at the appropriate time, his coffee or cold drink was brought to his chair. The daughter said he thought of himself as "King" in his home. This is an extreme example, but there are many bosses, husbands, wives, and associates who see themselves as kings or queens. They walk on people, manipulate them, and use them for their own purposes.

Even in churches and Christian denominations these days, we hear a lot about taking control. There is often plenty of jockeying for position, and sometimes there are brutal power politics. This kind of power grabbing is not the sole possession of any one group. It cuts across ideological and theological persuasions. Needless to say, it is unchristian and destructive wherever it is found.

Barnabas was not like that. He did not demand control or position. He seemed honestly concerned to serve in love. We need his kind everywhere today.

Another quality in the life of Barnabas that is sorely needed today is loyalty. Barnabas was loyal. He demonstrated loyalty to Paul on a number of occasions. He stuck by John Mark when Mark was on the ropes, so to speak. I'm certain he was just as loyal to others with whom he worked and associated. This quality—loyalty—is desperately needed today. It is, unfortunately, not that common.

I believe I have many friends and a few people who really love me. As I look back over my life up to this point, I can think of so many with whom I have worked, laughed, cried, shared, and walked. I am grateful for each one. Very few people have ever been unkind to me. I consider myself blessed in this regard. Yet I have observed something in the last couple of years that I had not thought of before. Many people walk into our lives and stay for a while. While they are there, the sharing is often very deep and special. Then, these people make an exit and become only a memory. Sometimes the reason is circumstances, sometimes distance, sometimes changing needs, and sometimes cost. But whatever the reason, they are gone, except from our remembrance.

But then there are those few people who walk into our lives and never leave. They are always there for us if we need them. We know they believe in us, pray for us, and love us. We know, too, that those people will do whatever they can for us. That's what I mean by loyalty. We need more people with that kind of attitude and love.

I once heard a man speak who had formerly been a pastor. He had ended his pastoral career when he experienced the breakup of his shaky marriage and divorce. He talked that day about how people had treated him since his divorce. He confessed that the most hurting reaction he had encountered was from some of his long-time friends and associates in the ministry. He lamented that many of these people had changed toward him. They were no longer warm toward him or available to him. The former pastor also said he did not expect these fellow ministers to agree with him, condone anything he had done, or in any way violate their convictions. But what hurt the most, he said, was: since his divorce they didn't even seem to know him. This man needed some Barnabas people who would be his friends, regardless of the circumstances. All of us need this.

I believe there are several levels of human relationships that call for different levels of loyalty. First of all, there are those relationships that are casual, chance, or temporary in nature. Every day all of us have encounters with many different people. These would include clerks in the store, waitresses, taxi drivers, customers, flight attendants, salespersons, and even the stranger who holds a door open for us. We never see many of these people again, or if we do, we encounter them only briefly and casually. The level of loyalty in these relationships is relatively low. We should certainly treat such persons with kindness, courtesy, and respect, but our lives aren't really involved with them, at least not at this point in time. We should not take these relationships lightly; however, sometimes we can make a person's life a little easier by simple kindness and friendliness. The writer to the Hebrews cautioned: "Remember to welcome strangers in your homes. There were some who did that and welcomed angels without knowing it" (Heb. 13:2). Whatever else that verse means, it certainly tells us that sometimes we do more than we realize when we are open and warm in everyday relationships.

Then, there are those relationships which might be thought of as contractural. These would include relationships at work. We may never become close friends with the boss or with other employees, but we do owe them a pretty high level of loyalty. We have kind of a contract with them. This contract may not be in writing, but it makes certain demands on us. Loyalty will require us to do our work, respect our fellow workers, and look out for the best interests of those for whom and with whom we work. In a sense we also have a kind of contract or covenant with fellow church members, too. We are not close and intimate friends with everyone with whom we worship, especially if we attend a larger church, but we have a responsibility to be loyal to them regardless. As brothers and sisters in Christ, we must be available to them and open to them, even if they are not in the circle of our closest friends.

A higher degree of loyalty operates in relationships that are deep and personal but not permanent or continuous. Sometimes we cross the path of a person who plays a very important role in our lives for a while. These may be people with whom we work on a special project, or it may be someone who shares a burden with us at a special time of need. I have always believed that God brings certain people into our lives just when we need them or just when they need us. Valuable and beautiful relationships are often brief. Circumstances, distance, time, or need may make a long-term friendship difficult, but these relationships are important. They should be cherished and remembered. We owe a high degree of loyalty to the people we encounter on this level. In some cases these relationships develop into lifelong friendships.

Finally, the highest loyalty is required for those relationships that wrap themselves around our lives forever. All of us have people in our lives who will always be there. Many times the very direction of our lives is determined by these relationships. These are the people who matter most of all to us. Included in this category would be family, loved ones, and our closest friends. We may give many things to these people, but most importantly, we love them, and we are loyal to them—no matter what.

Nothing is so painful as to feel that a person in this inner circle has shown disloyalty to you. It is important not to jump to hasty conclusions in this regard. We are often mistaken in our assessment of a situation. Love and loyalty would teach us to give our loved ones the benefit of the doubt. Loyalty also calls us to forgive our loved ones. Barnabas had to forgive Mark for quitting on him on the missionary journey. True love always includes the willingness to forgive. Loyalty, at this high level, also involves refusing to be petty and little. If we truly love someone, we must be more concerned with their feelings and needs than with our own. This is never easy. If we feel betrayed or left out, it is human and natural to feel hurt and anger. Loyalty calls us to deal with these quickly, and then go on loving the person even if we feel they have let us down.

Barnabas was a loyal person. We need people like him today. Our friends and associates should know they can count on us. We can give them that gift even if we have no other to give.

The positive way that Barnabas encouraged other people is another quality I admire. By now, you are familiar with the fact that this was the strong point of Barnabas's ministry. He made it his business to encourage. He was always positive in his dealings with others. We need people who will do that today.

One of my favorite Old Testament stories comes from the life of the prophet Elisha. The king of Syria was at war with Israel, but his plans were being spoiled because the king of Israel seemed always to know what was coming next. The king of Syria thought someone in his own ranks was giving information to Israel. When he called in his officers to confront them about this, one of them reported that it was the prophet Elisha who was able to predict what the Syrians were about to do. Elisha was giving the information to the king of Israel. The Syrian king was furious. He decided to go after Elisha and put a stop to his prophesying. Just to make certain that he got his man, the king sent a large contingent of soldiers, horses, and chariots. He completely surrounded the town where Elisha was staying.

Early the next day, Elisha's servant got up and walked out of the house where Elisha was staying. He was terrified when he saw that the Syrians had them completely surrounded. The servant ran into the house and announced to Elisha: "We are doomed sir! What shall we do?" (2 Kings 6:15).

What followed is thrilling. Elisha said to his frightened servant: "Don't be afraid. . . . We have more on our side than they have on theirs" (v. 16). The servant probably thought Elisha had taken leave of his sanity. Elisha had no soldiers, horses, or chariots. How could they possibly defend themselves against this siege? And how could the prophet even imagine that he had more forces than the Syrians?

Then Elisha prayed for his terrified servant: "O Lord, open his eyes and let him see!" (v. 17a). The old prophet's prayer was answered. When the servant looked up, he was amazed to see: "The hillside covered with horses and chariots of fire all around Elisha" (v. 17b). Obviously, the angelic forces were poised to defend the prophet. The Syrians were no match for them. I believe you will agree with me that Elisha gave his servant some positive encouragement. He helped him see that, even though the situation was serious, resources were available to meet the test. If the servant could only get his eyes opened, he would not need to be afraid. God used Elisha as an eye-opener for his servant.

As we relate to people, we can either focus on the dangers, difficulties, and problems; or we can help them see that there is hope, beauty, and the promise of victory. We can be spreaders of bad news or heralds of good news.

Positive encouragement can make the difference to people, and we have it in our power to give them that precious gift.

Do you know someone who always looks on the dark side of everything? Negative thinking and a gloomy outlook are powerful forces for evil. People who think and talk doom and gloom pull themselves and others down to discouragement, defeat, and even despair. How do you feel when you are with a negative, self-pitying person who is certain that nothing is going to work out?

On the other hand, do you know a positive encourager? Such a person does not ignore a problem but looks for an answer. This kind of person believes in the good and has confidence in God's power to help us work things out. The encourager finds hope in almost any situation. Most of all, a person like this believes in people and truly enjoys being able to help them. The word *hopeless* is not in the encourager's vocabulary. How do you feel when you are with this kind of person? If you are like most people, this kind of positive encouragement will give you the will and strength to give it your best even if the circumstances are rough.

A friend told me a story about a great college football coach who always seemed to be able to motivate his players to give super effort. The coach's team was playing one of its traditional rivals, but things were not going so well that Saturday. A series of early mistakes had permitted the opposing team to build a 21-0 lead by halftime. The game seemed almost out of hand and the lead insurmountable. At the halftime break, the great coach and his players filed into their dressing room. The things normally done at halftime were done: first aid for injuries, equipment changes, wrapping sprained ankles, and specific coaching instructions by assistant coaches. The head coach said nothing. He just walked around among the players and coaches and watched what was going on. Finally, just as it was time to go back to the field for the second half, the renowned coach made his brief and to-the-point speech. He looked at his discouraged players and said: "Let's get back out there, men. I believe we've just about got 'em." The team went to the field, dominated the second half of play, and won by a score of 35-21. Now that's positive encouragement.

All through the pages of this book we have examined the positive attitude of Barnabas—the Encourager. We have looked at the biblical passages that tell his story. These passages present an impressive picture of a man who was devoted to Jesus Christ and cared deeply for people. We must not get the impression that Barnabas was a perfect person—there aren't any of those. Yet, he was a man who cared so much that he filled his life with positive, loving, and affirming relationships.

The remaining pages of this book will have just one purpose. That purpose is to challenge all who read them to be Barnabas people.

By now, you know I believe we need people like Barnabas more than we need anything else in the area of human relationships. We have a rather good collection of superstars in our society. There are the top executives, famous entertainers, able athletes, and more than a few powerful religious leaders. We need all these people up at the top of the human mountain, but even more, we need Barnabas people at every level of life.

We hear a plenty these days about "looking out for number one," productivity, and even intimidation if that's what it takes to win. We start boys and girls out early with the win-at-any-cost mentality. Little boys and girls are introduced to competitive sports soon after they are old enough to walk. Many valuable lessons are learned in sports. You've probably guessed by now that I am an avid sports fan. We live in a competitive society, and sports is a way to teach youngsters to compete fairly. They learn how to win, but they also learn how to lose, and everyone will do both of those all through life. Yet, parents and coaches often put a terrible burden to perform and win on children. Too often they are taught that losing a game or making a mistake means they are failures. They are also permitted to "rub it in" when they win. Is it any wonder that we often see the disgraceful spectacle of a college or professional athlete standing over a vanquished opponent and taunting them? Recently, I even heard of a well-known college player who sometimes spits on a player after he tackles him.

This attitude carries over into every area of life. Some bosses and supervisors are tyrants. They push their people to the limit to squeeze every drop of productivity out of them. In many homes there are tyrannical husbands, self-indulgent husbands and wives, unreasonable parents, and disrespectful, self-centered children. Even in the churches, there are sometimes those who seem determined to have their own way.

The reason these things exist is a misunderstanding of the legendary "bottom line." If the "bottom line" is winning at any cost, making a profit, even if it means misusing people, getting one's own way, or even building a great religious institution, then we'll do whatever is necessary to get the job done. If that means using or hurting people, the end justifies the means.

If, however, the "bottom line" is people, that is far different. Winning will still be important. A profit will still need to be made. Self-actualization will still be desirable. Building a great church will still be a worthy goal. But none of these things will be done at the expense of other people. We will see that people are most important of all. We will try to look out for them, even as we try to take care of ourselves. Surely, this is what Jesus meant when He taught that we are to love our neighbor as we love ourselves.

The competitive pressures of our society are a reality. Like it or not, winning or making a profit is important. In many cases it is essential. You can't stay in business if you don't show a profit. Our society doesn't cheer very much for losers. But even so, we can put the priority on people. That is where it must be.

I recently talked with a man who worked for a large company for eight years. The pressures of his job—traveling, deadlines, and long hours—were very demanding. But the thing that finally brought this man down was that nothing he did was ever enough. His supervisor criticized everything he did. When things went well, there was never any praise. When something went wrong, he was subjected to a tirade. Finally the man became physically ill. Stomach disorders, hypertension, and even seizures turned him into a physical and mental basket case. His family life began to disintegrate. Finally his doctor told him that he had to get away from that job before it literally killed him.

Mercifully, a new job opportunity opened up for him. That was four years ago. This man still travels, he still works long hours, and he still has a lot of responsibility. But there is a big difference. The people he now works for value and appreciate him. They encourage and affirm him. They even insist that he take some time off once in a while. He now works for Barnabas-like people. The "bottom line" with Barnabas was people.

The good news is that every one of us can be a Barnabas person. We can't all be powerful executives, top-name entertainers, superstar athletes, influential politicians, or big church pastors; but we can all do what Barnabas did so well. We can be encouragers for others. Of course, the powerful people at the top can also be Barnabas people—and many of them are. But the point is that, even those of us who walk ordinary paths, can do what needs most to be done. We can care for others.

This is not to say that being a Barnabas person is easy.

It isn't easy at all. The person who wants to be an encourager has to guard against the all-too-human tendency to become self-centered. This is a battle we all have to fight. If we aren't careful, we can become more concerned about being loved than being loving toward others. Of course, we must be willing to receive from others what they want to give to us, but once we start loving in order to be loved, we become selfish. Barnabas living involves both giving and receiving. It ebbs and flows; that is, sometimes our needs are so great that we should take gratefully what others are willing to give us. At other times the needs of others will dictate that we do most of the giving while they receive. This reciprocity is vital to human relationships. It is not selfish to receive from others, but it is selfish and wrong always to expect others to meet our needs and desires.

Another thing that can make a Barnabas life-style difficult at times is that there are times when our love and encouragement are not accepted by others. Because they have been hurt or taken advantage of, some people wonder if we have a "hidden agenda" when we tray to give love to them. It hurts when our motives and intentions are doubted. We can't force our caring on anyone. About all we can do is to give as much of ourselves as the other person can accept. Then, we can hope that barriers of mistrust and cynicism can be broken down with time.

Then, of course, we are going to encounter people who are not easy to love. We are going to meet some people who are unpleasant or cruel. We are going to have some people disappoint us or let us down. Remember, you can only give what someone else is willing to receive. Modern-day Barnabas people are responsible to offer love, affirmation, and encouragement. They will look for the best and give people every possible opportunity to respond. But the way others receive the caring is their responsibility.

Really, there are only two necessary ingredients in a Barnabas style of living. One is a sincere commitment to Jesus Christ. This provides the spiritual dynamic for unselfish living. The second essential is a genuine concern for other people and a willingness to be sensitive to their needs. These qualities can be cultivated in every person's life. Anyone who is willing to pay the price can be a Barnabas.

My first year working at the Baptist Sunday School Board was very difficult. I had taken a sizable reduction in pay to come to Nashville. Then, to make matters worse, we were unable to sell our house in Louisville. Interest rates were very high, and the Louisville real estate market was at a virtual standstill. For almost a year I lived in one room in Nashville while Diann, my wife, remained in Louisville trying to sell the house. At one point, I got very discouraged with the situation. It seemed to me that nothing was ever going to work out. I began to question seriously my decision to come to Nashville in the first place. I was seriously considering just giving up and trying to find another job. In my discouraged state of mind, I was imagining that no one really cared what happened to me.

One day I was sitting in my office when my telephone rang. When I answered, the person on the other end of the line identified himself as one of the most influential and powerful men at the Board. He asked if he could come to my office to talk with me. I straightened up the clutter on my desk while I waited for him to arrive. When this important man walked into my office, he sat down across from me and told me he knew I was struggling. He complimented me for hanging tough and not giving up. (He didn't know how close I was to quitting.) He said he wanted me to know that he was concerned about my situation. He even gave me his home telephone number and said if I ever needed him I could call. Finally, just before he left, he asked if he could pray for me. His prayer was simple, caring, and sincere. When he walked out of my office, I sat at my desk for a long time just thinking about what he had said and done. His visit to me didn't sell our house in Louisville or put one dime into my pocket. It did far more than that. It gave me the courage to go on. How could I quit when someone believed in me? That man was my Barnabas that day.

I meet a lot of interesting people as I travel in my work. Sometimes brief encounters with people I'll probably never see again prove to be serendipities and make an imprint on my life. A recent flight from Nashville to Dallas provided me with such an experience.

I was a bit hurried and tired as I walked briskly through the boarding gate onto the airplane. It had been a busy week with tremendous pressure. I had just returned from

Baltimore the day before. Now I was on my way to Tucson, by way of Dallas. When I got to my assigned seat, 10B, it was filled with the belongings of the passenger seated in 10A, a young black woman. I pushed aside the temptation to be irritated that my seat was filled with all her stuff and instead offered to help her put it where it belonged. I put her bag in the overhead compartment and picked up her army uniform on a hanger draped across my seat and took it for her to the hang-up closet. Finally, I made my way back to 10B, stowed my own belongings overhead, and sat down beside the young woman. She smiled, thanked me for helping her, and explained that she was not accustomed to traveling on airplanes. I asked where she was headed, and she told me she was going to Fort Bliss, Texas, where she would be stationed. She had just completed her basic training in South Carolina and had been on leave in her small Kentucky hometown.

As she spoke, I heard her voice break a little bit, and when I looked at her face, I saw glistening tears on her cheeks. All at once I felt like she was my little sister or maybe the daughter I never had. (We have two terrific sons.) I touched her arm and told her I was sorry if I had said anything to upset her. She said she was just a little frightened about her new life in the army, so far away from home and from the special young man who had just told her good-bye at the airport.

As we talked for the next hour or so, I learned quite a bit about Alicia. I learned that she was afraid of flying because of terrorists. I learned that she worried about a possible war while she would be serving in the army. And I learned that she hoped to finish college while in the military. She was studying criminal justice. She said her interest was to understand why young people commit crimes and to help them in some way. She hoped, too, someday to marry the young man she had just left at the boarding gate in Nashville.

The pilot announced that we were making our descent into Dallas. We would be on the ground in a matter of minutes. When the big jet was parked at the gate, I helped Alicia gather her things up and told her I would help her find her gate for her flight to El Paso. We got off the plane together, found a representative of the airline, and asked for the gate numbers—Tucson for me, El Paso for Alicia. Alicia's gate was the next one over. Mine was ten minutes away. She said she would be OK, and I wished her well in her new adventure. I told her not to be afraid because she would make many new friends and learn many new things. She smiled, with a tear glistening in her eye, and said simply, "Thank-you." As I turned to go, Alicia reached and touched my arm. Then, she gently hugged me and walked away.

As I walked to my gate, I marveled at what had just happened. I am certain I'll never see the young woman soldier again, but for an hour or so, I had been her encourager and friend. It felt good to be a Barnabas.

And that's what Barnabas living is all about. It is giving what you can to help some fellow or sister pilgrim on the way. Then, it is opening your heart in gratitude as some modern-day Barnabas speaks just the word or gives just the touch you need so very much.

Be a Barnabas person. An old song of the early 1930s went:

> Give to the world
>   the best you have,
> and the best will come
>   back to you.

That's *a Barnabas Life-style*!

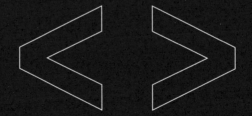

The MIT Press Essential Knowledge series

METADATA

JEFFREY POMERANTZ

The MIT Press | Cambridge, Massachusetts | London, England

MIT Press books may be purchased at special quantity discounts for business or sales promotional use. For information, please email special_sales@ mitpress.mit.edu or write to Special Sales Department, The MIT Press, 1 Rogers Street, Cambridge, MA 02142.

Set in Chaparral Pro by the MIT Press. Printed and bound in the United States of America.

Library of Congress Cataloging-in-Publication Data
Pomerantz, Jeffrey, author.

Metadata / Jeffrey Pomerantz.
    pages   cm.—(The MIT Press essential knowledge series)
Includes bibliographical references and index.
ISBN 978-0-262-52851-1 (pbk. : alk. paper) 1. Metadata. 2. Information organization. I. Title.
Z666.7.P66   2015
025.3—dc23
                                                                    2015030578

10   9   8   7   6   5   4   3   2   1

CONTENTS

SERIES FOREWORD

The MIT Press Essential Knowledge series offers accessible, concise, beautifully produced pocket-size books on topics of current interest. Written by leading thinkers, the books in this series deliver expert overviews of subjects that range from the cultural and the historical to the scientific and the technical.

In today's era of instant information gratification, we have ready access to opinions, rationalizations, and superficial descriptions. Much harder to come by is the foundational knowledge that informs a principled understanding of the world. Essential Knowledge books fill that need. Synthesizing specialized subject matter for nonspecialists and engaging critical topics through fundamentals, each of these compact volumes offers readers a point of access to complex ideas.

Bruce Tidor
Professor of Biological Engineering and Computer Science
Massachusetts Institute of Technology

PREFACE

This book was borne largely out of a massive open online course (MOOC) that I taught for the University of North Carolina at Chapel Hill on the Coursera platform, in the fall of 2013 and again in the spring of 2014, titled "Metadata: Organizing and Discovering Information." Online teaching and learning is not a new idea by any means, but MOOCs focused a great deal of attention on this form of pedagogy, both inside and outside the academy. I had been teaching online for many years when MOOCs hit the news in 2011, but the sheer scale of a MOOC captured my attention. I got to thinking about what teaching and learning in Information Science might look like, if it were entirely online. I believed then, and still do, that the first course in any Information Science curriculum should be a course on metadata: almost everything else in the field depends on metadata, and the subject provides a hook into most of the issues in the field. So when Carolina decided to launch its MOOC initiative, I was very excited to have the opportunity to launch a course on metadata, to put my ideas to the test.

I'm very pleased about how well the metadata MOOC was received. And I'm equally pleased that the course caused metadata to come to the attention of the editors of the MIT Press, as a topic worthy of being included in the

Essential Knowledge series. So my first thank you must be to Margy Avery, for first suggesting the idea of this book.

Naturally I also must thank the University of North Carolina at Chapel Hill, for launching its MOOC initiative in the first place, and for supporting us MOOC instructors during the production process. I must also express a great deal of thanks to my teaching assistant for the MOOC, Meredith Lewis.

I would like to thank the nearly 50,000 students who registered for the course... and especially to the 17,464 students who actually participated in the course across both sessions.

I recorded several interviews for the MOOC, with people who are doing interesting and cutting-edge things with metadata. This provided (I hope) useful supplementary material for the course, and saved the students from having to watch my ugly mug all the time. I learned a great deal in conducting these interviews, and that inevitably made it into this book as well. So let me thank my interviewees: Murtha Baca, of the Getty Research Institute; Robert Glushko, Adjunct Full Professor in the School of Information at the University of California at Berkeley; Steve Hogan, Music Analyst at Pandora; Hunter Janes, Data Analyst at Red Storm Entertainment; Clifford Lynch, Director of the Coalition for Networked Information; and Jason Scott, of the Internet Archive.

The interviews for the MOOC went so well that I decided to do some more, specifically for this book. Thanks to Mary Forster, Joel Steinpreis, and Joel Summerlin of Getty Images for a fascinating conversation about image metadata.

Thanks to Clifford Lynch, again, for bringing pen registers to my attention, and for pointing me in the right direction while researching the history of the word "metadata."

Thanks to Ted Johnson, of Studio 713, for helping me to understand music metadata.

Thanks to Jessamyn West, for helping me find images of catalog cards.

This book is dedicated to my daughters, Charlotte and Eleanor, who thought it was cool that I was writing a book.

INTRODUCTION

Metadata is all around us, all the time. In the modern era of ubiquitous electronics, nearly every device you use relies on metadata or generates it, or both. But when metadata is doing its job well, it just fades into the background, unnoticed and nearly invisible. And this is partly how, in the summer of 2013, metadata came to be a *cause célèbre*.

Edward Snowden, a subcontractor to the United States National Security Agency, flew to Hong Kong in May of 2013 to meet with journalists from *The Guardian*. There, Snowden handed over a large number of classified documents about the NSA's surveillance program within the United States. One of these programs, PRISM, included collecting data on telephone calls directly from telecommunications companies. Needless to say, this was very big news when *The Guardian* published the story.

Reactions in the US media to the Snowden revelations were varied, and their evolution was significant. The immediate reaction was anger that the NSA was collecting data on US citizens. This was quickly tempered by relief, when it became clear that the NSA was only collecting metadata about calls, and not the calls themselves—in other words, the NSA was not engaging in wiretapping. After that came punditry, as the media explored just how much information about individuals could be inferred from "only" metadata.

The MetaPhone study, conducted by researchers at the Stanford Law School Center for Internet and Society in late 2013, attempted to replicate the NSA's data collection of phone metadata. What they discovered was that a truly incredible amount of information can be inferred from "only" metadata. One example that the MetaPhone researchers report is of a study participant who called "a home improvement store, locksmiths, a hydroponics dealer, and a head shop." Perhaps this individual had perfectly innocent reasons for placing all of these calls, and perhaps these calls were entirely unrelated... but that's not the inference that most of us are likely to make.

A lot of metadata is associated with phone calls, particularly cell phone calls. Probably the most obvious pieces of metadata about a call are the phone numbers of the caller and the recipient. Then, of course, there's the time and duration of the call. And for calls made from smartphones—most of which have GPS functionality—there are the locations of the caller and the recipient, at least to the level of precision of the range of the cell phone towers in which the phones are located. There's more metadata than this associated with cell phone calls, but even this small amount is enough to give privacy advocates pause. Because your phone exchanges data with local cell towers, even when you're not on a call. And, of course, your phone is presumably being carried by you. A record of your location at any given moment, and your movements over time, may therefore be collected by your cell phone service provider ... and is in fact collected, as the Snowden revelations revealed.

Thus did the word "metadata" enter the public conversation. Though, given how pervasive metadata is, a public conversation about it is probably overdue; it deserves to be better understood. In the modern era of ubiquitous computing, metadata has become infrastructural, like the electrical grid or the highway system. These pieces of modern infrastructure are indispensible but are also only the tip of the iceberg: when you flick on a lightswitch, for example, you are the end user of a large set of technologies and policies. Individually, these technologies and policies may be minor, and may seem trivial... but in the aggregate, they have far-reaching cultural and economic implications. And it's the same with metadata. Metadata, like the electrical grid and the highway system, fades into the background of everyday life, taken for granted as just part of what makes modern life run smoothly.

As citizens of the modern world we all are familiar with and have a reasonable (though probably incomplete) understanding of the electrical grid and the highway system, and many other pieces of modern infrastructure. But unless you're an information scientist—or an intelligence analyst working for the NSA—the same is probably not true of metadata.

And so we arrive at the purpose of this book. This book will introduce you to the topic of metadata, and the wide range of topics and issues that metadata touches on. We will discuss what metadata is, and why it exists. We will look at a range of different types of metadata, for different users and use cases. We will talk about some of the technologies that make modern metadata possible, and we will speculate about the future of metadata. And by the end of the book, you will be seeing metadata everywhere.

It's metadata's world, and you're just living in it.

Invisible Metadata

When you picked up this book from your local bookstore shelves, you were using metadata. What attracted you to this book, to cause you to pick it up? Was it the title, the publisher, the cover art? Whatever it was, it almost certainly was *not* the content of the book itself. Of course, now that you are reading this, you have some information about the content of this book, but you did not have that information before you picked it up. You had to rely on other cues, other pieces of information about the book. Those other pieces of information are metadata: data about this book.

When metadata is doing its job well, it fades into the background, almost to the point of being invisible. You're so used to seeing books with titles and publishers and cover art, that it probably didn't even register with you that this book has those things too. It would probably only have registered if this book *didn't* have a title or publisher or cover art. We're so conditioned to metadata about books being part of our book-buying environment that we don't even think about it. We're so conditioned to metadata about lots of things being part of our everyday environment that we don't even think about it. How did it come to be this way?

A Brief History of Metadata

The word metadata only came into the English language in 1968, but the idea of metadata goes back to the first library. The word is a deliberate play on Aristotle's *Metaphysics*. Though Aristotle never called those particular works by that name, they have historically been collected together under that title, to indicate that they came after, or dealt with topics beyond the *Physics*. Similarly the word "metadata" indicates something that is beyond the data: a statement or statements about the data. Linguistically this is a loose translation of the Greek prefix "meta-," but it is consistent with what has become the everyday use of the word "meta," to indicate something at a higher level of abstraction.

Although the word "metadata" is only a few decades old, librarians have been working with metadata for thousands of years. Though what we now call "metadata" has historically just been called "information in the library catalog." The information in a library catalog is intended to solve a very specific problem: to help users of the library find materials in the library's collection.

The *Pinakes* is considered by historians to be the first library catalog, created by Callimachus for the Library of Alexandria, around 245 BC. Only fragments of the *Pinakes* have survived the intervening millennia, but here's what is known: works were listed by genre, title, and author's name, along with some biographical information about each author. Additionally a summary, and the total number of lines of a work were included. Fast-forward more than two thousand years, and we're still using many of the same pieces of information in library catalogs: author, subject, blurb, length.

To be fair, however, we now use more pieces of information in library catalogs than Callimachus did. The *call number* of the work is ubiquitous: a number or other alphanumeric string, according to some scheme (the Dewey decimal system, for example), that lets the library user locate a work on the shelves. Call numbers are especially critical for large collections, as users must navigate the correspondingly large physical space occupied by the collection to find individual items. It's difficult to imagine how Callimachus could have developed the *Pinakes* without also inventing call numbers, since the Library of Alexandria is said to have included half a million works, which is a fairly large collection even by modern standards.

The *Pinakes* was a set of scrolls. If you have ever read from the Torah in synagogue, you know that a scroll is not the most user-friendly interface: moving between sections is a challenge. Indeed there's an entire holiday in the Jewish calendar (Simchat Torah) that celebrates coming to the end of reading the Torah, and rolling the whole thing back to the beginning. If you've never read from the Torah, think about using other scroll-like technologies: an audiocassette, or a VHS tape. Indeed stickers exhorting us to "Be kind, please rewind" used to be common on rental VHS tapes. In short, the *Pinakes* could not have been a picnic from the standpoint of usability.

The codex—what we moderns just call *the book*—is in many ways a superior user interface to the scroll. Thus, inevitably, once the codex was invented, it was adopted for use as library catalogs. Library catalogs in book form were often what is called a "shelf list," which is exactly what it sounds like: a list of books on the shelves, often in the order in which they were acquired by the library. This order makes it easy to add new entries—just write them in at the end—but is still not very user-friendly when one wants to find an individual item in the list.

The library catalog made a great leap forward with the invention of the card catalog in France, around the time of the French Revolution. This innovation atomized the shelf list, making it simple to add or remove entries, as well as to find entries for individual items. A scroll or a codex cannot be easily edited once completed, but to add an entry into a card catalog, all you have to do is slip a new card into the correct spot.

The card catalog atomized the library catalog by making each record—each entry for a book—an individual object that could be manipulated independently. The pieces of data within each record, however—the title of the book, the author's name, and so on—had been atomized all the way back to the *Pinakes*. Even if the individual pieces of data on a catalog card are not labeled as title, author, etc., it's understood what categories each piece of data represents. Thus the catalog card is atomized along two dimensions: records for individual items, and categories of data shared by all items.

And with that atomization along two dimensions, we arrive at databases, and the modern approach to metadata. When you break up a dataset into records, where each

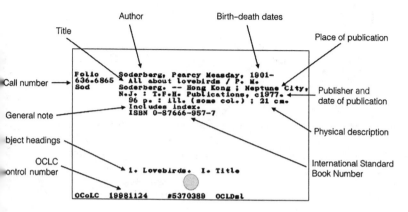

Figure 1

record represents an individual item, and records contain categories of data, where each category is shared across items, you have essentially just invented the spreadsheet.

Imagine a spreadsheet: each row is a record for a single object, and each column is a single characteristic of those objects. Now imagine a spreadsheet containing data about books. What would be the headers of our columns? Title, author, publisher, date of publication, place of publication, subject, call number, number of pages, format, dimensions, you name it. Each row, then, would be a record for a single book, containing all of these pieces of data about that specific book. Such a spreadsheet could be used as a library catalog.

Table 1

Title	Author	Date of publication	Subject	Call number	Pages
Intellectual Property Strategy	Palfrey, John	2012	Intellectual property —Management	HD53 .P35 2012	172
Open Access	Suber, Peter	2012	Open access publishing	Z286.O63 S83 2012	242
Memes in Digital Culture	Shifman, Limor	2014	Social evolution. Memes. Culture diffusion. Internet— Social aspects. Memetics.	HM626 .S55 2014	200

Ceci n'est pas une pipe

But why store data *about* an object, when you have the object itself?

The scientist and philosopher Alfred Korzybski is perhaps best remembered for his quote, "the map is not the territory" (a quote that is frequently misattributed to Marshall McLuhan). This quote has been analyzed and commented upon for nearly a hundred years, in both science and art (including by McLuhan). Korzybski first wrote this line in a paper about language, and it's language that will be discussed in this section.

Language is a map, according to Korzybski. Language is a means by which we collapse the incredible complexity of the world down into a much simpler form. The word for a thing is not the thing itself: the name Jeffrey is not me, in any meaningful way, but under some conditions it represents me. Language allows humans to understand things in the world, even if that understanding is merely a simplified representation of those things.

There are many kinds of maps: road maps, topographical maps, nautical charts, star maps; the list goes on and on. Different kinds of maps serve different functions, and they're not interchangeable: a nautical chart is well-nigh useless when planning a driving trip. So what do all of these different things called "map" have in common? Just this: they boil down the richness and complexity of the physical world to just the details that one needs in a particular situation. When you are driving, you need to know what roads go where and how they intersect, which roads are one-way, and how to get on the highway, and you probably don't need topographic information, or depth soundings. The map is not the territory because the map is both a separate object from the territory, and much simpler.

Similarly metadata is a map. Metadata is a means by which the complexity of an object is represented in a simpler form. The author of the novel *Moby Dick* is Herman Melville, it's about whaling, the original date of publication is 1851. This is a very thin representation of a lengthy and complex book. But it's probably enough to enable you to locate a copy of it, if you wished to do so.

Metadata is a map. Metadata is a means by which the complexity of an object is represented in a simpler form.

A roomful of books is not a library. In order to find a specific book in a library, one would not simply walk around and hope to spot it. Even a small library is too large an information space for that to be practical. Instead, libraries make use of a metaphorical map: the catalog. The catalog provides the library user with a simplified representation of the materials in the library collection. Within the catalog, the library user finds the record for the specific item she wants. The catalog record then provides the user with a critical piece of metadata: the call number. The call number corresponds to a location in the information space of the library, which enables the user to move from the record to the actual object described by the record.

Why store data about an object, when you have the object itself? Because without data about the objects contained in a space, any sufficiently complex space is indistinguishable from chaos. Even when an object is contained within a space, if you want to find it again in a timely fashion, you need metadata about it. If you have ever lost your keys in your own house, you understand how useful even a single piece of metadata can be.

Metadata, not Just for Libraries Anymore

Librarians have been in the business of describing things for more than 2,000 years, and have inevitably learned a thing or two. The discipline of Library Science has given the rest of the world a lot of insight into how to describe things effectively.

Thanks largely to librarians working out principles of description, it is now possible for anyone to apply those principles to anything that needs to be described. Furthermore, once the database was invented and it became possible to store structured data, it also became possible for anyone to create and maintain metadata electronically.

While libraries were early adopters of computer and database technologies, they were far from the only adopters. Prior to the development of the minicomputer, library metadata was stored in specialized and custom-built repositories, such as shelf lists and card catalogs. After the development of the minicomputer, library metadata was stored using the same technologies that everyone else was using.

With the advent of the database, it became possible to create and store structured data about anything, not just descriptive metadata about resources in library collections. Of course, businesses and governments, in particular, have always collected and stored structured data for more than descriptive purposes: ledgers of profit and loss, inventories, tax documents, censuses, and the like, have existed on paper—and even earlier technologies—for millennia. But these were never considered to be metadata; these were simply the documents generated by and that made possible the daily operations of businesses, governments, and other organizations. As these operations came to be performed using computers, however, it became possible not only to reference an object from a document about it (which, of course, you can do in a paper document, or even on a cuneiform tablet), it became possible to provide an actual link to that object in a file system. This functionality is so ingrained in modern life, as the web is so ingrained in modern life, that it's difficult to convey how radically this changed the way in which documents are managed.

What's It All For?

You're so conditioned to metadata being part of your everyday environment that you don't even think about it. Maps, signs, dashboards, web searches, ATMs, grocery stores, phone calls, the list could go on indefinitely. Metadata is central to how all of these things operate, and to how you interact with them. For most of us, it would be undesirable to have access to the full complexity of a banking system or the telephone network. Interacting with the complex systems of modern life requires a simplified interface between the system and us, and that interface usually relies on metadata.

This is particularly true where information systems are concerned. Prior to the advent of the web, if you were interested in, say, the life of Herman Melville—I heard he sailed on a whaling ship, is that true?—you needed to either own a copy of a biography of the man, or get one from a library. The same can be said for almost any information object. Nowadays, however, information objects are just a web search away. And doing a web search will fetch you more information objects than you want. A search for "Herman Melville biography" gets me hundreds of thousands of results, which is more than I can process in my lifetime.

The term for this in information science jargon is "resource discovery." Resource discovery is, as you might expect, the process of identifying information resources that might be relevant to my information need—in this case, information about the life of Herman Melville.

The idea of *relevance* is slippery though, as it's highly subjective: what's relevant to you, what information fulfills your information need, may not be the same as what's relevant to me, even if the questions that we articulate are similar. For example, I may be interested in knowing if Melville sailed on a whaling ship, you may be interested in whether he has any living heirs, but both of us might conduct a web search for "Herman Melville biography." Whether or not a specific information resource is relevant is a subjective judgment call, and therefore can only be made by an individual after having processed that information resource.

In general, however, metadata is not used to capture subjective interpretations of resources such as relevance, but rather to capture objective features of resources such as descriptions. Resource discovery relies on good metadata like this. If you were to go to a library to find a biography of Herman Melville, the success of your search (assuming that such a book exists in your local library) depends on the records for one or more resources containing the text "Herman Melville" in the subject field, and some indication that a book is a biography. To use our map metaphor: the simplified representations of information objects that are contained in the catalog must include data that will help you discover resources that you might find relevant.

This type of metadata is called *descriptive metadata*. This is exactly what it sounds like: metadata that provides a description of an object. In this book thus far, descriptive metadata is the only type of metadata that has been discussed, but it is not the only type there is. In fact there are several categories of metadata. *Administrative metadata* provides information about the origin and maintenance of an object: for example, a photograph might have been digitized using a specific type of scanner at a particular resolution, and might have some copyright restrictions associated with it. *Structural metadata* provides information about how an object is organized: for example, a book is composed of chapters, a chapter is composed of pages, and those chapters and pages must be put together in a particular order. *Preservation metadata* provides information necessary to support the process of preserving an object:

for example, it may be necessary to emulate a specific application and operating system environment in order to interact with a digital file. Both structural and preservation metadata are sometimes considered to be subcategories of administrative metadata, as data about the structure of an object and how to preserve it are both necessary to administer the object. Finally, *use metadata* provides information about how an object has been used: for example, the publisher of an electronic book might track how many downloads the book has received, on what dates, and profile data about the users who downloaded it.

All of these flavors of metadata will be explored in more depth as this book progresses. But first the terminology that will be used throughout the rest of this book will be defined.

DEFINITIONS

Information science, like any discipline, has its share of jargon terms. The word "metadata" is one of these, though it has crept into more common usage in the past few years. To investigate metadata, as this book does, inevitably also means to encounter other jargon terms. In this chapter we will explore these terms, and define them as best as possible.

The most common—and perhaps least useful—definition of metadata is that it is "data about data." As catchy as this definition is, however, it is entirely ambiguous. First of all, what is data? And second, what does "about" mean?

Information We Have Lost in Data

We will start by trying to understand what data is. This is, unfortunately, leaping into the deep end of the pool: *data* is such a nebulous concept that even information scientists, who have devoted their entire careers to this phenomenon, don't always agree.

T. S. Eliot's poem *The Rock* is a favorite among information scientists, for the following two lines:

Where is the wisdom we have lost in knowledge?
Where is the knowledge we have lost in information?

Eliot seems to posit a hierarchy: wisdom, knowledge, and information, in order of decreasing desirability. Information scientists tend not to feel quite so negatively about information, but we do often make use of this same hierarchy—though with the addition of *data* below information. This hierarchy—data, information, knowledge, wisdom—is invoked to explain levels of informativeness, or stages of information in the realm of human cognition. Data, according to this view, is the raw stuff: what is collected by instrumentation or machinery. The stream of bits sent to Earth by a Mars Rover, for example, is data. The signal carried by radio frequencies between your phone and the local cell tower is data. Information, then, is data that has been processed into a form that may be consumed by a human being: that stream of bits converted to an image, for example, or that signal modulated into sound. This is slippery ground, however: there's a philosophical debate to be had about whether something is information if it has only the *potential* to inform someone, or if it has to *actually* inform someone. (If a tree falls in the forest and no one is around, does it generate information?) But we will ignore that issue here, and refer the reader to the Further Readings section, for some articles that deal with this issue. Knowledge, then, is what you know, information that you have internalized. Wisdom is knowing what to do with that knowledge.

Data is stuff. It is raw, unprocessed, possibly even untouched by human hands, unviewed by human eyes, un-thought-about by human minds. We're not used to thinking of information objects in this way: we're used to thinking of information objects as things like books, or files on our computer, things that have been deliberately created by humans, and where human understanding is an integral part of their creation. However, think about the stream of bits sent to Earth by the Mars Rover, or a book in, for example, Lushootseed (or some other language that you neither speak nor read... and apologies if you actually do know Lushootseed): you may know that a stream of bits or a book in Lushootseed has some meaning embedded in it, but without some processing, that meaning is not accessible to you. Data is *potential* information, analogous to potential energy: work is required to release it.

Books are used as examples throughout this book, for the simple reason that they are well understood: chances are that if you're reading this book, you're familiar with the technology of books in general. The problem with using books as an example is that strictly speaking, a book is not data: a book is a *container* for data but is not the data itself. A book is fundamentally a lump of processed wood; the data are the words contained inside it. The words are the wine; the book is the bottle. (You could even go a step further and argue that the words are also a bottle and the wine is the ideas.) This container metaphor will serve us well, since almost everything that will be discussed throughout this book is a bottle, not wine. Metadata is data, but metadata cannot exist outside of a container: a metadata record must exist in some format, be it physical or digital. Likewise a metadata record is itself a container for data about an object. And that object may itself be a container for data, in the case of that object being a book or other information object. And so again, we're faced with the difficulty of differentiating between data and information... and again, we're going to ignore that issue. It is sufficient for our purposes to acknowledge that a metadata record is a container.

Describing Description

Let us now move on to the concept of *aboutness*. The word "about" is so commonplace that spending any time defining it seems as hairsplitting as debating what the meaning of the word "is" is. But there *is* a lot of debate about "about."

The word "about" indicates description. But that just pushes the inevitable question back: instead of asking what "about" means, now we're asking what "description" means. Unfortunately it's difficult to define "description" without being circular; even some dictionaries define "description" as "describing something." Fortunately, the commonsense definition is the right one here: a description tells you something about the thing being described. A description is a statement about a thing, providing some information about that thing. A description sets the described thing apart from all the other things that exist in the universe, to help you identify the described thing later. For example, the title of this book is *Metadata*. The author of this book's name is Pomerantz. This book has nineteen figures, et cetera.

Data such as name, or title, or page length, these are all relatively uncontroversial. To be sure, names are arbitrary... but once a name is given, it generally does not change. More controversial is *subject*. The subject of a book (or other creative work) is often a matter of interpretation. For example, what is this book about? I think we can all agree that it's about metadata. So one term that might be used to describe the subject of this book is "metadata." But what else is this book about? Is it about the semantic web? One chapter deals with that subject; is that enough to justify using that term to describe the subject of the entire book? The theme of networks runs throughout much of this book, though little space is dedicated to discussing it explicitly; is that enough to justify using that term to describe the subject of this book?

The process of asking and answering questions like these is referred to as *subject analysis*. Which is exactly what it sounds like: analyzing an object (such as a book) to identify what its subject is... what it is about. Obviously not everything has a subject: naturally occurring objects, for example, can't really be said to have a subject. What is Mount Rainier about? It's a meaningless question. Similarly some pieces of art don't have a subject—though, to be fair, some do. The fourth movement of Beethoven's Symphony No. 9 (usually referred to as the "Ode to Joy") is about friendship and the brotherhood of all humankind, but what are the first three movements about? Again, it's a meaningless question. Furthermore, even when objects *can* be said to be about something, subject analysis is often a matter of interpretation. What is the novel *Moby Dick* about? On the one hand, it's about a whale and whaling. On the other hand, it's about revenge and obsession. Which of these interpretations justifies assigning subject terms?

The answer, unsurprisingly, is "it depends." It depends on what you're trying to accomplish with your subject terms. Flip to the back of this book, and you will find several pages of index. An index is a list of words, names, and concepts that can be found in the text of this book, and the pages on which they can be found. These index terms were selected by a professional indexer to help you, the reader, easily find concepts in the pages of this book. Now flip to the front of this book, and look on the page after the title page. You will see a bunch of information about copyright and the publisher, and at the bottom of the page you will see some numbered terms. In the jargon of librarianship, these are what are called *subject headings*, and they describe what this book is about. (This description is necessarily at a very high level, since only a few subject headings are assigned for even the longest book.) These subject headings were selected by a professional cataloger to help the potential reader who is interested in books on this subject, find this particular book. Both index terms and subject headings were selected by human beings, to help other human beings accomplish specific types of tasks. But given the differences in these types of tasks, the terms that are considered useful are different.

The difference in the terms employed as subject headings versus in an index begs the question: Where do these descriptive terms come from? Do the indexer and the cataloger just make them up? Do they select them from some menu of terms? You may have already guessed the answer: the indexer, on the one hand, makes up terms, though generally these terms are selected from the words and concepts used by the author. The cataloger, on the other hand, selects terms from a large, but finite set of available terms. The nature of that set of available terms will be discussed further, below.

A Definition of Metadata

Now hopefully you can see why "data about data" is not a useful definition of metadata. Data is only potential information, raw and unprocessed, prior to anyone actually being informed by it. Determining what something is about is subjective, dependent on an understanding of that thing, as well as dependent on the available terms. Thus, not only is this definition of metadata not useful, it's almost meaningless.

This definition can be salvaged only if we understand the word "data" to mean "potential information," as discussed above. Data must be understood not as an abstract concept but as objects that are potentially informative. Then metadata can be defined as "a potentially informative object that describes another potentially informative object." This is better, but somewhat clunky. Or, since a description is a statement about something, we can define metadata as a statement about a potentially informative object. And while not perfect, this is the definition that we will stick with for this book:

Metadata Is a Statement about a Potentially Informative Object

As you'll see throughout the course of this book, this definition is useful in several ways. Specifically, it provides latitude along several dimensions that we'll be grateful for later: first, as to the nature of the object; second, as to the nature of the statement, and how that statement is made.

The Resource

Making a statement implies that we have (1) something to make a statement about and (2) something to say about it. Our "potentially informative object" is the something about which we are making a statement. This object is more commonly referred to as a *resource*. The description, then, is what we are saying about the resource.

A statement has 3 parts: First, we have the *subject* of our description, the resource: for example, the *Mona Lisa*. Second, we have a category of relationship between the resource and some other thing (called a *predicate*): for example, that the resource has a creator. Finally, we have another *object* that has the predicated relationship with the resource: for example, Leonardo da Vinci.

Please note that—confusingly—the way that the terms "subject" and "object" are used in the context of

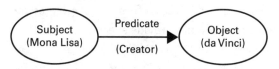

Figure 2

metadata is exactly the opposite of how they are used in the context of grammar. In grammar, the object of a sentence is the entity that is acted upon by the subject: for example, in the sentence "Leonardo da Vinci painted the *Mona Lisa*," *Leonardo da Vinci* is the subject and *Mona Lisa* is the object. In a descriptive metadata statement, however, these terms are defined very differently: the subject is the entity being described, and the object is another entity being used to describe the subject. This will be revisited in chapter 6, when we will discuss the Resource Description Framework, which is the data model according to which most metadata is currently structured.

Schemas, Elements, and Values

A metadata *schema* is a set of rules about what sorts of subject-predicate-object statements (called *triples*) one is allowed to make, and how one is allowed to make them.

Imagine that you are filling out a form: for a job application or at a doctor's office, for example. Forms have fill-in-the-blank spaces, which require you to write specific information in those spaces: the date, your name, your phone number, etc. Sometimes a form even specifies the format in which you should provide specific information: dates must be written as MM/DD/YYYY, for example. The form dictates the data that you are supposed to provide and how you are supposed to provide it.

A fill-in-the-blank form is not a metadata schema, but it makes for a decent analogy: one can think of a metadata schema as defining the blanks on a form. In the next chapter we will discuss Dublin Core, which is a metadata schema designed to enable description of any resource. A very simple Dublin Core record about the *Mona Lisa* might look like this:

Title: Mona Lisa

Creator: Leonardo da Vinci

Date: 1503–1506

In this example, title, creator, and date are the blanks that are filled in. These "blanks" are the predicates in subject-predicate-object triples: for example, Leonardo da Vinci (object) is the creator (predicate) of the Mona Lisa (subject). By defining a small set of predicates, Dublin Core has restricted the set of statements that one is allowed to make about a resource. In the context of a metadata schema, however, these predicates are usually called *elements*.

An element in a metadata schema is a category of statement that can be made about a resource; an element names an attribute of a resource. A *value*, then, is the data that is assigned to an element: "Leonardo da Vinci" is the creator of this resource, or "1503–1506" was the date of creation of this resource, for example. Together, you have an *element-value pair*, which is the totality of a single statement about a resource. If metadata is statements about a potentially informative object, the element-value pair is the irreducible particle of metadata.

By defining metadata as statements, a metaphor of language is clearly being invoked. It's an imperfect metaphor, and only one specific philosophy of language is being invoked—of language being a formal system of symbols—but it's a useful metaphor for our purposes.

A metadata schema, according to this metaphor, is the set of rules according to which a language operates. A metadata schema is therefore a very simple language, with a small number of rules.

Encoding Schemes

The rules of a language, no matter how simple, apply to a set of symbols that are used to convey meaning. Here we get into semiotics (where instead of "symbol," the term "sign" is used): a sign conveys meaning by signifying, or referring to, a signified. The set of letters "Jeffrey," for example, signifies me. The set of letters "Jeffrey" is not me, but under some conditions it is a sign that represents me. I am the signified; "Jeffrey" is the signifier.

Metadata schemas exert control over the kinds of statements that may be made. Metadata *encoding schemes* exert control over the way the signifiers used in those statements may be constructed. Encoding schemes are agnostic as to what types of things may be signified. What encoding schemes do is dictate how signifiers are constructed.

There are two ways in which signifiers may be constructed, in the context of metadata... two types of encoding schemes: for specifying syntax, and for specifying vocabulary.

Signifier Type 1: Syntax Encoding

A syntax encoding scheme is a set of rules that dictate how to represent, or encode, a specific type of data. Importantly, a syntax encoding scheme is specific to an individual metadata element.

For example, many metadata schemas recommend that when specifying dates, values should be encoded

Table 2

Metadata schema controls this	*Encoding scheme controls this*
Title:	Mona Lisa
Creator:	Leonardo, da Vinci, 1452–1519
Date:	1503–1506
Format:	Poplar (wood)

according to the ISO 8601 standard. ISO 8601 is a standard of the International Organization for Standardization, for representing dates and times. Let us take, as an example, the date 14 March 2015, which is of course Pi Day (3/14, in the month/day notation used in the United States). On that day, for one second, the date and time will be the first 10 digits of Pi: 3/14/15, 9:26:53. This date and time, encoded in ISO 8601, looks like this:

Date: 2015–03–14T09:26:53

ISO 8601 is a syntax encoding scheme, which means that it provides a standard for how to represent a specific type of data. A date may be an attribute of a resource (for example, of its creation); this encoding scheme is used to provide a standard for how dates are represented in metadata records. A syntax encoding scheme dictates a set of rules for how to construct a signifier to indicate a specific type of signified.

Signifier Type 2: Controlled Vocabulary

Like a syntax encoding scheme, a controlled vocabulary is a set of rules that dictate how to represent a specific type of data, and also is specific to an individual metadata element. The difference, however, is this: while a syntax encoding scheme dictates how a string describing a resource must be formatted, a controlled vocabulary provides a finite set of strings that may be used at all. Returning to our language metaphor, if a metadata schema exerts control over the kinds of statements that may be made, a controlled vocabulary exerts control over the words and phrases that may be used in those statements.

For example, the recommendation for the subject element in Dublin Core is that values be selected from a controlled vocabulary. One of the most widely used controlled vocabularies is the Library of Congress Subject Headings—which is, as you might expect, maintained by the Library of Congress. Subject headings from the LCSH have been used in every book published in the United States since the early 1970s. In fact subject headings from LCSH are used in this very book: take a look at the copyright page of this book (on the fourth page, opposite the dedication).

One of the LCSH terms used for this book is "metadata." What puts the *control* in *controlled vocabulary* is this: the term is "metadata," and not anything else. If you want to adhere to LCSH, you could not describe this book as being about "meta-data," or "data about data," or any other synonym. The term is "metadata," and "metadata" is the only acceptable term.

A controlled vocabulary is, in a sense, like Newspeak, the language from the novel *1984*. Newspeak is an artificial language, in which the number of available words has been dramatically limited, all synonyms and antonyms have been eliminated, and the scope of the meanings of those words that remain have been clarified and simplified. Replace "Newspeak" with "a controlled vocabulary," and the previous sentence remains accurate. Of course, it is not a thoughtcrime against the Library of Congress to use a term that is not in LCSH to describe a resource... but it would violate the practice of adhering to the standard in the first place.

The Library of Congress Subject Headings is, of course, only one controlled vocabulary out of many. But the LCSH is the granddaddy of controlled vocabularies: it's one of the oldest still in widespread use, having been developed at the Library of Congress in 1898, and one of the broadest, as it attempts to cover the entire range of human knowledge.

Attempting to cover the entire range of human knowledge, unfortunately, runs up against a rather large ontological problem. The universe is a big place, and there is, arguably, an infinite number of possible subjects in it. A controlled vocabulary, however, is by definition a finite set of terms. How can a controlled vocabulary possibly hope to be able to represent all possible subjects?

To be fair, the LCSH is enormous. As of this writing the most recent edition is the 35th, which is published in 6 volumes, weighs in at 6,845 pages, and contains over 300,000 subject headings. (As an aside, the 35th edition will be the final print edition, as the Library of Congress is transitioning to online-only publication.) In fact, though, the figure of 300,000 is misleading: LCSH contains rules to allow you to string subject headings together, to create what are called *subdivisions*. You could, for example, describe a work about the ferries that existed in Seattle at the time of the Great Fire as follows, using both geographic and chronological subdivisions:

Ferries—Washington—Seattle—1889

By remixing subject headings in this way, LCSH allows for a potentially infinite number of terms to emerge, out of what is otherwise a finite set.

Name Authority

Related to the controlled vocabulary is the *authority file*. Like a controlled vocabulary, an authority file provides a finite set of strings that may be used to describe a resource. A *name authority file*, then, is specific to names.

The Library of Congress, again, maintains one of the most widely used name authority files: the Library of Congress Name Authority File (LCNAF), which provides authoritative name data for people, places, and things. The LCNAF entry for Mark Twain, for example, is as follows:

Twain, Mark, 1835–1910

As with a controlled vocabulary, this string is the only acceptable term for referring to Mark Twain. Samuel Langhorne Clemens wrote under several pseudonyms, but if you are using the LCNAF as the source of values for a metadata element, there is only one valid way to refer to him. Indeed the LCNAF entry for "Clemens, Samuel Langhorne, 1835–1910" contains this note: "This heading is not valid for use as a subject. Works about this person are entered under Twain, Mark, 1835–1910." An authority file is a harsh mistress: it is very particular about what terms you are allowed to use, and issues a stern correction if you even consider using the wrong one.

While the LCNAF is one of the broadest authority files, it is far from the only one. The J. Paul Getty Research Institute has created two name authority files: the Cultural Objects Name Authority (CONA)®, which provides titles and other information about art objects, and the Union List of Artist Names (ULAN)®, which provides authoritative name data and associated information about artists and groups of artists. The ULAN entry for Mark Twain is slightly different than the LCNAF entry:

Twain, Mark (pseudonym)

Many other authority files exist. Authority files are often created by national libraries, which is only natural as national libraries generally have as their scope all materials published in, or relevant to, that nation. (As an aside, the Library of Congress is *not* actually a national library, it is Congress' library, though it serves as a de facto national library.) That large a scope, of course, inevitably ends up overlapping with the scope of other national libraries: how could the Library of Congress collect material on US history, for example, without duplicating materials also collected by European national libraries? And we've already seen that the authority files created by the Library of Congress and the Getty Research Institute overlap.

In order to minimize this sort of wheel-reinvention, and to the reduce the costs of maintaining authority files by spreading the work around, the Library of Congress, the German and French National Libraries (the Deutsche Nationalbibliothek and the Bibliothèque Nationale de France), and OCLC (an organization that will be discussed further in the next chapter) launched a project called the Virtual International Authority File (VIAF). VIAF has since grown to become a partnership of, as of this writing, 22 institutions from all over the world (including the Getty as the only contributor that is not a national library). VIAF is an uber-authority file, combining records from all participants into a single service, shared globally.

Thesaurus

Let us now back up slightly, to controlled vocabularies. A controlled vocabulary, like Newspeak, is a restricted set of terms that are allowable for use. But such a set of terms may simply be a list.

A *thesaurus* builds on the simplicity of the list, adding structure and hierarchy to the set of terms. This structure is not a grammar, however. A language is both a set of words and the grammatical rules that govern how those words may be strung together to form coherent sentences. (Of course, both the set of words in and the grammatical rules of a language evolve over time, but that's neither here nor there.) The grammatical rules of a language are a structure, to be sure, but of a different kind than the structure of a thesaurus. A thesaurus does not govern how words may or may not be used; a thesaurus governs the *relationships* among words.

Let's return to our Seattle ferries example. A controlled vocabulary might articulate, say, the set of allowable terms to refer to places in the United States: perhaps the 29,514 "incorporated places and census designated places" recognized in the 2010 US Census. But that would just be a list of terms.

A thesaurus would include the relationships between the entities named using these terms: *Seattle* would be a "child" of *Washington*, as would *Olympia*, *Spokane*, *Walla Walla*, and all of the other identifiable places within Washington state. Each of the 50 states would similarly have its list of child entities. This hypothetical thesaurus would only be two layers deep, but you could easily imagine a thesaurus that has many layers. Cities might have neighborhoods as child entities, which in turn might have streets as children. Instead of states, cities might have counties as their parents, the parents of counties would be states, then nations, then continents. In fact this is exactly how the J. Paul Getty Research Institute's Thesaurus of Geographic Names® is organized.

Washington is a classic example of why thesauri are useful. There are many Washingtons throughout the United States: the state of Washington, the US capitol city of Washington, a Washington county in no less than 30 different states of the Union, a city or town named Washington in at least 25 different states, and a host of other Washingtons besides. But it's a simple matter to represent this diversity of Washingtons in a thesaurus, since each one occupies a unique place in the hierarchy: there can be

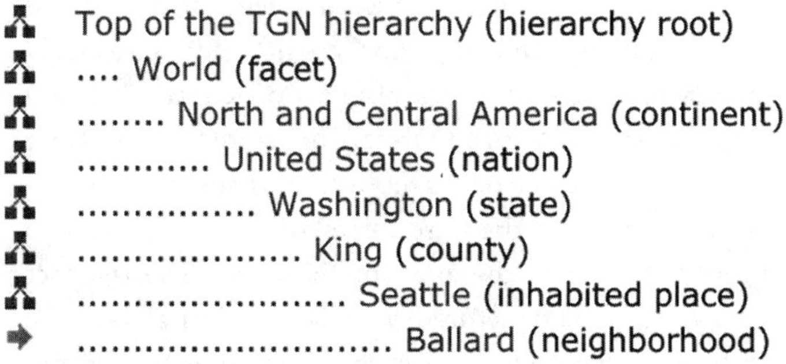

⚒ Top of the TGN hierarchy (hierarchy root)
⚒ .... World (facet)
⚒ .... North and Central America (continent)
⚒ .... United States (nation)
⚒ .... Washington (state)
⚒ .... King (county)
⚒ .... Seattle (inhabited place)
➡ .... Ballard (neighborhood)

Figure 3

no confusing Washington county, North Carolina with Washington county, Maine, because each Washington county has a different parent.

The type of thesaurus under discussion here is somewhat different than the common meaning of the term "thesaurus." One of the most popular thesauri in the English language is *Roget's Thesaurus*, which is a book (now also online, of course) that lists words, and provides synonyms and antonyms for each word. If we were to search for the word "control" in *Roget's Thesaurus*, for example, we would find that some of its synonyms are "regulation" and "restraint," while some of its antonyms are "chaos" and "lawlessness."

Roget's Thesaurus (like any thesaurus of a language) provides a set of words and their relationships. The relationships, however, are very simple: synonymy and antonymy. These relationships are made somewhat more complicated when you consider that most words have shades of meaning ("regulation" and "restraint" are not themselves truly synonyms, but both are synonyms of "control"). Every meaning of a word may therefore be treated as a separate entity, each with its own synonyms and antonyms. (Consider, for example, the word "blue," which has at least two separate meanings, the color and the mood.) This is in fact how WordNet is structured: WordNet is a lexical database of English that's widely used in information science and computer science. All that aside, however, in a language thesaurus there are two and only two relationships (synonymy and antonymy) regardless of how the thesaurus defines what a word is.

A thesaurus in the information science sense—that is, a thesaurus that provides values for metadata elements—might have different, and sometimes more complex, relationships between terms. Returning once again to our ferries example, LCSH uses "broader terms" and "narrower terms" to indicate hierarchical relationships. For example, "passenger ships" is a broader term than "ferries," and "water taxis" is a narrower term. Thus "ferries" is a subcategory of "passenger ships," and "water taxis" is a subcategory of "ferries." The relationship between terms here is *IS A*. In mathematical terms, this is an *asymmetric transitive relation*: if a water taxi is a ferry, then a ferry is not a water taxi (Y is a X, X is not a Y); and if a ferry is a passenger ship, then a water taxi is also a passenger ship (Z is a Y, Y is a X, therefore Z is a X).

This kind of hierarchical structure is commonplace, as it's the same structure as a family tree: a parent may have one or more children, who may in turn have one or more children, etc. As in a family tree, too, entities may have siblings, if a parent has more than one child. Thus *ferries*, *cargo ships*, and *ocean liners* are siblings, as they are all children (narrower terms) of *passenger ships*.

One further type of relationship is common in thesauri: "use for." The use of "use for" indicates that a specific term

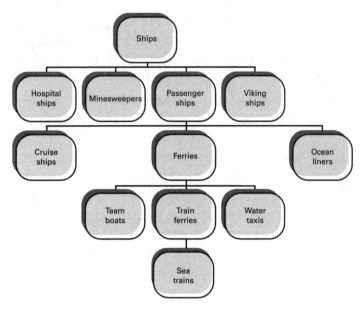

Figure 4

is the preferred term, which should be used instead of any specified alternative. In our Mark Twain example above, it was pointed out that the LCNAF entry for "Clemens, Samuel Langhorne, 1835–1910" points to the preferred term "Twain, Mark, 1835–1910." In the Getty Thesaurus of Geographic Names®, for another example, there are several names listed for the city of Casablanca—Dar el Beida, Ad-Dār Al-Bayḍā, Anfa—but "Casablanca" is listed as the preferred term. The relationship between these entities is a "use for" relationship: if you are using TGN, "Casablanca" should be used instead of "Dar el Beida" or any other name.

A Very Brief Foray into Network Analysis

A hierarchical structure is only one type of topology for a network. In mathematical terms, a network is a *graph*: a set of entities connected by relationships. Many fields deal with phenomena that form networks: computer networks, biological networks, telecommunication networks, social networks, and the like. Different fields use different terms to refer to the objects and links in a network; we will use the terms from graph theory and refer to these entities as *nodes*, and the connections as *edges*.

Topology, as a branch of mathematics, is the study of shapes and spaces, and what shapes are actually equivalent, in the sense that one may be deformed into the other (for example, a coffee mug may be deformed into a torus). The topology of a network is the "shape" of the network, in the sense of the structure created by the edges between nodes. Some simple network topologies include a ring (in which one node is connected to the next, which is connected to the next, etc., until the last node in the ring is connected to the first), and a star (in which all nodes are connected to one central node). A hierarchy, or family tree arrangement of nodes, is a *tree* topology.

Network analysis is a somewhat poorly defined term, given how diverse the fields are in which networks are applied. For our purposes, however, network analysis is the use of networks to study phenomena that may be more complex than their component parts. The World Wide Web, for example, is more than the sum of the servers that exist in the world, and it exhibits behaviors that no individual server exhibits. Similarly a social network is more than a set of individuals who are acquainted with each other.

Thanks to Facebook and Twitter and other social networking services—as well as news stories about the NSA collecting phone records—social network analysis has become very well known in the past few years. But social network analysis is only one type of network analysis: the analysis of connections among people, as opposed to the connections among computers, or neurons, or any of the many other entities that form networks. In the social network as represented by Facebook, for example, the nodes are people, places, and organizations, and the only relationships are "friend" and "likes." Facebook's social network is fairly flat: people, places, and organizations are all very broad categories, and not all of your Facebook "friends" are actually your friends. There are a host of names for the relationships that can exist among people: friend, acquaintance, neighbor, coworker, colleague, sibling, spouse, employer, employee, enemy, frenemy… the list goes on and on. Furthermore not every entity in a network—even in a social network—needs to be a person, place, or organization. For example, the NSA's analyses of social networks supposedly include such entities as phone numbers and email addresses.

Network analysis is a large and very interesting area of study in its own right, and we cannot do it justice here. Some books on various aspects of the topic are listed in the Further Readings section.

Two nodes connected by an edge is the most basic unit of a network; this three-part relationship was discussed above as the subject-predicate-object triple. The subject and object of a metadata description are thus both nodes, and the predicate is the edge.

In this example of a network, we very quickly move from the *Mona Lisa* to Allentown, Pennsylvania, two entities that usually have very little to do with one another. As more and more entities and relationships are added, a network grows rapidly. Indeed, as more and more entities and relationships accumulate, there's really nowhere to stop, short of mapping out the network of relationships between everything in the entire universe. Such mapping is, in most cases, not feasible. We will return to mapping in chapter 6, when we discuss linked data.

In short, a node in a network may be any type of entity, and an edge may be any type of relationship between entities. The nature of the network (computer, social, neural, etc.) naturally dictates both the type of entity and type

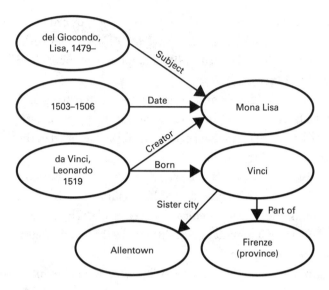

Figure 5

of relationships that may exist in the network. However, given that an edge may be any type of relationship, we must discuss ontologies.

Ontology

In philosophy, ontology is the study of the nature of reality and the categories of things that exist. In information science, an ontology is a formal representation of the universe of things that exist in a specific domain. What these two approaches to ontology share in common is that they both articulate a universe of entities and relationships between entities... even if it's a small universe.

A thesaurus is a hierarchy, but one in which the relationships between entities are usually fairly simple, often *IS A*: a water taxi is a ferry, a ferry is a passenger ship. Other common relationships in thesauri include *part of* (for example, Vinci is part of Firenze province, Firenze is part of Tuscany), *instance of* (John Tyler is an instance of President of the United States), and *part-whole* (the elbow is part of the arm). However, in principle, the relationships in a thesaurus may be anything at all.

An ontology builds on a thesaurus: an ontology is also a set of entities and the relationships between them, it is also organized as a hierarchy, it also often uses a controlled vocabulary or other encoding scheme for naming entities and relationships. In fact an ontology so closely resembles a thesaurus that the two terms are often used interchangeably, though it is incorrect to do so.

An ontology differs from a thesaurus in that an ontology includes a set of rules. As a straightforward hierarchical structure, a family tree makes a good example. An entity in a hierarchy may have children, and in a family tree this is literally a parent–child relationship. There are in fact two parent relations in a family tree, mother and father, and two child relations, daughter and son. Knowing this, we can create the following rules: if A is female, then A is the mother of B; or the inverse, if A is the mother of B, then A is female. *Female* is a characteristic that may be assigned to entities, and based on that characteristic an inference may be made about relationships between that entity and other entities. Or inversely, if we know the relationship between two entities, an inference may be made about the characteristics of one of more of those entities. Inferences are a layer on top of a thesaurus, a way to integrate knowledge about the world into an ontology.

This knowledge about the world may be encoded as rules for action, for example in software. For example, in a genealogy application the following rules might exist: If B is female, then the default relationship between B and any child entities is mother, and a ♀ symbol should be drawn next to B's name.

Metadata Gone Wild!

From encoding schemes to thesauri to ontologies, this chapter has moved from less to increasingly structured and information-rich mechanisms for creating or selecting values for elements in a metadata schema. This section, however, moves to the extreme other end of the spectrum, to a complete lack of structure.

In the novel *1984*, Newspeak restricts the words that even exist, on the premise that a limited vocabulary limits the concepts that it's possible to communicate, and even to think. Like Newspeak, an encoding scheme controls the terms that it's possible to use—either by limiting the number of allowable terms, as in a controlled vocabulary, or by specifying the structure of terms, as in a syntax encoding scheme. The premise behind encoding schemes is that natural language is often ambiguous, so control is necessary to limit the complexity of metadata records. This is a top-down, command-and-control approach to metadata.

What if, instead, one were to take a bottom-up, grass-roots approach to metadata? What if there were no control over the terms that it's possible to use? The beauty of the Internet is that it is uncontrolled. Yes, there are organizations in which certain functions are centralized, such as assigning IP addresses and emergency response. But there is no agency that dictates what kind of content you can put online.

The fact that the Internet is largely uncontrolled, makes it rich soil for the *uncontrolled vocabulary*. Where a controlled vocabulary provides a finite set of terms that may used as values for a particular element in a metadata schema, an uncontrolled vocabulary allows any term to be used. And any term really does mean *any*: not only is the entire range of words in your chosen language fair game, but an uncontrolled vocabulary allows terms to be invented on the spot.

What committee developing a name authority file for book titles could have anticipated *How to Avoid Huge Ships*, or *The Stray Shopping Carts of Eastern North America*?

Some elements, of course, lend themselves naturally to this lack of control. The Title element, for example, is probably best uncontrolled, since it should be possible for the creator of a resource to name it anything they want. What committee developing a name authority file for book titles could have anticipated *How to Avoid Huge Ships*, or *The Stray Shopping Carts of Eastern North America*? Yet some elements benefit dramatically from being controlled. The Date element, for example, is probably best controlled, as there are so many ways to write a date. A simple example of this is the month-day-year format common in the United States, versus the day-month-year common in Europe.

Between these two extremes, there are many elements that can swing either way. Subject is perhaps the most notable of these. As discussed above, Subject is host to perhaps the largest controlled vocabulary in existence, LCSH. On the other hand, Subject also lends itself extremely well to being uncontrolled. If you have ever created a blog post, or uploaded a video to YouTube, or saved a book to Goodreads, you know that you can assign any tags to it that you want.

These tags serve a double purpose. For you, the user of a service, these tags are a way of organizing your own materials. You can create any tag you want, no matter how idiosyncratic, so that you can search and browse and find your own materials. If you want to use the tag "to read" on a book in Goodreads, that's fine, even if that book is on no one else in the world's To Read list. If you want to use the tag "turlingdrome" to describe a photo on Flickr, that's fine, even if you're the only person in the entire world to use that tag. Tags are individualized terms, and need only be meaningful to their creator.

Nevertheless, it turns out that most users will use the same or similar tags for a specific piece of content. For example, some of the most common tags in Goodreads for the book *The Hitchhiker's Guide to the Galaxy* are "science-fiction" and "humor." (Goodreads calls tags "custom shelves.") By aggregating the tags used idiosyncratically by thousands of independent users, Goodreads has accurately surfaced the genres of this book. So if a future Goodreads user goes searching for science fiction books to read, or humor books, or humorous science fiction, she will find *The Hitchhiker's Guide*.

This is precisely what tags are good for: allowing users to search or browse for content online, using terms that reflect the way people actually think about searching and browsing. The LCSH are terrific, but the subject headings assigned to *The Hitchhiker's Guide to the Galaxy* probably do not reflect the way most people would search for that book:

Prefect, Ford (Fictitious character)—Fiction

Dent, Arthur (Fictitious character)—Fiction

These subject headings are accurate, in the sense that these two are characters in the book. But probably few people would think to search for the book that way.

In addition to the tag "science-fiction" in Goodreads, other very popular tags for *The Hitchhiker's Guide to the Galaxy* include "sci-fi," "scifi," and "sf." This variation re-opens the issue of the value of idiosyncrasy. If tags are supposed to be good for allowing searching and browsing in a commonsensical way, doesn't the existence of variant tags interfere with that usefulness?

On the one hand, yes. If a user is browsing for "sf," it's true that she will not find books that are tagged "scifi." On the other hand, if the number of tags is large enough, chances are that there will be significant overlap: the same books will be tagged "sf" by some users and "scifi" by others. So variability may reduce some of the usefulness of tags, but not completely.

While most users will use the same or similar tags for a specific piece of content, some users and some tags are more idiosyncratic. One Goodreads user, for example, has tagged *The Hitchhiker's Guide* with "xxe" and another with "box-8." What do those tags mean? Who cares! The tag "xxe" isn't wrong... it makes sense to someone, just not to me. There is no such thing as a bad or a wrong tag: if a tag is useful to even one person, then it's a good tag... just one that won't be used a lot.

And that is the fundamental difference between controlled and uncontrolled vocabularies. A controlled vocabulary provides a standardized set of terms to describe some set of objects, while an uncontrolled vocabulary allows any and all terms to emerge. A controlled vocabulary exerts control to restrict the range of options; an uncontrolled vocabulary lets a hundred flowers bloom.

Of course, it's human nature to want to simplify the complexities of the reality around us. Thus communities of users often arise around services that make use of tags, dedicated to normalizing tagsets. This is very common in Wikipedia, for example; there are entire groups dedicated to organizing and defining the scope of the categories within subject areas in Wikipedia. Thus there is constant pressure on uncontrolled vocabularies toward a greater degree of control. And, of course, even controlled vocabularies change over time, as new terms are created and obsolete terms are dropped, in an effort to reflect changes in the state of knowledge about the entities within their scope. There is no such thing as a pure controlled or uncontrolled vocabulary: all actual vocabularies are somewhere along a spectrum of greater or lesser degrees of control.

The Record

A metadata schema is a set of rules about what sorts of subject-predicate-object statements are possible to make.

An element is a category of statement that can be made according to the schema, and a value is the data that is assigned to an element, according to the schema's rules for that element. We have now concluded the lengthy section of this chapter devoted to how to create or select values, and we will move on to the metadata *record*.

A metadata record is simply a set of subject-predicate-object statements about a single resource. In a spreadsheet, a single row is an entry for a single entity, containing all data about that entity, the categories of which are specified in the column headers. Likewise a metadata record is specific to a single resource (for example, the *Mona Lisa*), containing all metadata about that resource (Leonardo da Vinci, 1503–1506, etc.), the categories of which are specified by the elements in the schema (creator, date, etc.).

An important characteristic of metadata records is as follows: There should be one and only one metadata record for a single resource. This is, in fact, so important that it's known as the One-to-One Principle: one resource, one record. This principle was originally articulated for Dublin Core metadata records, but it is applicable outside of that context as well.

In practical terms, the One-to-One Principle specifies that there should be one and only one metadata record for the *Mona Lisa*. This seems perfectly reasonable on the face of it. But there are a great many works that are derived from the *Mona Lisa*. No one is likely to argue that, for example, Marcel Duchamp's work *L.H.O.O.Q.* is a resource distinct from the *Mona Lisa*, and therefore deserves its own metadata record. But what about, for example, a high-resolution digital photograph of the *Mona Lisa*, created and maintained by the Louvre, and intended to be the definitive surrogate for the original? Should this be considered to be a resource distinct from the *Mona Lisa*, with its own metadata record? Yes, it should. A digital photograph of the *Mona Lisa* is not the *Mona Lisa*.

Many metadata schemas include elements to deal with situations such as this. Both Dublin Core and VRA Core (a schema for describing works of visual culture, created by the Visual Resources Association), for example, include elements named *Relation*, and the CDWA (the J. Paul Getty Trust's Categories for the Description of Works of Art) includes an element named *Related Works*. The Louvre's high-resolution digital photograph of the *Mona Lisa* is a resource related to the *Mona Lisa*, as is *L.H.O.O.Q.* Both of those resources might share an element-value pair in common, indicating the relation to the *Mona Lisa*, establishing a relationship between those resources and the resource from which they are derived. Thus the One-to-One Principle is maintained: each resource has its own metadata record, but an important relationship between resources is captured.

The One-to-One Principle has one significant shortcoming, however: there are many metadata schemas to choose from. It is at this point that the One-to-One Principle breaks down.

In fact the One-to-One Principle could reasonably be renamed the One-to-One-to-One Principle: there should be one and only one metadata record for a single resource, *for a single metadata schema*. The *Mona Lisa*, a digital photograph of the *Mona Lisa*, and *L.H.O.O.Q.* all should have unique metadata records using elements from Dublin Core. But they might also all have unique metadata records using elements from CDWA, and yet a third set of unique records using elements from VRA Core.

Why one might want a DC record or a CDWA record or a record in another metadata schema, for a particular resource, depends on the use case. What are your resources? Who are your users likely to be? What are they likely to want to do with your metadata records? The pros and cons of different metadata element sets, and possible values that can be assigned to elements, will be discussed in the next several chapters.

Location of Metadata Records

There should be one and only one metadata record, in a single metadata schema, for a single resource. This, however, begs the question: Where is this record? The answer is that there are two places that a metadata record may be located: inside and outside. That is, embedded within the resource to which the record refers or separate from the resource.

We've already seen examples of records in these two locations: On the one hand, the Library of Congress Cataloging in Publication data, subject headings, and other metadata located on the copyright page of this book, is a metadata record about this book embedded inside this book. A card in a library catalog, on the other hand, is a metadata record about this book (containing much of the same information) that is a separate object from this book.

In both the physical and the online worlds, inside and outside exhausts the universe of possibilities for where something can be: a physical or a digital object can contain metadata about itself, or a metadata record may exist separate from the object. This raises the question: Which is preferable? The answer, unsurprisingly, is: It depends. For the most part, it depends on what the use case is.

Metadata embedded in an object is generally produced with the object. Consider schema.org, which will be discussed further in chapter 7. Schema.org is a standard that enables structured data to be embedded in HTML files, which are otherwise usually unstructured. This internal metadata is therefore likely to represent the authority of the creator of the website. However, metadata embedded in an object is likely to be difficult or impossible to change. You, as a user, cannot change the markup in a webpage, for example; only the website administrator can do that. Internal metadata is authoritative but static.

Metadata external to an object may be produced with the object, but it may just as easily be created after the fact. Consider a metadata record about a published article, stored in a database. For example, I once discovered that a journal article that I wrote was incorrectly attributed to another author in an online database. In other words, the metadata record about that article had been assigned the incorrect value for the Author field. I contacted the database vendor and they corrected the record within hours. This story ends happily for me, and reflects well on the database vendor. But metadata external to an object inevitably raises the question of who created that metadata, and how trustworthy the process of creation is. Furthermore external metadata may be customized for specific use cases: the metadata record created for a commercial database of scholarly literature may be different than the record created for Google Scholar, may be different than the record created by a citation management application. External metadata is flexible but may be of questionable authority.

With digital files, it can sometimes be difficult to identify exactly where the metadata record about a resource is located, and in fact the location of a record can change. The company Gracenote maintains the CDDB (Compact Disc Database), which is, as the name indicates, a database of descriptive metadata records about CDs and the music files on them. The CDDB is online, and any licensed music player application may access these records to display this metadata to the user of the application. In other words, the CDDB is a collection of external metadata records. The CDDB was originally developed because early CDs did not contain any metadata about their contents; later the CD-Text specification was developed to store this metadata on CDs. This CD-Text data, however, is stored in a different location on the CD than the music files it describes. CD-Text records on a CD are therefore still external metadata records, in the same sense that the metadata located on the copyright page of a book is external to the actual content of the book. When a CD is "ripped" (the files on it copied and often reformatted), however, many applications also rip the CD-Text data for the audio files on the CD. In other words, the CD-Text metadata for a digital audio file is internal to the file.

If a metadata record is internal to an object, then it's obvious that the record describes that object. The metadata on the copyright page of a book clearly describes that specific book; the schema.org markup in a webpage clearly refers to that specific webpage; it would be nonsensical otherwise. But if a metadata record is external to the object that it describes, then how are those two things connected? How can we know where a metadata record for an object is? Conversely, how can we know what object a record refers to? The answer to this question is, quite simply: More metadata.

A metadata record about a book will contain elements such as the title and author. These two elements alone will generally be enough to uniquely identify a book: there's more than one book in the world with the title *Metadata*, but only one is by Jeffrey Pomerantz. Any additional metadata that's provided about a book is just icing, for the purposes of uniquely identifying a book: there's certainly not going to be more than one book titled *Metadata*, by Jeffrey Pomerantz, published by MIT Press, in 2015.

Rather than rely on multiple elements in combination to uniquely identify an object, however, it is often preferable to have a single element. For books in a library this is the call number, for example Library of Congress Classification. Shortly after its publication this book, like all books published in the United States, was assigned an LCC call number. When this book is placed on a shelf in a library, it will be placed according to its call number, which will—conveniently for library users—put it near other books on similar topics. Of course, LCC is only one system for creating call numbers for books; another common scheme is the Dewey Decimal Classification. And, of course, outside of the context of libraries, publishers have yet another scheme for uniquely identifying books: the International Standard Book Number (ISBN).

This call number appears in metadata records that are external to this book: in the library catalog record. But for the call number to be useful, it must also exist internal to the book itself. The call number of a book is printed with the Cataloging in Publication data on the copyright page, and in libraries it is often attached to the book spine as a sticker. In other words, the call number is added to the book as a piece of internal metadata (even if it's in fact on the outside of the object). The existence of this piece of metadata allows a librarian to know where to place the book on the shelves, and a library user to know where to find it.

Thus, for external metadata records to be useful, they must rely on the existence of internal metadata. So, if internal metadata must necessarily exist, then why have external metadata at all? This is because external metadata saves the user's time. One of the most important uses of metadata, as discussed in chapter 1, is resource discovery. External metadata is far more useful for resource discovery than internal metadata: a library catalog is much smaller and easier to search than an entire library.

Unique Identifiers

A unique identifier is exactly what it sounds like: something that identifies an entity uniquely, without any confusion with other entities. Usually a unique identifier is a name or an address. And in fact, when discussing unique identifiers, the distinction between the two tends to break down.

Take, for example, the address of the White House:

1600 Pennsylvania Ave NW
Washington, DC 20500

Washington, DC, is the largest geographic area, then the zip code, then the street name, then the building number on the street. This address is sufficient to uniquely identify a single building: there's only one Pennsylvania Avenue NW in Washington, DC (though there is a Pennsylvania Ave SE), and there's only one 1600 on Pennsylvania Ave NW. It may be obvious, but it's worth pointing out that this is the entire point of the postal addressing system: to uniquely identify buildings.

Many encoding schemes exist to create unique identifiers for specific types of resources: ISBNs and call numbers for books, the Digital Object Identifier (DOI) for online publications, the International Standard Recording Code (ISRC) for sound recordings, GPS coordinates for points in physical space, ISO 8601 for dates and times, Social Security numbers for citizens of the United States. There is even a system to create unique identifiers for academic researchers, the ORCID identifier.

It's especially important to be able to uniquely identify entities online, for two reasons. First, there are many technologies that can be used to access objects online. HTTP has emerged as the standard protocol for exchanging data online, but this was not always the case. Even today, there are many web browser applications, and it's important that when you type a URL into Chrome, it takes you to the same webpage as if you type it into Safari or Firefox. Second, objects on the web can be moved fairly easily, for example, if an

http://mitpress.mit.edu/books/metadata/

Scheme   Domain   Path
name

Figure 6

organization's server infrastructure is changed. So it's critical to be able to indicate that even though some particular web content has changed location, that it's still the same content.

The way this is accomplished is by using a uniform resource identifier (URI). The uniform resource locator (URL) is a typical web address, and a type of URI. A URI specifies a unique identifier in the network space of the web, though you could also think of it as a unique address, since one and only one object may exist at that address.

A URI is to resources on the Internet what a postal address is to buildings in the physical world: an identifier that uniquely specifies one and only one object. A URI (and a postal address) is also metadata internal to the object. Or perhaps it would be more accurate to say that a URI (and a postal address) is metadata *inherent* in the object, since moving the former will change the latter. And it is this fact—that a unique identifier may be inherent in a resource—that makes it perhaps the most important single piece of metadata, providing the address (or name, or location) to which any external metadata record may point.

DESCRIPTIVE METADATA

Standards are like toothbrushes, everyone agrees that they're a good idea but nobody wants to use anyone else's.

—Attributed to Murtha Baca, Getty Research Institute

In this chapter we will explore what is arguably the simplest kind of metadata, and was certainly the first kind of metadata to be extensively developed: descriptive metadata. To do this, we will explore in depth one descriptive metadata schema that was designed to be able to describe literally anything: Dublin Core.

Dude, Where's My Core?

The Dublin Core is not, as you might expect, named after Dublin, Ireland. Rather, it's named after Dublin, Ohio, a city just outside of Columbus. Dublin, Ohio, is the headquarters of the Online Computer Library Center, Inc. (OCLC), a nonprofit organization that develops and licenses many tools for information organizations, and in particular is a major player in the library market. Why is the Dublin Core named after the city in which OCLC is headquartered? To answer that question, believe it or not, we need to go back to the origin of the World Wide Web.

In November 1993, the National Center for Supercomputing Applications (NCSA) released Mosaic version 1.0. Mosaic was the first application capable of simultaneously displaying both text and image files on the Internet. This is, of course, how we are now used to seeing the web. But prior to the release of Mosaic, tools for accessing files on the Internet could only display one file at a time. In 1993, the functionality to display text and images side-by-side made Mosaic a "killer app," and in large part is responsible for the popularization of the web. Within months, Mosaic had a user base of millions worldwide, and by early 1995 the web, and its critical enabling technology, the Hypertext Transfer Protocol (HTTP), had passed all other Internet-based services for the volume of data being moved. (We hardly think about these other services any more, but once upon a time, FTP, Gopher, Telnet, WAIS, and other services with now-odd-sounding names were very popular ways to transfer data.)

In March 1995, the NCSA and OCLC hosted an invitation-only workshop in Dublin, Ohio, to discuss metadata for the web. At that time Google did not yet exist, was not yet even a research project. There were, however, several search engines in existence, though none that had achieved much in the way of market dominance. These search engines were effective, for the time, though somewhat primitive by current standards. The computer scientists and information scientists who participated in the 1995 workshop recognized that searching the web was becoming "siloed": no search engine indexed the entire web, and search engines often provided the user with no description of the files indexed beyond their names. Worse, some tools (FTP, Gopher, etc.) allowed searching only of files made available using those protocols. Thus the 1995 workshop was convened "to advance the state of the art in the development of resource description (or metadata) records for networked electronic information objects."

In other words, the consensus at the workshop was that for web search tools to continue to be useful, files on the web needed to be better described. (Subsequent developments in information retrieval, network analysis, and related fields open this up for debate. But that's a discussion for another book.) Thus one of the goals of the workshop was to reach consensus "on a core set of metadata elements to describe networked resources."

A core set of metadata elements, from Dublin, Ohio. If you'll forgive pushing the metaphor in the quote at the start of this chapter to its logical, yet disgusting extreme: the Dublin Core was developed to be *everyone's* toothbrush.

Cost of Adoption

The Dublin Core metadata element set was created as a lowest common denominator. This is not meant disparagingly, it was in fact a deliberate design decision: calling something *core* carries with it the assumption that it is core for everyone, for all use cases. It doesn't do anyone any good for one group to create a core set of something, only to have some other group decide that isn't the right set, and create their own core set. That only leads to a proliferation of standards.

Therefore, if the goal is to create a core set of something, that set must be so appealing that everyone will use it. To be a success, the Dublin Core metadata element set had to be adopted widely, indeed adopted by everyone who might have any kind of a need for it. So how to create a new tool that will be adopted by everyone who might need it?

Fortunately, scholars have been studying that very question for decades. The book *Diffusion of Innovations*, by Everett Rogers, is one of the most-cited works of social science, and has spawned an entire discipline. This book develops a model of how and why and how rapidly innovations are adopted into society as a whole. The figure here shows the S-shaped curve of the rate of adoption of several common household technologies. An innovation may be a technology (for example, smartphones) or an idea (for example, hand-washing as a strategy for improving public health). Rogers, and the many researchers who have followed him, have articulated several factors that affect the adoption or rejection of an innovation. The important one of these, in the current context, is *simplicity*: in order to be adopted, an innovation must be perceived as being simple to use. Or, to state this in reverse: if those who might find an innovation useful perceive it as being too complex, then those potential users will never become actual users.

Complexity raises the cost of adopting an innovation. Cost, of course, may mean financial cost, and new technologies are often quite expensive. But it may also mean other types of costs, such as time expended, or risks assumed. If I adopt a new and complex piece of technology, it will take me some time to learn to use it, and the time that I spend scaling that learning curve is a cost to me. Think about learning to drive a car: that's very costly in terms of the amount of time it probably took you to learn to do it well (and probably also in the amount of stress you caused your driving instructor). Furthermore new technologies are often unstable: when a new and improved version is released, early adopters of a new technology are

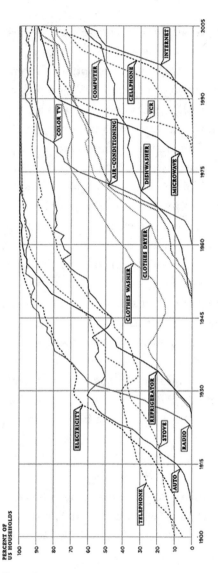

Figure 7

out the time and money that they sunk into that earlier version. Think about media for digital video: early adopters adopted videodiscs, which were completely supplanted by DVDs, which were supplanted by Blu-ray discs... all of which is currently in the process of being supplanted by on-demand streaming media services.

15 Elements

Dublin Core was designed to be simple and low-cost, easy to learn and easy to use. The intention was that it would therefore be widely adopted, and would become ubiquitous on the web. This was a very ambitious goal, especially given how new the web was, and how rapidly it was evolving, when work on Dublin Core began. What is perhaps most remarkable is that it worked.

The participants in the 1995 OCLC / NCSA workshop set out to develop a core set of descriptive metadata elements that could be applied to any and all resources on the Internet. That goal, paired with the equally ambitious goal of simplicity, forces the question: What descriptive metadata elements are absolutely necessary? What is the irreducible set of metadata elements necessary to describe literally any resource that exists, or might ever exist on the web?

It took several years for the Dublin Core metadata element set to stabilize. But in the end, 15 elements emerged as core:

Table 3

Element	Definition
Contributor	An entity responsible for making contributions to the resource.
Coverage	The spatial or temporal topic of the resource, the spatial applicability of the resource, or the jurisdiction under which the resource is relevant.
Creator	An entity primarily responsible for making the resource.
Date	A point or period of time associated with an event in the lifecycle of the resource.
Description	An account of the resource.
Format	The file format, physical medium, or dimensions of the resource.
Identifier	An unambiguous reference to the resource within a given context.
Language	A language of the resource.
Publisher	An entity responsible for making the resource available.
Relation	A related resource.
Rights	Information about rights held in and over the resource.
Source	A related resource from which the described resource is derived.
Subject	The topic of the resource.
Title	A name given to the resource.
Type	The nature or genre of the resource.

Note that the Dublin Core was developed to describe *online* resources, but the Format element refers to the "physical medium, or dimensions of the resource." Obviously neither physical medium nor dimensions is applicable to digital resources. But it's a short step from describing anything that exists on the web, to describing anything that exists, period. As the Dublin Core metadata element set evolved, it did not take long for the scope of the Format element to expand to include physical description. The Dublin Core metadata element set was created to describe networked resources, but by virtue of being a lowest common denominator, it is low enough, so to speak, to also describe physical resources.

Elements and Values

Now that we have seen that the Dublin Core metadata element set may be used to describe any type of resource, we need to revisit the idea of an *element*. What does it mean for Dublin Core to be a metadata element set?

Let us return to our working definition of metadata:

Metadata is a statement about a potentially informative object

Recall that a resource may be literally anything. Anything that can be either physically or electronically pointed to (a painting, or a digital file of that painting) is considered a resource.

Each of the 15 Dublin Core elements names an attribute or a characteristic of a resource, and enables the description of that attribute. In other words, each element is a category of statement that can be made about a resource: the Creator of this resource is X, the Title of this resource is Y, etc. Take this familiar piece of art as an example.

The first descriptive statement about this work of art is the following: the Title of this resource is *Mona Lisa*. But the *Mona Lisa* isn't called that in Italian; it's called *La Gioconda*. Which Title should be used? Answer: Both. The description of the Dublin Core element Title specifies that it is "A name given to the resource"... it doesn't specify that it is "*the* name." The freedom to repeat the same element with different values—to make more than one of the same *kind* of statement about a resource, but saying different things—will be explored further below.

This painting is called *La Gioconda* after the subject of the painting, Lisa Gherardini, wife of Francesco del Giocondo. And so another statement about this painting is the following: the Subject of this resource is Lisa Gherardini.

Yet another statement about this work is the following: the painter of this resource is Leonardo da Vinci. There is, of course, no *Painter* element in Dublin Core. However, Leonardo da Vinci is certainly "an entity primarily responsible for making" the *Mona Lisa*. Since the Dublin Core was

Figure 8

designed to allow description of literally any networked resource, by necessity it's agnostic as to the format of the thing being described. Someone who creates a painting is called a painter; someone who creates a book is called an author, someone who creates a movie is called a filmmaker, someone who creates a dance is called a choreographer, etc. Many names exist for individuals who engage in different forms of creation, and these names are meaningful in natural human language. But these shades of meaning are irrelevant for lowest common denominator description. Dublin Core simply collapses all of these forms of creation into one single category: Creator. The fact that semantics are shared across domains—that subtleties of meaning are flattened out so that the element definitions are as unambiguous as possible—is both one of the greatest strengths and one of the most serious limitations of Dublin Core.

Finally, it is thought that Leonardo da Vinci painted the *Mona Lisa* between 1503 and 1506. And so five statements can now be made about this resource, five element-value pairs that compose a Dublin Core record:

Title: Mona Lisa

Title: La Gioconda

Creator: Leonardo da Vinci

The fact that semantics are shared across domains—that subtleties of meaning are flattened out, so that the element definitions are as unambiguous as possible—is both one of the greatest strengths and one of the most serious limitations of Dublin Core.

Subject: Lisa Gherardini

Date: 1503–1506

Dublin Core, like many metadata schemas, includes rules for the selection or construction of values. Recommended best practice for the Date element, for example, is to use an encoding scheme such as ISO 8601. Recommended best practice for the Subject element is to select a value from a controlled vocabulary; recommended best practice for the Format element is to select a value specifically from the controlled vocabulary of Internet MIME types. Recommended best practice for the Identifier element is to use a value conforming to a formal unique identifier system; recommended best practice for the Relation and Source elements is to identify the related resource using a unique identifier. There is no recommended best practice for the Creator element, though in practice often a name authority file will be used.

Descriptive Records

A Dublin Core record describes a resource. There are several purposes to which a descriptive metadata record could be put. But one of the most important of these is *resource discovery*, discussed in chapter 1.

A resource discovery tool is a piece of technology that enables users to (obviously) discover resources: a web search engine, for example, or a library card catalog. And it is the element-value pairs in a metadata record that make that discovery possible. Each element-value pair is what's called an "access point": a way in, if you will, to discovering the resources described by the records available via the discovery tool. For example, if you're interested in finding a work of art called "Mona Lisa," some metadata record must contain the value *Mona Lisa* for the element *Title*. If you're interested in finding work by Leonardo da Vinci, some metadata record must contain that name as the value assigned to the element *Creator*.

This is one of the most important characteristics of a metadata record: that it includes all element-value pairs that might be useful. Of course, "usefulness" is highly subjective: one user might be interested in finding work by Leonardo da Vinci, while another user might be interested in finding Italian Renaissance portraiture; the element-value pairs that might be useful for these users might be quite different. When creating a metadata record, it is critical to consider all possible use cases, and include all possibly relevant element-value pairs. Of course, for a resource such as the *Mona Lisa*, this might mean repeating an element with different values: Title: Mona Lisa, Title: La Gioconda, Title: La Joconde. And so, in a Dublin Core record, all elements are repeatable, with different values:

more than one of the same *kind* of statement may be made about a resource, but saying different things.

The flip side of this particular coin is another important characteristic of Dublin Core metadata records: all elements are optional. If an element is irrelevant to a resource, then it is not included in a record about that resource. For example, while Leonardo da Vinci spoke Italian, that's really not relevant to describing the Mona Lisa itself. So the Language element could just be left out of any Dublin Core metadata record created to describe the *Mona Lisa*.

Artifacts, such as art objects or digital files, are generally going to have a Creator, and a Title, and a Format, and a Date. Characteristics of artifacts may be deliberately assigned to them by their creator (such as title), or inherent in the process of their creation (such as format), and all of these characteristics may be captured in a metadata record. On the other hand, what about natural objects: leaves, rocks, insects, anything not created by human agency? In this case many of the elements from Dublin Core would seem to make less sense. A leaf doesn't have a language. A rock doesn't have a date of creation, or at least not one that can be known with the degree of accuracy that the date of creation of an artifact can be known. An insect doesn't have a creator, or at least not without invoking theology—and then everything that exists would have the same Creator, which is actually not very useful from the standpoint of resource discovery. In order for Dublin

Core to be a lowest common denominator, for it to be able to describe anything and everything, not only are all elements repeatable, but also any irrelevant element may be left out of a record.

Qualified Dublin Core

As mentioned above, Dublin Core was developed to be a lowest common denominator metadata element set. The problem with the lowest common denominator, however, is that sometimes it's too low. For some use cases, more than 15 elements may be necessary. There are therefore three ways in which the Dublin Core element set can be extended.

The core of Dublin Core, so to speak, is the 15 elements discussed above. But the Dublin Core metadata element set also includes a larger set of *Terms*. These incorporate the core 15, but also include such Terms as *modified* (the date of modification), *hasPart* (a related resource included in the described resource), *isPartOf* (a related resource of which the described resource is a part), *audience* (a category of entity, human or otherwise, for which the resource is intended), and many others besides. It is not necessary to list all of the Dublin Core Terms here. The point is that, even while attempting to arrive at a core set of metadata elements to describe any resource, those involved in the development of Dublin Core recognized that the minimal set would be insufficient, for at least some uses. The first extension of the Dublin Core element set is this set of 40 terms, in addition to the core 15 elements.

The second mechanism for extending Dublin Core is by using a *qualifier*. A qualifier is specific to an individual element, and specifies a narrower interpretation—a refinement—of the element. For example, imagine an interoffice memo: the first draft was written on the 1st of December 2014, and it was edited twice, once on the 3rd and again on the 5th. Further this memo pertains to the first quarter of 2015, before which it should be embargoed, and after which it will be irrelevant. All of these—the writing of the first draft, the two edits, the embargo, and the drop-dead date—are dates, and so can be described using the Dublin Core Date element. But the Dublin Core Date element is nonspecific: "A point or period of time associated with an event in the lifecycle of the resource." More detail is needed to cover these more specific types of dates. This detail can be achieved by appending qualifiers to the Date element, like this:

Date.Created = 1 December 2014

Date.Modified = 3 December 2014

Date.Modified = 5 December 2014

Date.Valid = 1 January 2015–31 March 2015

In fact all of these qualifiers exist as Dublin Core Terms: *Created*, *Modified*, and *Valid*. These specific refinements to the Date element are so useful that they were among the first qualifiers to be invented after Dublin Core was developed, and therefore in time were folded into the set of Dublin Core Terms. This is the history of the development of Dublin Core Terms: qualifiers to existing elements and new elements developed for specific use cases, that proved to be popular and useful, get folded into the set of Terms. Some of these use cases include version control (which provided the Terms *replaces* and *isReplacedBy*), education (*audience*, *educationLevel*, *instructionalMethod*), and intellectual property (*license*, *rightsHolder*, *accessRights*). The set of Dublin Core Terms is thus always evolving.

What enables this evolution is that all Dublin Core Terms and elements and qualifiers must be constructed according to the Dublin Core Abstract Model. The Abstract Model is a data model for subject-predicate-object statements, specifying the concepts behind these subjects, predicates, and objects, and how these may be combined into graphs. This logical model is based on the Resource Description Framework (RDF), which will be discussed in chapter 6.

The cleverly named Darwin Core provides an example of a use case that has not (yet?) been folded into the set of Dublin Core Terms. Darwin Core is a metadata schema for providing descriptive biodiversity information. The Darwin Core includes such elements as *continent*, *country*, *island*, and *waterBody*, which build on the Dublin Core term *location*, as well as domain-specific elements such as *kingdom* and *phylum*. Darwin Core elements are constructed according the Dublin Core abstract model, and therefore could be folded into Dublin Core; the question of whether or not they ever will be may rest on whether these elements are of sufficiently broad applicability to justify inclusion.

Finally, the third mechanism for extending Dublin Core is by using an encoding scheme, as discussed in the previous chapter, to clarify the interpretation of the value for an element. If we were to encode our memo's date metadata in ISO 8601, for example, it would look like this:

Created = 2014–12–01

Modified = 2014–12–03

Modified = 2014–12–05

Valid = 2015–01–01/2015–03–31

Use of encoding schemes has also been folded into the set of Dublin Core Terms. As discussed above, recommended best practice for many Dublin Core elements (as well as for many Terms) is to select or construct a value using a specific controlled vocabulary or syntax encoding scheme.

Webpages

Perhaps the most common type of object online is the webpage: a document composed primarily of text, though often with images, videos, or other media embedded in it, and encoded in the HyperText Markup Language (HTML) for display in browsers. Just like anything else, a document on the web may contain metadata within itself, or metadata about a web document may live elsewhere.

As it happens, HTML has contained functionality to enable metadata to be embedded in webpages since the specification for version 2 was first published in 1995. The <meta> element is a child of the <head> element—in other words, it is contained inside the head section of a webpage. The head section contains a variety of metadata about a webpage, including the document title and stylesheet information. The <meta> element, then, contains metadata about a webpage not otherwise specified in other child elements of <head>. In other words, <meta> is a bucket of miscellaneous items.

The <meta> tag has several attributes, but only two are relevant here: *name*, the equivalent of a metadata element, and *content*, the value assigned to that element.

There are five standard values for *name* in HTML5: author (self-explanatory), description (also self-explanatory), generator (the application with which the webpage was created), application-name (the name of the web service of which the webpage is a part, if any), and keywords (tags or uncontrolled vocabulary terms). Thus, if a webpage were created of this chapter, the metadata might look like this:

< meta name="author" content="Jeffrey Pomerantz" >

< meta name="description" content="Chapter 3 of the book Metadata, published by MIT Press"

< meta name="keywords" content="metadata, Dublin Core, Darwin Core, unique identifiers, meta tag, ISO 8601, Essential Knowledge Series" >

Author, description, generator, application-name, and keywords are the values for *name* that are officially recognized in the HTML5 specification document. However, any value may be assigned to the *name* attribute… it's possible to simply make up your own.

Of course, we're already familiar with the problem of making up your own values: being so idiosyncratic that no one knows what you're talking about, like the Goodreads user who tagged *The Hitchhiker's Guide to the Galaxy* with "xxe." Fortunately there is a middle ground between being incomprehensible and being restricted to a mere 5 choices, and that middle ground is to import a preexisting metadata schema. For example, Dublin Core is frequently used in the <meta> element, so the Dublin Core element becomes the value for the *name* attribute, and the value assigned to the element becomes the value for *content*. To continue to use the same example, the metadata for a webpage of this chapter might look like this:

< meta name="dc.creator" content="Jeffrey Pomerantz" >

< meta name="dc.description" content="chapter 3 of the book Metadata" >

< meta name="dc.publisher" content="MIT Press" >

< meta name="dc.language" content="en" scheme="ISO 639" >

< meta name="dc.identifier" content="978-0-262-52851-1" scheme="ISBN" >

< meta name="dcterms.dateCopyrighted" content="2015" scheme="ISO 8601" >

```
< meta name="dcterms.bibliographicCitation"
content="Pomerantz, J. (2015). Metadata.
Cambridge, MA: The MIT Press." >
```

In short, the elements from any schema, and values
from any encoding scheme, may be embedded right into
an HTML document. This certainly seems like the realiza-
tion of the goal of the 1995 workshop that gave rise to the
Dublin Core: to advance the state of the art of descriptive
metadata for online resources. We can declare victory and
move on. Right?

Search Engine Optimization

Wrong.

Because values for *name* and *content* can be invented
uniquely for individual webpages, the HTML <meta> tag
is unfortunately quite easy to abuse... and abused it was.
"Keyword stuffing" used to be a fairly common "black hat"
(that is, unethical) search engine optimization strategy.
Search engine optimization is a set of strategies, constantly
evolving as web search engine technology evolves, for increasing the visibility of one's website in a list of search
engine results. In general, the more lists of results a site
appears in, and the closer to the top of the list, the more

likely it is that search engine users will visit that site. There are, of course, many legitimate search engine optimization strategies, but keyword stuffing is not one of them. Keyword stuffing is the use of lots of irrelevant terms in the meta tags in a webpage, in order for that webpage to be retrieved by a search engine for as many searches as possible. As a result of widespread keyword stuffing, Google—and most other search engines—started to simply ignore meta tags in webpages in the mid-2000s.

More recently Google—and probably most other search engines—has started to use meta tags again, though in a limited way. Google still ignores any content associated with keywords in meta tags (in other words, any tag like this: < *meta name="keywords" content="..."* >). But Google does use the content associated with the description: when displaying a list of results in response to a search, Google may use the description in a meta tag as the snippet to display for a webpage.

Conclusion

Using Dublin Core as an example makes it easy to illustrate many principles of descriptive metadata. As ubiquitous as descriptive metadata is, however, Dublin Core itself is not all that widely used. But Dublin Core was developed to be a metadata core for the web. So what went wrong? Is Dublin Core a failure?

Yes and no. As should be clear to anyone who has ever created a webpage, there is in fact no metadata core to the web. As discussed above, the thinking at the 1995 OCLC workshop in Dublin, Ohio, was that descriptive metadata was necessary for the success of web search tools. Improvements in full-text searching, and the development of tools such as Google that take advantage not only of text but of the network structure and other features of the web, have subsequently shown that that is not in fact so.

Nevertheless, as one of the earliest and largest scale centralized efforts to develop metadata for the web, Dublin Core set the tone for much later metadata development. The Resource Description Framework, mentioned briefly above, predates the development of the Dublin Core Abstract Model, but Dublin Core was perhaps the first metadata initiative to implement the RDF data model, thus promoting the idea that metadata development should be a rigorous and formalized process. As metadata is increasingly understood to be central to the success of large-scale collaborative projects managing information resources, initiatives such as the Digital Public Library of America and Europeana and dbpedia are developing their own metadata schemas, but these schemas rest on the Dublin Core element set and terms. Using Dublin Core as an example makes it easy to illustrate many principles of metadata, for the simple reason that those principles were worked out by the groups that developed Dublin Core in the first place.

Throughout the rest of this book, we will explore metadata schemas that build on these principles—even if not on Dublin Core explicitly. In particular, descriptive metadata will reappear in chapter 7, with our discussion of the semantic web, and the metadata that enables it.

ADMINISTRATIVE METADATA

The nice thing about standards is that there are so many of them to choose from.

—Admiral Grace Hopper

A picture may be worth a thousand words, but a thousand words are not worth much as a metadata record. A thousand words are equivalent to approximately 3 1/2 pages of this book, which may not seem like a lot of data but would make for an exceptionally rich metadata record. So exceptional is this in fact that metadata records of that size rarely exist. One of the functions of a metadata record is to be a proxy for an object, and for a proxy to be effective, it generally must be simpler than the original object.

A proxy may serve a variety of purposes. One simple and obvious use of a metadata record as a proxy for a resource is as a stand-in for discovery. In the previous chapter we looked at descriptive metadata: metadata that simply provides descriptive information about characteristics or attributes of a resource. A primary use of descriptive metadata records is for resource discovery. Discovery is not the only reason that information about characteristics or attributes of a resource might be useful, however; such descriptive metadata may also be useful for informing the maintenance of a resource. Metadata about the origin of a resource, its history, current state, and plans for its future may inform the "care and feeding" of a resource.

In this chapter we will look at administrative metadata: metadata schemas that provide information about the full life cycle of a resource, information that may be used in the administration of resources. It probably goes without saying that there are a great many administrative metadata schemas in existence, so naturally we will be able to look at only a small fraction of them: this chapter will explore schemas for only a few types of common objects. The goal of this chapter is not to provide you with an exhaustive view of administrative metadata schemas for any need, but instead to introduce you to the range of use cases for which administrative metadata is a solution.

Administrative metadata is a very big umbrella. It is so big that some texts separate out as entirely independent categories some types of metadata that are treated here as subcategories of administrative metadata: specifically, technical and preservation metadata. These are treated here as subcategories of administrative metadata because there is considerable overlap in the function and uses of these types of metadata: preservation metadata, for example, provides information to support the processes involved in ensuring that a resource continues to exist over time, and surely such care and feeding is a form of administration. Rights metadata provides information that may be used to control who gets access to a resource, under what conditions, and what they can do with it, and surely such access control is a form of administration.

We will begin with technical metadata, which is the flavor of administrative metadata that is perhaps simplest to understand. Technical metadata provides information about how a system functions, or system-level details about resources.

Technical Metadata: Digital Photography

Digital photography is one of the most familiar situations in which technical metadata plays a role—and the data is often created entirely automatically. Most modern digital cameras and smartphones embed a rich metadata record into the image file that is a photograph. That metadata comes along with the file when the image is downloaded from the camera, moved to another computer, or uploaded to a photo-sharing site such as Flickr or Instagram.

The metadata schema used by most modern digital cameras is the Exchangeable image file format (Exif). An

Exif record contains a fairly large number of elements and values. These are of three distinct types. Values that are set by the manufacturer, and are consistent over the lifetime of the device include the Manufacturer and Model. Values that are configurable by the user include X- and Y-Resolution and Exposure. Values that change from one photograph to the next include the Date and time, Orientation (landscape or portrait), whether or not the flash fired, and GPS coordinates. Figure 9 shows some of the Exif data associated with a photo uploaded to Flickr.

All this metadata is generated at the moment of creation of a digital photograph, and embedded in the image file—and the person holding the camera does not need to do anything. After purchasing a digital camera, a photographer will probably set the internal clock, and will probably change the exposure or resolution of photos under different conditions. But it is possible that most casual photographers are not even aware of the existence of this metadata, as it is created automatically and invisibly at the moment of creation of the digital object itself.

Several software applications and websites exist that allow you to view and edit Exif data. Image management and processing applications such as iPhoto and Adobe Photoshop, and photo hosting services such as Flickr and Instagram, display Exif data. There are websites and plugins for web browsers that will expose this metadata for images on the web. Third-party services can also extract

Canon EOS
Digital Rebel XTi

f/20.0   10.0 mm

30   ISO 100

Flash (off, did not fire)   (i) Hide EXIF

JFIFVersion - 1.01

X-Resolution - 72 dpi

Y-Resolution - 72 dpi

Viewing Cond Illuminant - 19.6445 20.3718 16.8089

Viewing Cond Surround - 3.92889 4.07439 3.36179

Viewing Conditions Illuminant Type - D50

Measurement Observer - CIE 1931

Measurement Backing - 0 0 0

Measurement Geometry - Unknown (0)

Measurement Flare - 0.999%

Measurement Illuminant - D65

Make - Canon

Orientation - Horizontal (normal)

Date and Time (Modified) - 2012:06:04 15:53:38

ISO Speed - 100

Exif Version - 0221

Date and Time (Original) - 2012:06:04 15:53:38

Date and Time (Digitized) - 2012:06:04 15:53:38

Components Configuration - -, -, -, Y

Exposure Bias - 0 EV

Metering Mode - Average

Flashpix Version - 0100

Color Space - sRGB

Focal Plane X-Resolution - 4433.295455

Focal Plane Y-Resolution - 4453.608696

Focal Plane Resolution Unit - inches

Custom Rendered - Normal

Exposure Mode - Manual

White Balance - Manual

Scene Capture Type - Standard

Camera ID - 68

Camera Type - Digital SLR

Figure 9

this metadata from digital images to make use of it in a variety of ways. The project *I Know Where Your Cat Lives* (iknowwhereyourcatlives.com) makes use of GPS data embedded in Exif records to position photographs of cats from web-based photo hosting services on a world map; the project *Photosynth* (photosynth.net) takes this a step further and stitches together multiple photos taken near the same location into panoramic views.

Exif records are, of course, only one form of technical metadata, and moreover are specific to one type of resource, digital image files. Technical metadata is generated, often automatically, at the time of creation and modification of all digital files. I am writing this chapter in Microsoft Word, for example, and by viewing the properties of this file, I can see the date and time on which I first created this file (about six months ago), the date and time of the last saved modification to this file (about a minute ago), the number of minutes this file has been open for editing (more than I care to admit), and many other pieces of technical metadata besides.

Even if this data was not embedded in this Word document, it would be possible to extract some of it from the file system on my computer. All computer operating systems display some technical metadata about the files on a computer: the date and time of creation, the last modified date and time, the size of the file. The UNIX operating system goes a step further and displays information about the access permissions to files: rights metadata, which will be discussed below. Technical metadata captures information about the characteristics of a resource, and as such has considerable overlap with descriptive metadata: the size and type of a file, for example, may be considered descriptive or technical metadata, depending on the context. The characteristics of a resource captured by technical metadata, however, are those that require no human judgment to identify, which allows technical metadata to be captured automatically by software. Naturally, as algorithms for machine processing of digital files improve, the greater the number and types of characteristics of resources that it will be possible to capture automatically.

Structural Metadata: MPEG-21

If digital photography is one of the most familiar situations in which technical metadata plays a role, then digital video is one of the most familiar situations in which structural metadata plays a role. MPEG-21 is a standard from the International Organization for Standardization (ISO) that defines an open framework on which applications can be built to serve and display multimedia files. The heart of the MPEG-21 standard is the *Digital Item*, a structured digital object that may include videos, images, audio tracks, or other resources, plus data describing the relationships between these resources.

The Digital Item Declaration Language (DIDL) describes a set of terms and concepts for describing digital items. Among these are *Container*, which may contain a number of child entities, including a descriptor, items, and other containers. An *Item* is a digital item that may be displayed to a user via a multimedia player application; an item may contain sub-items (as a music album contains individual songs), descriptors, and conditions. A *Descriptor* is descriptive metadata about a Container or an Item. A *Condition* defines a test that must be performed by a multimedia player prior to displaying a file (for example, what file format to display). The DIDL includes many other elements as well, which collectively determine the contents of a multimedia object and how it will be displayed in a range of software and rights environments.

Structural metadata captures information about the organization of a resource. A very simple structural metadata record might describe a book, providing information about the order of chapters, and the order of sections within each chapter. An MPEG-21 record provides similar information about multimedia files: which digital items must play in what order, which audio track must play alongside which video item, etc.

Provenance Metadata

Digital files are easily duplicated. It takes little effort to make a copy, and storage space is cheap. Indeed copying is so easy that entire technology stacks literally cannot operate without it: every time you view a resource on the web, for example, your browser creates a copy of that resource. In economic terms, the marginal cost of production for digital resources is nearly zero. Because of this, data about the provenance of resources is more important in the online world than perhaps it ever was in the physical world, where duplication is far more time-consuming and expensive.

The provenance of a resource, according to the World Wide Web Consortium (W3C) Provenance Incubator Group, is "a record that describes entities and processes involved in producing and delivering or otherwise influencing that resource." In other words, provenance means not just the history of a resource but the relationships between that resource and other entities that have influenced its history.

In 2007 a tool called WikiScanner was launched, which identified the individuals and organizations responsible for editing any specified Wikipedia article. WikiScanner captured the history of a Wikipedia article, cross-checked the IP addresses in the history with the Whois service (a reverse phone directory for the Internet, so to speak, that allows one to look up to whom an IP address is registered), and displayed that list. It should come as no surprise that many controversial edits were uncovered using WikiScanner: edits to the Wikipedia page about Pepsi made from IP addresses registered to the Pepsi Corporation, edits to the Wikipedia page about the Exxon Valdez oil spill made from IP addresses registered to ExxonMobil, edits to Wikipedia pages about Australian politics from IP addresses registered to the Australian Department of Prime Minister and Cabinet, among many others. Perhaps these edits were perfectly legitimate—after all, who knows more about Pepsi than the Pepsi Corporation?—but it's clear that some investigation is justified.

Sadly, WikiScanner is now defunct. (Though a new service called WikiWatchdog replicates much of the same functionality.) But the short happy life of WikiScanner throws into sharp relief why data about the provenance of a resource is absolutely critical. Electronic resources are both easy to duplicate, and easy to edit—some (like wikis) easier than others. WikiScanner makes it abundantly clear that knowing the history of an online resource is necessary but not sufficient; to be able to trust in the validity and reliability of a resource, it is also necessary to know what entities have influenced that history.

If metadata is a statement about a resource, that begs the question of who is making that statement. Metadata is an assertion that someone makes about something. But how trustworthy or reliable or accurate is that assertion? The Internet is a big place, and it is not possible to know everything about the entities that created or otherwise influenced the history of a resource. Provenance metadata is a mechanism to provide data about those entities, and their relationships to the resource and to other entities. In short, provenance metadata is a way of situating a resource in a social network, to provide context that a user might need to evaluate a resource. In the very large network space of the Internet, provenance metadata is a proxy for the more direct and first-hand knowledge about entities that could inform a user's decision about the trustworthiness of a resource.

Several provenance metadata schemas currently exist; the standardization that has occurred in other domains and for other use cases (Dublin Core for general use, Getty thesauri for art objects, Exif for digital images, etc.) has yet to emerge for provenance. These provenance schemas share many characteristics: they are all composed of sets of elements that identify characteristics of the resource or of entities that have influenced it, and they all categorize relationships between resources and entities. Work by the W3C to develop a provenance data model nicely illustrates this. The three "core structures" in this data model are *entity*, *agent*, and *activity*, consistent with the W3C Provenance Incubator Group's definition: an entity is a resource, an agent is an entity that has influenced the life cycle of that resource, and an activity is the nature of that influence. Entities may be *derived from* other entities, or *attributed to* an agent; entities may be *generated by* or *used in* activities; et cetera.

The W3C put a great deal of excellent work into developing recommendations for provenance standards.

If metadata is a statement about a resource, that begs the question of who is making that statement.

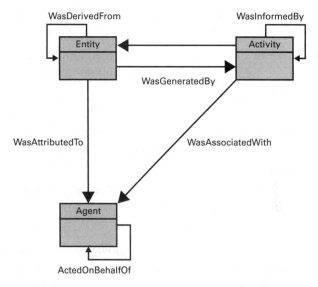

Figure 10

Much of this work has been folded into the development of PREMIS, an even broader schema for capturing metadata about the preservation of resources.

Preservation Metadata: PREMIS

Perhaps the most fully developed metadata schema for supporting preservation is another standard from the Library of Congress: Preservation Metadata Implementation Strategies. PREMIS was developed to be a core set of metadata elements for the preservation of digital objects. The use of the word "core" here is meant in the Dublin Core sense: the PREMIS element set is intended to be the minimum necessary to capture data about how to preserve digital objects over time.

According to the PREMIS documentation, preservation metadata is "the information a repository uses to support the digital preservation process." The definition of "repository" is left slightly ambiguous, but it can be understood to be an online collection of resources that's managed over the long term. There are several categories of information that a repository uses to support the digital preservation process: viability, renderability, understandability, authenticity, and identity. In other words, a repository must ensure that a digital object continues to exist over time, that it remains possible to display and use it, and that the original or canonical version can be identified, versus copies or modified versions.

The PREMIS data model defines four entities of importance to the preservation process: *objects* (digital resources, which may be abstract intellectual entities such as the collection of representations of the *Mona Lisa*, or specific resources such as a specific digital photograph of the *Mona Lisa*), *agents* (people or organizations that may influence the object), *events* (time-stamped actions performed by agents on the object), and *rights statements* (permissions such as intellectual property rights). Each of

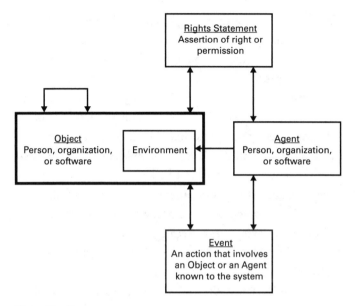

Figure 11

these entities contains a set of "semantic units," which in other metadata schemas would be called elements.

PREMIS specifies a large number of semantic units for these four entities. Semantic units for Objects include some familiar ones, such as *size*, *format*, and *creatingApplication*, as well as some less familiar, such as *significantProperties* (characteristics of a resource that are important enough to be preserved) and *preservationLevel* (the preservation functions to be applied to an Object). Other semantic units are likewise familiar: *name*, *type*, and *identifier* for Agents; *date*, *description*, and *identifier* for Events; etc. PREMIS also suggests how to create or select values for some semantic units, though these suggestions are often even less prescriptive than Dublin Core's "recommended best practice": while Dublin Core recommends use of an encoding scheme such as ISO 8601 for the Date element, PREMIS merely suggests that the value for the semantic unit *dateCreatedByApplication* "should use a structured form." In other areas, however, PREMIS is far more precise than almost any other metadata element set, in order to provide as much detail as possible to support the digital preservation process. Recall, for example, that recommended best practice for the Dublin Core Format element is to select a value from the controlled vocabulary of Internet MIME types. PREMIS makes this same recommendation, with such an additional degree of specificity that there are actually 9 format-related semantic units, including *formatName*, *formatVersion*, and *formatRegistry* (a link to or a unique identifier for the full format specification).

Rights Metadata

The issue of copyright looms large over any initiative that deals with digital resources, so it was probably inevitable that several metadata schemas to capture data about rights have been developed. The first of these is of course Dublin

Core. Recall from the previous chapter that one of the core 15 elements of Dublin Core is *rights*, the value for which should be "a statement about various property rights associated with the resource." Three additional Dublin Core Terms qualifying the *rights* element also exist: *license* (a legal document), *rightsHolder* (an individual or organization), and *accessRights* (what rights a rightsHolder has to access a resource, based on policies that are presumably laid out in the license). Dublin Core provides a minimal number of terms for capturing data about rights, all of which are quite broad, with no recommended best practices for how to select or construct values. This leaves the door open to richer schemas for declaring rights metadata.

One of the more widely used of these is the Creative Commons Rights Expression Language (CC REL). Creative Commons is a project to enable sharing of creative work, through the development of standardized legal licenses that allow creators to selectively keep some of the several different rights bundled together under the heading of "copyright," while allowing some uses of their work. In order to accomplish this, Creative Commons has inevitably had to parse copyright exceedingly fine. As a result Creative Commons has articulated in detail the entities and relationships involved in copyright. The specification for CC REL identifies two classes of properties: properties of a work, and properties of the license for that work. Work properties include *title*, *type*, and *source*, which are drawn directly from Dublin Core. Work properties also include the original *attributionName*, "the name to cite when giving attribution when the work is modified or redistributed," and *attributionURL*, the URL to provide for that attribution, preferably a unique identifier. License properties are the following: *permits*, *prohibits*, *requires*, *jurisdiction* (the legal jurisdiction in which the license applies), and *legalCode* (the text of the license). A small controlled vocabulary provides values for these properties: the possible values for *permits*, for example, are Reproduction, Distribution, and DerivativeWorks, while CommercialUse is the only possible value for *prohibits*. The Creative Commons makes use of CC REL in their standardized legal licenses, and even provides a tool on their website that guides the user through the process of deciding which of their several licenses is most appropriate for a resource.

The last rights metadata schema that will be addressed here is the METSRights Rights Declaration Schema, or RightsDeclarationMD. This schema was developed to be an extension to the Metadata Encoding and Transmission Standard; METS will be discussed in more detail below. RightsDeclarationMD has three top-level elements: *RightsDeclaration* (the rights associated with a resource), *RightsHolder* (an individual or organization), and *Context* (a description of what rights holders have what rights, and under what circumstances). Each of these top-level elements has attributes: one attribute of RightsDeclaration, for example, is *RightsCategory*, which may be populated with the values from a small controlled vocabulary that includes copyrighted, licensed, public domain, etc. The Context element is fairly complex, and includes several attributes and subelements. One subelement of Context is *Permissions*, which also has a small controlled vocabulary associated with it, including such values as discover, display, copy, modify, and delete.

Copyright is a large and complex area of law; it therefore lends itself to multiple mechanisms for reducing that complexity. The rights metadata schemas here are all attempts to reduce the complexity of copyright to a metadata schema of manageable size. These schemas have arrived at similar, yet slightly different solutions to this problem. As mentioned above, the arena of provenance metadata schemas is still in flux, unlike other areas such as art and digital images, where standards have emerged. The arena of copyright sits somewhere in between these: multiple rights metadata schemas exist, and these schemas, in principle, may be more or less interchangeable but, in practice, have become standard for certain use cases. Creative Commons licenses, for example, are widespread on the web, while RightsDeclarationMD has narrower use in the library and archive community, which is where the Metadata Encoding and Transmission Standard originated.

Meta-Metadata

This chapter has addressed several metadata schemas, for a variety of types of resources and use cases. But now it is time to discuss the one metadata schema to rule them all: METS, the Metadata Encoding and Transmission Standard.

METS was developed in response to the increase in the early 2000s in digital resources on the web from libraries, archives, museums, and cultural heritage institutions of all types, and the concomitant increase in metadata schemas for those resources. At that time there was also an increase in the number of repositories in which digital resources were being stored: universities were developing institutional repositories for publications, disciplinary repositories were emerging outside of universities (such as arxiv.org), cultural heritage institutions were developing digital libraries for their collections, and software (such as DSpace, eprints, and Fedora) was being developed to enable institutions to easily create institutional repositories and digital libraries. In order to deal with this proliferation of content and functionality, METS was to provide a standard structure for metadata about resources, as well as to ensure that metadata could be exchanged between repositories. METS is a metadata schema that enables the creation of a container—called a "document"—for metadata records. (As previously discussed, what is considered data and what is metadata is largely a matter of your point of view. METS places this issue squarely in the forefront, as the metadata records contained within a METS document must be considered the data to METS' metadata, the Subject to a METS document's Object.) A METS document is, according to the METS documentation, "a mechanism for recording the various relationships that exist between pieces of content, and between the content and metadata that compose a digital library object."

A METS document has 7 parts:

The *Header* contains metadata about the METS document itself, rather than about the resource described in the document. In other words, if METS is metadata about metadata records, the Header section of a METS document is a metadata record about the metadata about metadata records. Elements in the Header include the date of creation of the document, date last modified, and the role of agents associated with the document (Creator, Editor, Archivist, Intellectual Property Owner, etc.).

The *Descriptive metadata* section contains, unsurprisingly, descriptive metadata. Like PREMIS, METS is agnostic as to which descriptive metadata schemas are used in a document, since there are so many of them to choose from; in fact METS allows multiple descriptive metadata sections, so that multiple schemas can be used to describe a single resource. The Descriptive section does not provide any elements native to METS for describing a resource; all description is provided by metadata records in other schemas that are either "wrapped" in or linked from the METS document. Elements that are provided in the Descriptive section, however, include the type of metadata record "imported" into the Descriptive section, the date of creation of that record, the size of the record, and a unique identifier for the record.

The *Administrative metadata* section is subdivided into four sections that accommodate four different types of administrative metadata: technical, intellectual property rights, source, and provenance metadata. Like the Descriptive section, the Administrative section does not provide any native elements for describing the administration of a resource, but allows records from other administrative metadata schemas to be wrapped in or linked from the METS document.

METS employs this approach, of allowing metadata records in other schemas to be either wrapped in the METS document or linked to from it, in several sections. Both approaches have their pros and cons. When metadata records are linked to from the METS document, it is the *File* section that keeps the inventory. Elements in the File section include the unique identifier of the "element" of the METS document (that is, the metadata record linked to), and the date of creation, size, and MIME type of that element.

The *Structural map* section provides a mechanism for organizing the elements of the METS document identified in the File section, and is in fact the only required section of a METS document. Perhaps the most important element provided in the Structural map section is the Type of structure, which allows for both physical objects with physical structure (for example, a book divided into pages that must be in sequence) or digital objects with logical structure (for example, an album divided into tracks), or both. Other elements in the Structural map section include labels and identifiers for each section.

The *Structural link* section of a METS document is mercifully simple: it is simply a mechanism for specifying links between different sections of a METS document. For example, if a METS document describes a webpage, the Structural link section specifies the links between that webpage and any image files embedded in it.

The *Behavior* section is the part of a METS document in which these rules for action may be represented, by associating executable software code with other elements in the METS document. Recall from chapter 2 that an ontology builds on a thesaurus: an ontology is a set of entities and their relationships, as well as a set of rules, which may be rules for action.

Conclusion

As mentioned at the start of this chapter, Administrative metadata is a very big umbrella, with many subtypes, and often multiple schemas exist for each of these subtypes. The nice thing about standards is that there are so many of them to choose from.

That said, though, there is only one function for administrative metadata, in all its forms: to provide information that may be useful in the management of a resource, throughout its life cycle. Since resources are diverse, however, the life cycle and management of resources is equally diverse.

There is inevitably some overlap between administrative and descriptive metadata schemas, as it would be difficult, if not impossible, to manage a resource without first having some descriptive information about it. Thus, while descriptive schemas may contain administrative elements, administrative schemas must necessarily contain descriptive elements. In the next chapter, yet a third broad category of metadata schemas will be explored, one that serves a very different function than either descriptive or administrative schemas: use metadata.

USE METADATA

What was the last phone number you called? Where were you when you placed that call? What was the last thing you bought from Amazon, and what other items were part of that same order? How much money did you withdraw the last time you used an ATM, and was that ATM part of your bank's network? What were the last 25 websites that you visited?

These are all fairly simple questions about what are likely to be your everyday behaviors, but some of them are probably difficult for you to answer: an unfortunate quirk of memory is that everyday occurrences are sometimes the most difficult things to remember. It is, however, possible for others to answer these questions about you. As discussed previously in the context of the NSA's collection of phone metadata, your cell phone carrier collects data about all the numbers you call and that call you, as well as the location of your phone. I personally have been using

Amazon since 1996, and if I were so inclined, I could view a complete history of every order I've made. I do not have access to a history of all of my ATM transactions, but my bank surely does. And both my browser and my Internet service provider have records of every website I've visited. And since I've been using the Chrome browser for several years, Google probably also has a record of every website I've visited in that time.

You may find all of this data collection ominous; many people do. That, however, is an issue for another time: the politics of use metadata will be explored in the final chapter of this book. This chapter, however, explores the variety of types of use metadata.

"We Kill People Based on Metadata."

General Michael Hayden made this rather alarming statement in the panel debate "Re-evaluating the NSA," at Johns Hopkins University in April 2014. And General Hayden is a former Director of *both* the National Security Agency and the Central Intelligence Agency, so it's a pretty sure thing that he knows what he's talking about.

How is death by metadata even possible? Although anything from *Assassinations* to *Zombie art* may be described by the Art & Architecture Thesaurus, no one is going to kill anyone over a controlled vocabulary.

We kill people based
on metadata.

The answer is that metadata can be incredibly revealing. In particular, the type of metadata known as use metadata captures a great deal of data about individuals and individuals' behaviors. Further, not only can use metadata reveal information about individuals, it can also provide rich data about social networks, and the connections between individuals, places, and organizations. Human beings are social animals, so when describing a person, it's almost inevitable that you'll wind up describing that person's relationships with other people. And it should be clear from the very brief foray into network analysis in chapter 2, that once you start discussing relationships, you're discussing networks.

The game Six Degrees of Kevin Bacon provides a silly but nevertheless illuminating example. The goal of this game is to start with any actor or actress, and to connect him or her to Kevin Bacon in six or fewer steps, a step being defined as who was in a movie with whom. For example, Max Schreck (who played the vampire Count Orlok in the 1922 silent film *Nosferatu*), was in *Boykott* with Wolfgang Zilzer, who was in *Lovesick* with Elizabeth McGovern, who was in *She's Having a Baby* with Kevin Bacon—thus giving Max Schreck the surprisingly low Bacon number of 3. The game Six Degrees of Kevin Bacon was obviously based on the idea of "Six Degrees of Separation," made famous by the stage play and movie of the same name, that anyone in the world is connected to anyone else through no more than six other people—provided that you can identify the correct six. ("Six Degrees of Separation" was, in turn, influenced by Stanley Milgram's 1967 "small world experiment," which was one of the first empirical studies of social networks.) Variations on this idea are relatively common. Another popular example is the Erdős number, named after the mathematician Paul Erdős, who collaborated and co-authored papers very widely. Erdős' co-authors (511 of them) have an Erdős number of 1, their co-authors have an Erdős Number of 2 (9,267 people), and so on. (Amusingly, Paul Erdős has a Bacon number of 4, as he was the subject of a documentary, *N Is a Number*. Kevin Bacon, however, has an Erdős number of infinity, which means that there is no connection, as Kevin Bacon has never published a mathematics paper.)

The graphs that make Six Degrees of Kevin Bacon and calculating someone's Erdős number possible are quite simple: the nodes in these graphs are actors or mathematicians, and the edges are "was in a movie with" or "co-authored a paper with." Facebook has taken this idea of a dramatically simplified social network and built a business model on it. Nodes in Facebook are people, places, and things, and edges are "friend" and "likes," thus making Facebook's social graph somewhat more complex than the Bacon or Erdős graphs, but still a simplified version of reality.

Now imagine a social graph that actually attempts to capture the complexity of interpersonal relationships in the physical world. Nodes will still be people, places, and things, but there may be categories of each: cities, songs, buildings, food items, what have you. Edges may have a wide range of values: between people you might have friend, acquaintance, sibling, parent, spouse, neighbor, coworker, employer, employee, etc.; between people and places you might have resides, used to reside, born, works, went to college, etc. The possibilities are not infinite, but are certainly very large, as the variety of human behavior and relationships is very large.

When building a social network—when attempting to categorize nodes and label edges—it's probably futile to attempt to exhaustively capture every variety of person, thing, and relationship, as it is too large a set. The critical task is to decide what the important categories of nodes and labels for edges are, for the network you're attempting to create. These are very simple in Six Degrees of Kevin Bacon, which makes it easy for anyone to play the game. Facebook is somewhat more complicated, with more variety of nodes and edges. But Facebook has a software interface that presents these options to you, and algorithms behind the scenes that manage your network for you. These are important features of Facebook, and an important point about networks in general: the more complex the network, the more critical it is for computing to be involved in its management, and particularly in its analysis. Robin Dunbar first found a correlation between the size of primates' brains and the size of those species' average social groups. Based on these findings, Dunbar proposed that the maximum size of a human individual's social community—that is, the number of people with whom one can maintain stable social relationships, and understand everyone's relationships with everyone else—is approximately 150. Later researchers have debated this number, but estimates do not go much higher than 250. In short, humans can keep in mind a fairly large social network, as long as we are embedded within that network—but analyzing a larger network, or a network outside of one's own social sphere, requires computing.

This brings us back to General Hayden. The type of metadata he was referring to, the metadata that we kill people based on, is exactly this type of data about individuals and the networks in which they are embedded.

It's difficult to get complete information about this. Edward Snowden released a large number of classified documents about the NSA's surveillance program to the press, but even so, not all of those documents are (as of this writing) easily available for the average citizen to review. Still, it's possible to put together a decent understanding of the intelligence community's collection and use of metadata from other sources.

The NSA collects metadata about phone calls, directly from phone carriers. As discussed at the very beginning of this book, this is quite a lot of metadata: the phone numbers of the caller and the recipient, the time and duration of the call, the locations of the caller and the recipient, etc. If the NSA has reason to believe that a particular phone number is associated with a "person of interest," a database of phone metadata can be queried, to identify the numbers with which the phone of interest has had calls, and the numbers with which those phones have had calls.

Simply who calls whom is, of course, not sufficient for any self-respecting intelligence analyst. But the network of phone calls is a social network, which can be used to enrich other social network data that the NSA presumably also maintains. Entities (that is, nodes) in this social network include things like phone numbers, email addresses, and IP addresses, and presumably also individuals, geographic locations, and organizations such as banks. In stories about the Snowden case, various news outlets have reported that edges in this network include relationships such as *employs*, *travelsWith*, and *sentForumMessage*. One can imagine other labels for edges, such as *calls*, *sent email to*, *travels to*, and *visited*.

What did General Hayden mean when he said that we kill people based on metadata? Just this: that metadata about a social network and an individual's place in it, combined with metadata about an individual's actions, provides enough information to justify taking military action against that individual, according to the burden of proof currently required by the US intelligence community.

Data Exhaust

On the one hand, this sounds terrifying. On the other hand, this is no different than what many organizations do that we voluntarily interact with every day. Except for the killing people part.

Amazon, for example, collects a great deal of metadata about its users. In order to purchase anything on Amazon, you must create a profile, which at a minimum includes a credit card number and an address to ship items to. Amazon then captures additional data about you: what items you buy, what items you look at, any reviews that you write, etc. This is not unique to Amazon, of course; all online vendors collect similar types of data.

Aggregating this sort of data over time can allow alarmingly incisive inferences to be made. Perhaps the most famous example of this is the case in which Target predicted that a customer was most likely pregnant based on her purchasing patterns, and sent her a flyer with coupons for baby-related items. This might have simply been a good marketing strategy, had it not turned out that this customer was a minor, and Target had just announced her pregnancy to her parents, before she had.

The data that is produced—and that can therefore be collected—as one goes about one's day-to-day activities is often referred to as "data exhaust." This is a good term for it, because the word *exhaust* captures the idea that this kind of data is the by-product of other processes. The fact that this kind of data is separate from the process that produced it lends itself to being called metadata—though this is a slightly different definition than how the word has been used throughout this book. Up to this point, "metadata" has meant data that was created deliberately; data exhaust, on the contrary, is produced incidentally as a result of doing other things.

Paradata

When using online resources, data is produced incidentally as a result simply of using those resources. Often this data is in the form of web server logs. Web servers run software that generally is never seen by users, that collects data about all of the activities performed by the server. One of these types of activities is fulfilling requests for files on the server: for example, to serve up webpages and the images or other media that are embedded in them. These *access logs* contain a great deal of information about the "client" that made the request: the date and time of the request, the application that issued the request (usually the type and version of the web browser), the IP address of the client, even the identity of the user if a login was required.

Web server access logs are useful to enable a system administrator to track the use and health of a server, but

The data that is produced—and that can therefore be collected—as one goes about one's day-to-day activities is often referred to as "data exhaust."

they are limited to descriptive data. Increasingly systems are therefore being designed to collect specific types of data about users' use of a system. One area where this type of use data is becoming increasingly important is in online teaching and learning.

Paradata is a relatively new term for use metadata about learning resources. This term was adopted in the context of the National Science Digital Library (NSDL), as a way to refer to data about users' use of the digital learning objects within the NSDL. The NSDL, originally a project of the US National Science Foundation, is a collection of metadata about and links to high-quality online educational resources, with a focus on the STEM disciplines: sciences, technology, engineering, and mathematics. These resources are distributed across the web, on the websites of such organizations as NASA, the Public Broadcasting Service (PBS), the American Museum of Natural History, and many others with an educational mission. The NSDL is a portal, providing search and browsing functionality across these many diverse collections, to enable users to easily find quality resources for STEM education.

The NSDL does not itself host any educational resources; all resources are hosted on other organizations' websites. The NSDL is comprised entirely of descriptive metadata about educational resources and the organizations that host them. In addition to this metadata, however, the NSDL also collects metadata about the use of these resources: how often they are downloaded, tweeted about, included in other collections, used in curricula, modified, and many other indicators of use. In its documentation about paradata, the NSDL makes it clear that paradata is intended to be a supplement to, and not a replacement for, descriptive metadata. The descriptive metadata hosted by the NSDL aids users in searching and browsing for educational resources; the paradata collected by the NSDL provides feedback to the NSDL and participating organizations about how, why, and by whom those resources are being used.

As of this writing, the NSDL seems to be the only organization that is using the term "paradata" to mean "use metadata about educational resources." The NSDL is, however, certainly not the only organization to collect paradata. Over the past few years, "dashboards" have become a common tool for the presentation of data about websites and other online systems. Google Analytics, for example, is a well-known system for collecting detailed use data about websites. Many "learning management systems"—platforms for hosting online course content and discussions—collect data about students' use of the materials, and progress through the course. This figure, for example, shows some dashboard data from a massive open online course (MOOC) about metadata that the author taught through Coursera. Dashboards in some other education platforms present even more finely grained user data so that, for example, a teacher can identify individual

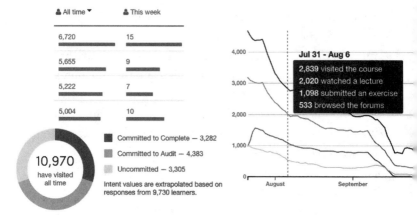

Figure 12

students who may be falling behind their classmates as well as specific lessons those students are having trouble with.

Referring to use data as use *metadata* is a fairly new development, and in fact slightly problematic. Collecting data about the use of resources is, of course, nothing new: web server software has included functionality to collect logs for almost as long as web servers have existed. Prior to the existence of web server logs, libraries collected data about books checked out, museums collected data about foot traffic through galleries, grocery stores collected data about which items were purchased and with which other items, etc. All of these are varieties of use data, but no one refers to them as use *metadata*.

This may be why terms such as "data exhaust" and "paradata" have been coined: to refer to use data, while simultaneously making it clear that such data is separate from the more traditional conception of metadata. "Data exhaust" is a useful term, but it is not very widely used, and it is not yet clear if the term "paradata" will come to be widely used. It is clear, however, that use metadata is a large and growing topic of interest, and that we are currently seeing rapid change in this arena, as software is developed to capture and analyze the wide variety of types of use metadata. As this development progresses, there will be an increasing need for clarity around terminology for use metadata: in the context of web servers this data is often called "logs," in the context of other online resources it is often called "analytics." In the context of still other services, it is often simply called "data."

ENABLING TECHNOLOGIES
FOR METADATA

This chapter will address technologies that underlie much of the metadata used on the web, and that underlies almost all semantic web-related metadata. Up to this point, only metadata schemas that already exist have been discussed. It may seem entirely obvious that whatever schema or thesaurus is being used, whether a metadata record is embedded in or external to the resource, that schema or thesaurus already exists. In this chapter, we will see how metadata schemas are created in the first place.

The technologies that will be discussed in this chapter are complex, and deserve much longer treatments than will be attempted here. There are, of course, many books and online tutorials that provide these longer treatments, and some of these are listed in the Further Readings section. This chapter will brush lightly over these technologies, exploring them only insofar as is necessary to explain their role in the creation of metadata schemas.

Structured Data

Question: What kind of a message is this?

> Lorem ipsum, Dolor sit amet, consectetur adipisicing elit, sed do eiusmod tempor incididunt ut labore et dolore magna aliqua. Ut enim ad minim veniam, quis nostrud exercitation ullamco laboris nisi ut aliquip ex ea commodo consequat. Duis aute irure dolor in reprehenderit in voluptate velit esse cillum dolore eu fugiat nulla pariatur.

Answer: It's impossible to tell; it's not written in a way that conveys any actual meaning. More important for our purposes here, it's presented as an undifferentiated block of text, so the formatting does not provide us with any clues.

Next question: What kind of a message is this?

> Lorem ipsum,
> Dolor sit amet, consectetur adipisicing elit, sed do eiusmod tempor incididunt ut labore et dolore magna aliqua. Ut enim ad minim veniam, quis nostrud exercitation ullamco laboris nisi ut aliquip ex ea commodo consequat.
> Duis aute,

Answer: Again, the words are meaningless. But its format suggests a letter, with a greeting at the top, the text of the letter in the middle, and a sign-off at the end. It's possible to identify this text as a letter because it's laid out on the page in a familiar form.

Finally: What kind of a message is this?

Lorem: ipsum
Dolor: sit amet
Consectetur: adipisicing
Elit: sed do eiusmod tempor incididunt
Ut labore et dolore magna aliqua. Ut enim ad minim veniam, quis nostrud exercitation ullamco laboris nisi ut aliquip ex ea commodo consequat.

Answer: Its format suggests a memo or an email, with the header at the top (To, From, Date, and Subject) and the text of the email below. Once again, it's possible to identify this text because it's laid out in a familiar form.

Formatting is useful to human readers who have learned what different genres of writing look like on the page: because we are familiar with the genre of email messages, we "see" the To, From, Date, and Subject lines in the third text, above. Formatting can also be used by software to automatically detect the genre of a text. In other words, formatting is a form of structure, and this particular form of structure helps us identify the category of a text, even when the writing itself is meaningless.

Text on a page has structure, as formatting. At a deeper level, language itself has structure: different languages use letters with different frequencies, different languages are more or less flexible about word order, individual writers have different styles of word use, etc. Thus any piece of writing in a natural language has inherent structure. This is of course why automatic tools for language translation (for example, Google Translate) and stylometry (authorship analysis, for example, to determine if Shakespeare was the author of a particular piece of writing) are able to work at all.

Of course, texts are not the only thing that has structure. Indeed all data is structured. Only pure randomness is unstructured, and then there's an argument to be made that pure randomness is noise, and not data anyway.

Text in natural language—that is, writing like this, intended for human consumption—is the classic example of unstructured data. Yet, as just discussed, even natural language texts have some structure, such as formatting and the statistical distribution of letters and words. Often the unstructured data has structure embedded in it that can be brought to light with some effort. Network analysis has already been discussed, and thanks to services such as Facebook and Twitter, it's commonly understood that something as seemingly unstructured as a social network has a great deal of inherent structure. In particular, the web, though it may be the most unstructured repository

All data is structured.

of files in existence, displays structure when viewed at a large scale.

Any and all data may be represented in a structured fashion. This is what enables databases to exist. A database allows a dataset to be decomposed into a set of statements, and stored as a set of values assigned to a set of shared fields. This should sound familiar. These statements have in fact the same structure as subject-predicate-object statements: in a dataset about art objects, for example, the shared fields might include Title, Creator, and Date of creation, and each individual record about a different art object would assign different values to these fields. Such a table is not a database but a spreadsheet—though, for readability, it's often easier to represent a database as a spreadsheet.

Another way to represent a database is relationally. In a relational database, a relationship may be established between a field and a tabulated set of values, in order to control what values can be assigned to that field. In other

Table 4

Title	Creator	Date of creation	In the collection of
La Gioconda	Leonardo da Vinci	1503–1506	Musée du Louvre
L.H.O.O.Q.	Marcel Duchamp	1919	Musée National d'Art Moderne
Eagle	Alexander Calder	1971	Seattle Art Museum

words, the table that a field refers to becomes a controlled vocabulary, and values that are assigned to cells in that field may only be assigned from that controlled vocabulary. Relational databases are especially useful for ensuring data quality: name authority files, for example, prevent names from being misspelled, eliminate ambiguity about different individuals with the same name, etc. Ensuring data quality is one of the primary functions of name authority files, and one of the primary reasons why every entity in a name authority file has a unique identifier.

Data quality is an especially important issue where metadata records for resource discovery are concerned. Resources can be rendered essentially invisible due to poor

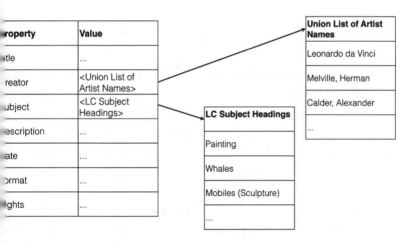

Figure 13

data: if a value in a record is different than the term that a user employs in a search—due to different terminology being used, or simply due to a misspelling or other error—then that record may not be retrieved for that user's search, and that user may never discover a relevant resource.

The existence of metadata is partly predicated on the existence of structured data. Structured data is organized according to a *data model*, which is a representation of the types of entities described by the data, the properties of those entities, and the relationships between them. Again, this should sound familiar. There are many data models in existence, but the data model central to most metadata work is RDF.

RDF

RDF, the Resource Description Framework, is a framework for describing resources. This, to be fair, is a tautology. But it is actually more useful as a definition than tautologies usually are. RDF is a data model: in other words, it's a framework, a logical structure according to which data is organized. A framework for what? For describing resources. What resources? Any resources at all, though generally RDF is used to describe resources on the web. In short, RDF is a generic data model for making descriptive statements about entities.

Recall the 3-part subject-predicate-object relationship discussed in chapter 2. This 3-part relationship is at the heart of RDF, and is referred to as a *triple*. A set of RDF triples is a *graph*, as discussed in the very brief foray into network analysis, in chapter 2.

An important feature of RDF is that the subject of a triple *must* be identified by a uniform resource identifier (URI), so that it can be referred to unambiguously in triples or by online services. Say that Frédéric D. Vinci is a photographer employed by the Louvre, who took a digital photograph of the *Mona Lisa*, and that file is stored online. The RDF triple representing that relationship would look like figure 15.

Mssr. Vinci might himself have an identifier that can be used as the canonical means to identify him online (the

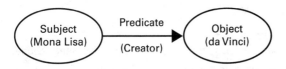

Figure 14

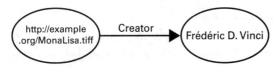

Figure 15

URL for his personal website, for example), and that relationship would be another triple. Creator, of course, is a Dublin Core element, and as such defined on the Dublin Core website: another triple. Anything can be a resource, and any resource identified by a URI may be the subject of a triple. Thus RDF triples may "link up" to form graphs.

RDF is a framework for describing resources. But in the arena of metadata, usually the resources and relationships of interest fall within a narrow domain: art objects, music, resources on the web, etc. RDF is the framework according to which most metadata schemas are built... according to which the types of entities, and relationships between those entities, that exist in the universe of a metadata schema are defined.

DCMI Abstract Model

The types of entities, and relationships between those entities, that exist in the universe of Dublin Core, for example, are defined in the Dublin Core Metadata Initiative Abstract Model, which is built on RDF.

While the DCMI Abstract Model is the framework on which the Dublin Core metadata schema is built, it was developed to be more broadly applicable than just the Dublin Core. The DCMI Abstract Model was in fact developed to be a *universal* abstract model for metadata schemas. Even though it's called the *Dublin Core Metadata Initiative* Abstract Model, it was developed to be independent of any specific syntax or semantics for encoding entities and relationships. In short, the DCMI Abstract Model was developed to be a generic model: the model on which Dublin Core is built, and a model on which *any* metadata schema may be built.

Why develop a generic abstract model? Because doing so actually increases Dublin Core's usefulness. Recall that the Dublin Core element set was created to be a lowest common denominator: so simple to use that everyone not only could, but would use it. The trade-off for this radical simplicity, however, is that Dublin Core would not be sufficient for every use case. The developers of Dublin Core understood this, and understood that the ability to extend Dublin Core was necessary for its success. Qualifiers were developed as the mechanism for extending Dublin Core: enabling elements to be refined (Date.Created, Date.Modified, etc.) and entirely new elements to be developed (the elements *continent*, *country*, *island*, etc. from the Darwin Core). The fact that Dublin Core can be used as a foundation, and easily built on using a generic abstract model, promotes the use of Dublin Core, which in turn promotes the outcome for which Dublin Core was originally developed: "to advance the state of the art in the development of resource description (or metadata) records for networked electronic information objects."

This "modular" approach to developing metadata schemas is possible when all schemas recognize the existence of the same types of entities and relationships. As a negative example, Dublin Core recognizes *Creator* as an entity primarily responsible for the creation of a resource, while the W3C's provenance schema recognizes *Agent* as an entity that has any influence in the life cycle of the resource. Not only do these entities have different names, but they are conceptualized differently and incompatibly. This is a basic problem of ontology (in the philosophical sense): communication is a challenge when the parties don't recognize the same categories of entity in the universe. The DCMI Abstract Model is fundamentally a mechanism for pinning down the ontology of metadata schemas.

The DCMI Abstract Model pins down the ontology of metadata schemas in a way that will be familiar. The described resource is the subject of an RDF triple (for example, the *Mona Lisa*). The described resource is described using a property-value pair. A property-value pair is composed of exactly one property and exactly one value (for example, the creator is Leonardo da Vinci). There are two types of values: literal and nonliteral. A nonliteral value is an entity, and a literal value is a string of characters that represents that entity (for example, the name *Leonardo da Vinci* is a literal value that represents the nonliteral, actual person who went by that name). Both the described resource and the nonliteral value are resources. In other words, any entity that can be described, can be the subject of an RDF triple.

There is more to the DCMI Abstract Model: the model also describes how metadata records are constructed, how unique identifiers stand in for entities, and how resources are described by encoding schemes. But this diagram is enough to convey the point that the generic model on which any metadata schema can be built, is itself built on the logic of RDF. RDF articulates the structure of triples and networks of triples. The DCMI Abstract Model explores that structure in more detail, but it makes use of that structure.

XML

This is where XML enters the picture. It was mentioned above that the DCMI Abstract Model, as a generic model,

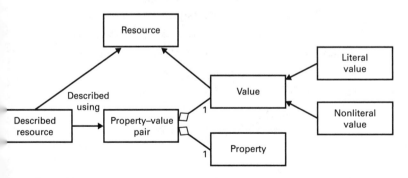

Figure 16

does not specify any specific syntax or semantics for encoding the entities and relationships in a metadata schema. In practice, however, the syntax and semantics of many metadata schemas are encoded in XML.

Even though this section is titled XML, it will start with HTML, the HyperText Markup Language. A markup language is not truly a language but rather a controlled vocabulary that allows instructions to be embedded in the text of a document, so that there is a clear separation of the text and the instructions. HTML is designed to be embedded in (as you might expect) hypertext documents: that is, documents on the web. And what makes the web a *web* is that documents may contain hyperlinks: thus the documents may be considered nodes and the links edges.

The instructions that HTML conveys are mostly concerned with formatting: this text is bold, this is italic, this is a heading, this is a link, etc. Your web browser interprets these instructions, so that the webpage you see is formatted as the creator of that webpage intended. HTML is metadata only in the sense that it describes the formatting of a document. We need not get into HTML any further, but if you're curious what this markup looks like, see the <meta> tag example from chapter 3, or this simple example:

```
<h2>This text is a heading</h2>
```

```
<b>This text is bold</b>
```

```
<a href="http://example.com/">This text is a link</a>
```

XML stands for the Extensible Markup Language. (And no, *extensible* doesn't start with the letter X. What can I tell you?) Again, XML is not a language but a set of instructions. However, where HTML is a set of instructions for specifying the formatting of a web document, XML is a set of instructions for specifying other markup languages.

In chapter 2 we invoked language as a metaphor: a metadata schema is a simple, structured language, and a metadata record is a set of statements made in that language. This is a useful metaphor, but like any metaphor, it can't be pushed too far... and XML is where this particular metaphor breaks down. XML is a structured language in which you can create other structured languages—an idea that simply doesn't make sense when talking about human languages.

It makes sense when talking about XML, though. You can, for example, create HTML in XML. This has in fact been done, and is called XHTML. HTML5, the latest version of HTML as of this writing, is also built on XML—though previous versions of HTML were built on a different markup language, the Standard Generalized Markup Language (SGML).

DTD

Your web browser interprets the HTML in a webpage, and displays the contents of that page: this text is bold, this italic, etc. But how does your web browser know how to interpret HTML? How does it know that <b> means "make this text bold," and not anything else?

The answer is a document type definition (DTD). A DTD is a document that declares and defines all of the elements that exist in a markup language. Different versions of HTML have different DTDs. But, since the elements in HTML are fairly stable across versions, these DTDs are fairly similar. A DTD for a version of HTML therefore contains definitions for all the markup elements that exist in that version of HTML. For example, the declarations for headings and font styles in the DTD for HTML 4.01 are as follows:

< !ENTITY % heading "H1 | H2 | H3 | H4 | H5 | H6" >

< !ENTITY % fontstyle "TT | I | B | BIG | SMALL" >

All 6 levels of heading, and all font styles (teletype or monospaced, italic, bold, etc.) are declared in these DTD statements. The definitions of *heading* and *fontstyle* are declared elsewhere in the DTD.

This is a simple example from the DTD for HTML. But the beauty of DTDs is that they can be used to define elements for any markup language. The Dublin Core metadata element set, for example, is also declared in a DTD. The following line declares all 15 elements:

```
< !ENTITY % dcmes "dc:title | dc:creator | dc:subject
| dc:description | dc:publisher | dc:contributor
| dc:date | dc:type | dc:format | dc:identifier |
dc:source | dc:language | dc:relation | dc:coverage |
dc:rights" >
```

And then these lines declare the *title* element in detail:

```
< !ELEMENT dc:title (#PCDATA) >

< !ATTLIST dc:title xml:lang CDATA #IMPLIED >

< !ATTLIST dc:title rdf:resource CDATA #IMPLIED >
```

Briefly, the element *title* requires data of a particular type (Parsed Character Data), and the attributes (ATTLIST) of *title* are derived from XML and RDF, and must be of a different data type (Character Data).

It is not necessary to delve further here into the creation of a DTD. As mentioned above, some resources that provide more detail are listed in the Further Readings section, below. These very simple examples nevertheless show that it is possible to declare any element in a DTD. A DTD that declares multiple elements therefore declares an entire markup language—an entire metadata schema.

It is also not necessary to delve further into DTDs because DTDs are becoming less common. Because HTML5 is not built on SGML, elements in HTML5 are not declared in a DTD. Instead, HTML5 elements are declared in a Document Object Model (DOM), which contains all elements that exist in HTML5, organized in a hierarchical tree structure. All modern web browsers contain functionality to refer to this DOM, and thus interpret the elements used in an HTML document. Thus at a very high level a DTD and a DOM may be considered to be analogous, as both declare the elements and the attributes of elements in a markup language. As of this writing, Dublin Core has not yet been revised, or a new version of Dublin Core developed, to accommodate this trend of DTD-lessness.

To conclude: All data is structured, and it is useful to keep the basics of database design in mind when thinking about the creation of metadata schemas. RDF allows the structure of a dataset to be articulated as a graph of triples. Entities may be both the subject and the object of multiple triples, which allows the graph to grow. A relationship between entities—the predicate—is the equivalent of a column header in a spreadsheet: a category of statement that can be made about that relationship. The terms that may be used to specify the object of a triple may be derived from a thesaurus. The syntax and semantics of the set of relationships, and the way in which thesaurus terms are specified, is specified using XML DTDs.

This chapter addressed a set of technologies that underlie much of the metadata on the web. A set of technologies used together to enable a specific set of functionalities is often referred to as a *technology stack*. The technology stack discussed in this chapter is in fact part of the World Wide Web Consortium (W3C) technology stack for the web—but only part. RDF and XML appear at the base of the W3C stack. Building on that base are technologies for mobile, voice, and other web services that are beyond the scope here. Also building on that base are technologies that rely on metadata: specifically, the semantic web.

THE SEMANTIC WEB

If suitable terms can be found in existing vocabularies, these should be reused to describe data wherever possible, rather than reinvented. Reuse of existing terms is highly desirable.

—Tom Heath and Christian Bizer (2011), *Linked Data: Evolving the Web into a Global Data Space*

Not content with merely inventing the World Wide Web, Tim Berners-Lee later went on to articulate a vision of a "web of data." This data would, of course, be consumable by human users of the web, as the current web is. But this data would also be capable of being processed by software, so that applications could perform tasks on behalf of users. Berners-Lee and colleagues wrote in 2006 that their vision was then unrealized, and it remains so today.

We are, however, getting closer to realizing this vision, as various standards, technologies, and other tools emerge that enable it. Many of these tools are metadata schemas and vocabularies, and the technologies that these are built on.

The semantic web is a complex subject, in terms of the technology that it encompasses. Some of these technologies are metadata-related technologies, but many are not. However, this is a book about metadata, not a book about web-related technologies generally. Consequently, in order to focus on what is specifically related to metadata, the same caveat from the start of the previous chapter also applies here: this chapter will brush lightly over lots of technologies that are involved in the semantic web, exploring these only insofar as is necessary to explain the metadata aspects, and some longer treatments of these topics will be listed in the Further Readings section.

Introduction to the Semantic Web

Metadata is not all there is to the semantic web, but metadata is a critical part of the operation of the semantic web. In order to understand how metadata fits in to the semantic web, it is first necessary to understand the vision of the semantic web and what problem the semantic web is attempting to solve.

In the original 2001 article in which a vision of the semantic web is laid out, Berners-Lee and colleagues state that the semantic web "will bring structure to the meaningful content" of the web, and that software agents will be able to use this structure to "readily carry out sophisticated tasks for users" (p. 36).

As discussed in the previous chapter, all data is structured to some extent. However, not all structure is accessible to algorithms. The statistical structure of the English language, for example, may be analyzed algorithmically, which is how stylometry works... but this sort of structure is implicit, which opens up room for debate about whether Shakespeare was in fact the author of *A Funeral Elegy for Master William Peter* (current consensus among literary scholars is that he is not). In order for software agents to be able to readily carry out sophisticated tasks for users, data on the web must be explicitly structured.

Software Agents

The idea of the software agent has been somewhat co-opted by the image of Agent Smith, from the movie *The Matrix*. While many of us might enjoy having our computers speak in Hugo Weaving's voice, Agent Smith is not what Berners-Lee and colleagues meant by "software agent." Rather, the semantic web vision of a software agent is more akin to email filters than to a malicious rogue computer program bent on subjugating all of humanity.

In their original article Berners-Lee and colleagues use the scheduling of a series of medical appointments as an example of the sort of tasks that software agents should be able to perform in a semantic web-enabled future. In this example, your agent retrieves data from your doctor's agent about the prescribed treatment, then finds lists of providers, checks which are covered by your insurance, which have acceptably high ratings, filters by their distance from your home, and finally interacts with the providers' agents to schedule appointments at times that fit into your calendar.

In order for this example to work in reality, several pieces of data would have to be provided by several entities: the treatment and details thereof from your doctor's office; a list of covered providers from your insurance company; ratings from the providers themselves or from some third party; calendars from the providers; your home address, and a personal calendar from you.

The calendar is perhaps the simplest part of this example. As discussed previously, ISO 8601 is a standard for representing dates and times, so assume that all calendars in this example are encoded according to ISO 8601. Events on your calendar will have dates and times associated with them, so your calendar agent can search for dates and times with no associated event, and share that list of dates and times with another agent.

It is not necessary for your calendar agent to share your entire calendar, or any of the events on your calendar. All that is necessary for your agent to share is some metadata about your calendar: the set of dates and times for which there are no associated events. In this example, software agents are not truly making use of the "meaningful content" of the web: they are not passing digital resources back and forth. Instead, software agents are passing metadata *about* those resources back and forth. In other words, this vision of the semantic web relies on software agents using the structure imposed by metadata on the meaningful content of the web.

Introduction to Linked Data

The semantic web requires more than putting structured data online; it requires creating links between the structured data. The fact that links exist between webpages is what makes it a *web*. Similarly it is links between structured data online that enables software to make connections between datasets.

In their book on linked data, Tom Heath and Christian Bizer state that "the basic idea of Linked Data is to apply the general architecture of the World Wide Web to the task of sharing structured data on global scale." While the web is a complex information space, that complexity arises from a fairly simple set of rules. These rules were proposed by Berners-Lee, in which he articulates a set of design principles for the web. Berner-Lee's rules are not requirements, but suggestions, for how data should be structured—though adhering to these rules ensures that new technologies for the web will be interoperable with existing infrastructure. Adhering to these rules also ensures that structured data on the web can be linked. To paraphrase these rules:

1. Use URIs as identifiers for resources.

2. Format URIs according to HTTP, so that resources can be found easily, using established technology.

3. Use standards such as RDF to provide both the resource and metadata about the resource.

4. Provide links along with this metadata to other URIs, so that more resources can be found.

All of the technologies invoked by these rules have already been addressed in previous chapters. A URI is a unique identifier for a resource online. The semantic web requires that a resource have a URI, so that it can be referred to unambiguously by other resources or online services. A resource that's accessible at a URI is called "dereferenceable."

HTTP is the preferred mechanism for referring to URIs because it is the most common protocol on the web, and therefore allows URIs to be dereferenced by a wide range of software and services. When the resource at a URI is a webpage, for example, and that URI is dereferenced by a web browser, what's passed back to the browser is that webpage. The vision of linked data is that any type of resource can be dereferenceable by software, and that what's passed back to the querying agent is not just the resource, but also metadata about that resource.

RDF is a framework for describing resources, making use of subject-predicate-object triples. The resource described by the triple (the subject) is uniquely identified by a URI, making it possible for that resource to be dereferenced. The object in the triple is also a resource and is likewise dereferenceable, creating a relationship between two uniquely identified resources. When a resource is dereferenced, the resource itself is provided to the querying application, along with any metadata records that exist about that resource. Included in that metadata is a list of other resources to which the original resource is linked: the objects in any triples of which the resource is the subject, and any other resources that are the subject of triples in which the original resource is the object. If a user were to query a semantic web search engine for the *Mona Lisa*, for example, a digital image of the *Mona Lisa* and descriptive metadata about it might be provided, along with links to further data about Leonardo da Vinci, Lisa del Giocondo, and the Louvre Museum: in short, data to help the user put the resource in context.

Europeana has created an excellent video about linked open data and its uses. Europeana is a portal to cultural heritage materials in the collections of (as of this writing) almost 150 "memory institutions" of various types (galleries, libraries, archives, museums, etc.), across the European Union. The digitized resources themselves are hosted by the providing institutions; what Europeana provides is shared mechanisms for users to access those resources. The example provided in this video is of a search for "Venus." What is the user searching for: the planet, the goddess, the tennis player Venus Williams, the *Venus de Milo*, the Botticelli painting *The Birth of Venus*? By providing linked open data about these resources, cultural heritage institutions enable the creation of tools that can disambiguate this search to help the user. For this search the search tool dereferences resources matching the term "Venus," and provides these to the user. Along with these resources comes metadata about the resources, and links to other resources that provide context. From this additional contextual information, the user who conducted the search will be able to identify the many meanings of the term "Venus" and decide which is the most relevant.

Everything Is Connected

The predicate in an RDF triple is what puts the *link* in Linked Data. Any resource can be either the Subject or the Object of a triple: Leonardo da Vinci (subject) was born in (predicate) the town of Vinci (object), for example, but Vinci (subject) is a part of (predicate) Firenze Province (object). When resources are dereferenceable, a network of triples between resources is created. It is this network of triples that makes linked data *linked*, that gives structure to the web of data, and that makes it possible for software agents to use this structure to carry out tasks. Linked data is a way of structuring data on the web so that it's (1) structured enough to be useful by software and (2) uses shared standards that can connect data from one provider with data from other providers.

It has been 15 years since Berners-Lee and colleagues wrote their original article about the semantic web, and software agents have not emerged quite as they envisioned. Instead of semi-autonomous agents interacting with web services, web services mostly interact directly with each other, serving and ingesting structured data via application programming interfaces (APIs). What metadata is being served and ingested by these APIs? The answer to that question, of course, depends on the application. But it may be anything and everything.

Calendars provide a good example. The websites of many organizations for which events play a significant role (schools, theaters, etc.) provide an iCalendar feed. These are common on the web, and often appear as a URL with the extension *.ics*, usually accompanied by a calendar-shaped icon. The iCalendar standard encodes event metadata, using elements such as start and end time, a summary, contact information for the event organizer. An iCalendar feed is a URL; many calendar applications allow that feed URL to be added to the calendar, which will then display all events encoded in that feed. Because the feed is a URL, it may be updated by the provider. Thus, if I subscribe to the iCalendar feed for the Boston Red Sox, for example, my personal calendar will always include the Sox's schedule.

Another good example of metadata being served and ingested via APIs is Exif data available from photo hosting services. Recall the projects *I Know Where Your Cat Lives* and *Photosynth*, from chapter 4: these services query the APIs of photo hosting services such as Flickr and Instagram for photos that match certain criteria (the photo contains a cat, or a specific landmark), and that contain GPS data in the Exif record. The API for a map application is then used to import this GPS data, and place these photos on a map.

There is no restriction to what can be put on the web. This is both the good and the bad of the web: on the one hand, you do not need permission to start a website or a blog or a Tumblr or a Pinterest board on whatever esoteric topic you happen to be interested in. On the other hand, someone out there has almost certainly started a website or a blog or a Tumblr or a Pinterest board on whatever topic you find most offensive. There are organizations that control certain aspects of the web—the Internet Corporation for Assigned Names and Numbers (ICANN) oversees the Domain Name System (DNS), for example—but no organization exerts control over the content that may be put up online. Of course, some organizations, such as some authoritarian governments, attempt to exert control over what users can access. And search engines exert de facto control over what users can access, by making resources more or less visible in lists of search results. But both of these are filters after the fact, not control over what is put online in the first place.

Likewise there is no restriction to what metadata can put on the web. This is as it should be, since the possible number of statements that may be made about a resource is nearly infinite.

Linked Data for Art

The types of statements that are in fact made about a resource, however, tend to be limited, as the scope of individual metadata schemas tends to be domain specific. The domain of art makes a good example here, as it is quite broad and encompasses many different types of entities and relationships.

The work of the J. Paul Getty Research Institute has already been mentioned. The Getty Institute has in fact developed four vocabularies to describe material culture: the Art & Architecture Thesaurus (AAT)®, the Thesaurus of Geographic Names (TGN)®, the Cultural Objects Name Authority (CONA)®, and the Union List of Artist Names (ULAN)®. Note that the AAT and TGN are both thesauri, and therefore have a hierarchical structure, like the figure accompanying the example of parent–child relationships for *Seattle* in chapter 2. CONA and ULAN are both name authority files.

The Getty vocabularies predate the idea of linked data: AAT, the oldest of the four, dates to the 1970s. Given their domain-specific scope, however, these vocabularies naturally lend themselves to being interconnected. As of this writing, the CONA hierarchy is still in pilot release, and the *Mona Lisa* is not yet included online. But another Leonardo da Vinci piece is currently online: *Caricature of a Man with Bushy Hair*, CONA ID number 700002067. The CONA record for this object includes several elements for which the values come from other Getty thesauri. The *Work Type*, for example, is *drawing*, AAT ID 300033973, and the *display materials* are pen and ink, AAT IDs 300022452 and 300015012, respectively. The creator of this work is, of course, Leonardo da Vinci, who naturally is an entity in ULAN, ID 500010879. This work is in the collection of the

Getty Center, ULAN ID 500260314, but it apparently used to reside in England, TGN ID 7002445.

Each ID number mentioned above is a unique identifier. The Getty Research Institute has created a unique identifier for every entity in all four of their thesauri. The Getty is a prominent player in the art world, and it has dedicated significant effort to developing these thesauri and other standards related to art. Many museums and other cultural heritage organizations therefore use the Getty's products. It is important nevertheless to note that these IDs are assigned by Getty. A URI is inherent in a resource once it's on the web, but Getty's unique identifiers are arbitrary, assigned according to whatever mechanism has been developed by the Getty, though nevertheless widely used. In turn these IDs correspond to a URI on the Getty's servers: the TGN ID 7002445, for example, corresponds to the URI http://vocab.getty.edu/tgn/7002445. At that URI is to be found a record containing a table of predicate-object pairs, all of which are two parts of triples with England as their subject (for example, the predicate *placeType* and the object *countries (sovereign states)*).

Every entity in the Getty vocabularies has a unique identifier, from which a URI is created. Every entity record may connect to any number of other entity records, via these unique identifiers. As a result the Getty vocabularies are tightly interconnected, as the example of Leonardo's *Caricature of a Man with Bushy Hair* demonstrates.

Even more important is the fact that a record from *any* thesaurus or metadata schema may connect to entity records in the Getty vocabularies, via these unique identifiers. Similarly any entity record that has a unique identifier, in *any* thesaurus or metadata schema, may be connected to. The Library of Congress, for example, provides their Subject Headings and Name Authority File, as well as several other vocabularies, via The Library of Congress Linked Data Service—in which every entity of course has a unique identifier, corresponding to a URI. (The URI for Leonardo da Vinci, for example, ishttp://id.loc.gov/authorities/names/n79034525.html.) The Virtual International Authority File (VIAF) was discussed briefly in chapter 2: VIAF is an authority file that combines records from multiple sources into a single service. The sources of VIAF records include, among others, the Library of Congress and the Getty Research Institute; VIAF records list all of the sources from which data was compiled, with links back to the original records. Every VIAF record, of course, has a unique identifier corresponding to a URI (the VIAF URI for Leonardo da Vinci ishttp://viaf.org/viaf/24604287).

Recall the One-to-One Principle, discussed in chapter 2: there should be one and only one metadata record for a single resource, for a single metadata schema. The "for a single metadata schema" part is important. No less than three records for Leonardo da Vinci have been mentioned in this section alone. Each of these records serves a different purpose, however: one of the primary purposes of the Library of Congress Name Authority File is to provide a controlled form of names, while the Union List of Artist Names provides not just names but biographical and other information. VIAF combines data from multiple sources into one record, to reduce the cost and increase the usefulness of authority files. While multiple records for a single resource may exist, all of these serve a dual function: to be a definitive record that can be dereferenced by an application or service, and to provide further links to related resources that can themselves be dereferenced.

DBpedia

Enter DBpedia. As the name indicates, the DBpedia dataset is derived from the content of Wikipedia. Wikipedia natively contains a great deal of structured data (beyond the structure of language and the layout on the page), including links, GPS data, and categories. Perhaps the most visible structured data in Wikipedia, however, is the Infobox: the sidebar in the upper right corner of many Wikipedia articles, containing summary information about the subject of the article. The Infobox about Leonardo da Vinci, for example, contains the element *Style*, with the value "High Renaissance," and the element *Notable work(s)*, with multiple values. This Infobox also contains the element *Born*, with three implied elements: *birth name*, *birth date*, and *place of birth*, each with appropriate values. A great deal more data could be extracted from the text of the Wikipedia article about Leonardo da Vinci, but it would require processing to structure it usefully, where the data in the Infobox is already structured.

A single Wikipedia article corresponds to a single entity (a person, place, thing, or idea). There can, of course, be debate about what constitutes "a single entity," which is why Wikipedia articles split and merge over time. But the ebb and flow of articles notwithstanding, there is a DBpedia entry corresponding to every entity with an article in, as of this writing, 125 different language versions of Wikipedia, for a total of over 38 million entries.

A DBpedia entry is a metadata record for an entity, containing a large set of elements and values. Not every record will contain the same elements, of course: a record for an individual will contain a *birthplace* and *birth date*, for example, while a record for a city would not. Moreover a record for a city might contain the element *birthplace of*, and a list of individuals who were born there, while that would not be included in records for other types of entities. A single DBpedia entry may not contain all, but will certainly contain a great deal of, the data about an entity that could be extracted from all the language versions of Wikipedia. So, for example, the entry on Leonardo da Vinci contains not only his name, places, and dates of his birth

Leonardo da Vinci

Portrait of Leonardo by Francesco Melzi

Born	Leonardo di ser Piero da Vinci April 15, 1452 Vinci, Republic of Florence (present-day Italy)
Died	May 2, 1519 (aged 67) Amboise, Kingdom of France
Known for	Diverse fields of the arts and sciences
Notable work(s)	*Mona Lisa* *The Last Supper* *The Vitruvian Man* *Lady with an Ermine*
Style	High Renaissance
Signature	 *vi leonardo de vinci*

Figure 17

and death, and notable works, but also artists who influenced him, ships named after him, and works of fiction in which he appears.

The formation of networks from subject-predicate-object triples has been explored previously: the subject (Leonardo da Vinci) is the resource being described, a category of relationship between the resource and some other entity is the predicate (for example, birthplace), and the object is the entity that has the predicated relationship with the resource (for example, Vinci). Leonardo da Vinci is the subject of further triples and the object of others, Vinci is itself both the subject and object of other triples, ad infinitum. In this way, were we so inclined, we could map out the network of relationships between everything in the entire universe.

Of course, even Wikipedia is finite. So, in using Wikipedia to map out a network of relationships between entities, eventually one would reach the edge of the known universe, so to speak.

Enter the *sameAs* element. Every DBpedia entry contains the *sameAs* element, and list of associated values, which are the URIs of other records about the same entity. Many of these are DBpedia entries in other languages, but some are from different sources, such as the Wikidata database, the New York Times' linked open data vocabulary, or the Cyc vocabulary. The *sameAs* element indicates that all URIs listed dereference records that refer to the

Property	Value
dbpedia-owl: abstract	Leonardo di ser Piero da Vinci (Italian pronunciation: [leo'nardo da v'vint∫i] About this sound pronunciation ; April 15, 1452 – May 2, 1519, Old Style) was an Italian Renaissance polymath: painter, sculptor, architect, musician, mathematician, engineer, inventor, anatomist, geologist, cartographer, botanist, and writer. His genius, perhaps more than that of any other figure, epitomized the Renaissance humanist ideal.Leonardo has often been described as the archetype of the Renaissance Man, a man of "unquenchable curiosity" and "feverishly inventive imagination". He is widely considered to be one of the greatest painters of all time and perhaps the most diversely talented person ever to have lived. According to art historian Helen Gardner, the scope and depth of his interests were without precedent and "his mind and personality seem to us superhuman, the man himself mysterious and remote. Marco Rosci states that while there is much speculation about Leonardo, his vision of the world is essentially logical rather than mysterious, and that the empirical methods he employed were unusual for his time.Born out of wedlock to a notary, Piero da Vinci, and a peasant woman, Caterina, in Vinci in the region of Florence, Leonardo was educated in the studio of the renowned Florentine painter Verrocchio. Much of his earlier working life was spent in the service of Ludovico il Moro in Milan. He later worked in Rome, Bologna and Venice, and he spent his last years in France at the home awarded him by Francis I. Leonardo was, and is, renowned primarily as a painter. Among his works, the Mona Lisa is the most famous and most parodied portrait and The Last Supper the most reproduced religious painting of all time, with their fame approached only by Michelangelo's The Creation of Adam. Leonardo's drawing of the Vitruvian Man is also regarded as a cultural icon, being reproduced on items as varied as the euro coin, textbooks, and T-shirts. Perhaps fifteen of his paintings have survived, the small number because of his constant, and frequently disastrous, experimentation with new techniques, and his chronic procrastination. Nevertheless, these few works, together with his notebooks, which contain drawings, scientific diagrams, and his thoughts on the nature of painting, compose a contribution to later generations of artists rivalled only by that of his contemporary, Michelangelo. Leonardo is revered for his technological ingenuity. He conceptualised flying machines, a tank, concentrated solar power, an adding machine, and the double hull, also outlining a rudimentary theory of plate tectonics. Relatively few of his designs were constructed or were even feasible during his lifetime, but some of his smaller inventions, such as an automated bobbin winder and a machine for testing the tensile strength of wire, entered the world of manufacturing unheralded. He made important discoveries in anatomy, civil engineering, optics, and hydrodynamics, but he did not publish his findings and they had no direct influence on later science.
dbpedia-owl: alias	Leonardo di ser Piero da Vinci (full name)
dbpedia-owl: birthDate	1452-04-15 (xsd:date)
dbpedia-owl: birthName	Leonardo di ser Piero da Vinci
dbpedia-owl: birthPlace	dbpedia:Vinci,_Tuscany dbpedia:Republic_of_Florence
dbpedia-owl: birthYear	1452-01-01 (xsd:date)
dbpedia-owl: deathDate	1519-05-02 (xsd:date)
dbpedia-owl: deathPlace	dbpedia:Clos_Lucé dbpedia:Amboise dbpedia:Kingdom_of_France
dbpedia-owl: deathYear	1519-01-01 (xsd:date)

Figure 18

same entity—just as your home address, work address, cell phone number, and Social Security number are all understood to refer to the same entity, you. Or, perhaps a better example, as a 10-digit and a 13-digit ISBN number are both understood to refer to the same published book.

The *sameAs* element is what enables a network of relationships between entities to extend not just to the edge of what Wikipedia knows about but to the edge of human knowledge. There is sure to be overlap in the content of different language versions of Wikipedia. But it is probably safe to say that there are topics that are covered in one language version of Wikipedia and not covered in another. As of this writing, for example, the entry on Leonardo da Vinci in the Italian language Wikipedia contains a far

owl:sameas   fbase:Leonardo da Vinci
              http://purl.org/collections/nl/am/p-10456
              http://fr.dbpedia.org/resource/Léonard_de_Vinci
              http://de.dbpedia.org/resource/Leonardo_da_Vinci
              http://cs.dbpedia.org/resource/Leonardo_da_Vinci
              http://el.dbpedia.org/resource/Λεονάρντο_ντα_Βίντσι
              http://es.dbpedia.org/resource/Leonardo_da_Vinci
              http://eu.dbpedia.org/resource/Leonardo_da_Vinci
              http://id.dbpedia.org/resource/Leonardo_da_Vinci
              http://it.dbpedia.org/resource/Leonardo_da_Vinci
              http://ja.dbpedia.org/resource/レオナルド・ダ・ヴィンチ
              http://ko.dbpedia.org/resource/레오나르도_다_빈치
              http://nl.dbpedia.org/resource/Leonardo_da_Vinci
              http://pl.dbpedia.org/resource/Leonardo_da_Vinci
              http://pt.dbpedia.org/resource/Leonardo_da_Vinci
              http://wikidata.org/entity/Q762
              http://wikidata.dbpedia.org/resource/Q762
              http://www4.wiwiss.fu-berlin.de/gutendata/resource/people/Leonardo_da_Vinci_1452-1519
              http://sw.cyc.com/concept/Mx4rwAvMqZwpEbGdrcN5Y29ycA
              http://yago-knowledge.org/resource/Leonardo_da_Vinci

Figure 19

more extensive biography than exists in the English language Wikipedia, as well as sections on Leonardo's library and manuscripts, which are entirely absent in the English language article. Once it is established that the Italian language Wikipedia article and the English language Wikipedia article are about the same entity, however, two isolated networks may be linked together. And the longer the list of URIs associated as values for the *sameAs* element, the more data from more networks can be linked.

Linked Open Data

This is, of course, why many organizations have made their datasets available as linked open data: because the more records about more entities that can be connected together, the richer the knowledge represented online can be.

What makes linked open data *open* is that an organization will publish a dataset on the web, using the structure of RDF triples within the dataset, as well as between entities within and external to the dataset. Organizations can of course use RDF triples in proprietary datasets, and leverage other organizations' efforts. But many organizations recognize that publishing their dataset openly, and thus expanding the growing network of linked open datasets, benefits them. A rising tide lifts all boats.

The more records
about more entities that
can be connected to-
gether, the richer the
knowledge represented
online can be.

As of this writing, the J. Paul Getty Research Institute is currently working on publishing all four of their vocabularies, discussed above, as linked open data: the Art & Architecture Thesaurus and the Thesaurus of Geographic Names were published in 2014, and the other two vocabularies will follow in 2015. Every record in the AAT and the TGN (for example, "sofas") currently includes a "Semantic View," which is a set of statements in which the resource exists as the subject, predicate, and/or object: in other words, all of the parent terms (furniture, multiple-seating furniture, etc.) and child terms (canapés, chesterfields, etc.) in the hierarchy, as well as the dates of creation and modification of the term, the unique ID for the term in English and other languages, etc. Some URIs from the Getty vocabularies have been included in DBpedia, thus linking this very rich network to others.

The *New York Times*' linked open data vocabulary was mentioned in passing, above. In 2010, The *New York Times* began publishing their "Times Topics" subject headings, a list of approximately 30,000 terms covering topics reported on in the newspaper. As of this writing, the *Times* has published approximately 10,000 of these. The URIs for at least some of these have been included in DBpedia, thus linking the very rich data provided by the *New York Times* to that extracted from Wikipedia.

The Library of Congress Subject Headings, Name Authority File, and other vocabularies have been made available as the Library of Congress Linked Data Service. Some unique identifiers from the Library of Congress have been included in DBpedia.

As discussed above, the Library of Congress has joined with several other nations' national libraries, the Getty Research Institute, and OCLC, to develop VIAF™, the Virtual International Authority File. Many unique identifiers from VIAF have been included in DBpedia.

Even Facebook, a company that has a reputation for being fairly restrictive about providing access to their data, has published a schema: the Open Graph protocol is a set of elements (called "properties": title, type, image, url, etc.) and recommended values (article, music.song, music.album, video.movie, etc.), that allows any resource on the web to "become a rich object in a social graph." When a video or a news article, for example, is embedded in a status update on Facebook, the title and description are imported via OGP.

There are in fact dozens or hundreds of organizations and services that make their data available as linked open data: the Linking Open Data cloud diagram shows many (though probably not all) of these, and connections between them. In total, the datasets in the current version of this diagram contain over 20 billion subject-predicate-object triples. Over time, more and more datasets have been made available as linked data, and more will no doubt be made available in the future.

More Is More

Enriching knowledge by connecting networks together sounds like a good idea. After all, described that way, we could be talking about the Internet itself, and it would be difficult to argue that the Internet wasn't a good idea. The technologies that have arisen from the Internet are familiar, however, and their use in daily life are reasonably well understood. It's less clear how linked data might be used.

Shortly after Tim Berners-Lee and colleagues first articulated their vision of the semantic web, Bijan Parsia wrote an excellent brief article titled "A simple, prima facie argument in favor of the Semantic Web." (Sadly, and somewhat ironically, this article has vanished from the web, along with the site that published it, and is now only available through the Internet Archive's Wayback Machine.) To paraphrase, Parsia's simple, prima facie argument goes like this: web links, as they currently exist, are "untyped"— that is, a link is simply a pointer from webpage A to webpage B; a link contains no data to provide context for why it exists between those two pages. Nevertheless, network analysis is a powerful tool, even when the network contains only untyped links... and by making use of network analysis, Google has created remarkable tools and services. Therefore, Parsia argues, if web links were typed, Google (and other tools that rely on network analysis) could create even more remarkable tools and services. To make Parsia's simple argument even simpler: more data is better.

It's certainly possible to argue with a "more is more" argument: the availability of increasingly more data has led to discussions of a "data deluge" (among other terms that get used for this phenomenon) for over a hundred years. But the availability of increasingly more data makes it possible for tools and services to be built that make use of that data. Search engines like AltaVista and Excite were ticking along happily in the mid-1990s, relying on full-text indexing, when suddenly Google came along with an algorithm that made use of more data: by layering network analysis on top of full-text indexing, Google shifted the entire search engine marketplace. Innovations that leverage data that exists online, but that no one had previously thought to use in quite that way, seem to be the bread and butter of the Internet. When data is available, someone somewhere will figure out how to use it. It may not be in a way that you are happy with (few people outside of the intelligence community are probably happy with the NSA's use of cell phone metadata), and it may even destroy your business model (as Google did to AltaVista). But more is indeed more, on the larger scale of creating an environment that encourages innovation.

Schema.org

One particularly important project to simplify the task of putting structured data on the web is schema.org. Schema.

org is something of a rare beast: a collaboration between Google, Microsoft, and Yahoo, companies that probably rarely collaborate on anything. But as companies with significant business interests in search technology, schema.org serves all of their interests very directly.

Schema.org is based on microdata, which is a specification for embedding metadata inside a webpage. The <meta> tag, discussed in chapter 3, allows metadata to be included in the <head> section of a webpage. Microdata—and schema.org—go further than that, and allow metadata to be included anywhere in a webpage.

An entire book longer than this one could be dedicated to a How To for schema.org. (The same could be said of all of the schemas and vocabularies that are brushed over so quickly in this book.) That said, here is a very brief overview of the mechanics of schema.org, using this book as an example.

Schema.org relies heavily on the HTML <div> tag, which specifies a section or division of a webpage. For the sake of this example, assume that the webpage on the MIT Press site for the Essential Knowledge series, of which this book is a part, contains a section for this book. That section might look like this:

```
<div>

<img src="metadata-bookcover.jpg">
```

```
<h1><a href="http://mitpress.mit.edu/books/
metadata">Metadata</a></h1>

<span>by <a href="http://mitpress.mit.edu/authors/
jeffrey-pomerantz"> Jeffrey Pomerantz</a></span>

<span>Everything we need to know about metadata,
the usually invisible infrastructure for information
with which we interact every day.</span>

</div>
```

To parse this markup, this section contains an image of the book cover, a title that is also a link to a webpage about the book, the author's name that is a link to a webpage about the author, and a brief blurb about the book. Here is that same section, marked up with schema.org metadata:

```
<div itemscope itemtype="http://schema.org/Book">

<img itemprop="image" src="metadata-bookcover.
jpg">

<h1 itemprop="name"><a href="http://mitpress.mit
.edu/books/metadata">Metadata</a></h1>
```

```
<span itemprop="author">by <a href="http://
mitpress.mit.edu/authors/jeffrey-pomerantz">
Jeffrey Pomerantz</a></span>

<span itemprop="description">Everything we
need to know about metadata, the usually invisible
infrastructure for information with which we interact
every day.</span>

</div>
```

The *itemscope* element in the opening *div* tag declares that the section is about an item. The *itemtype* element declares the type of item that the section is about (in this case, a book), and indicates that the declaration of that type in schema.org is at the URL provided. Now any application that parses this webpage—that can also interpret schema.org metadata—will be able to interpret the properties of the item type Book, because those are enumerated at that URL.

Schema.org declares many properties for the item type Book. Some of these are image, name, author, and description, which are used above. Every property expects data of a specific type: name and description expect a string of text, author expects a person or an organization, image expects a URL. Each data type also has properties: a person, for example, may have dates of birth and death (of data type *date*), an affiliation (data type *organization*), and an address (data type *postal address*).

Types in schema.org form a hierarchy: a person, for example, is a type of *Thing*, which is the highest level entity in schema.org. A *PostalAddress* is a child entity of *Contact-Point*, which is a child of *StructuredValue*, which is a child of *Intangible*, which is a child of *Thing*. Child entities inherit properties from their parents, so a postal address, for example, must have a *description*, because that is a property of *Thing*. This is the same kind of hierarchical structure as was illustrated in the Seattle example in chapter 2.

This is all well and good. But again, how would schema. org actually be used in practice? Fortunately, it is simpler to answer this question about schema.org, than it is to answer this question about linked open data generally.

And the answer is: Search in Google for "MIT press metadata." Chances are, you will get a link to this book on MIT Press' website as your first result. Do not click through to that page: instead, look at the 2-line snippet of text below the link. Note that that snippet is similar to the *description* above from the example of schema.org markup. Why is that text showing up in Google search results? It is because the HTML markup for the webpage for this book on the MIT Press website indicates the section where the description is located. Google's web crawler then simply grabs that text, assuming that the markup is telling the truth.

This is a trivial example, as only the content of the *description* appears in these search results. Many organizations make use schema.org markup much more extensively, however, which enables Google (and other search tools) to provide much more refined search results. A particularly rich example of this is to search for recipes. Search in Google for "chocolate chip cookie recipe," or for a recipe of your choosing. Below the search box, you will see a *Search tools* button: click it, and several menus drop down, including *Ingredients*, *Cook time*, and *Calories*. Say you have a nut allergy: you can restrict the list of ingredients in the recipes retrieved for your search so that recipes with nuts are not included. Say you're on a diet: you can restrict the list of retrieved recipes to include only those that produce cookies of less than 100 calories.

How does Google do this? The short answer is: schema.org. Probably every one of the recipes retrieved for this chocolate chip cookie search is marked up with schema.org metadata. Every element of a recipe can be specified using schema.org, including ingredients (itemprop="ingredient"), preparation instructions (itemprop="instructions"), yield (itemprop="yield"), number of calories (itemprop="calories"), etc.

There are two pieces to schema.org: a set of entities and their properties, and a syntax for embedding data about these entities into webpages. When this structured data is embedded in a webpage, Google, Bing, Yahoo, and any other search tool that can parse schema.org, can make use of it to enable the user to create highly customized and filtered searches. Searching in Google for "chocolate chip cookie recipe no nuts less than 100 calories" might retrieve some useful results, but using the *Search tools* menus is likely to be more accurate.

Ultimately, this is the promise of the semantic web, and the validation of Parsia's "more is more" argument. The more data that exists on the web, and specifically the more data that's embedded in webpages, the more web services can do with that data to help the user navigate the very large information space that is the web. And when that data is openly available, in open formats, it's possible for new applications to be built to provide new services. Often it is the big players on the web—Google, Microsoft, and Yahoo, for example—that develop these new services, but this is not always the case. Open data creates an environment that encourages innovation, in which anyone, anywhere, can potentially build useful tools and services.

Conclusion

The vision of the semantic web is of a "web of data" that can be used by algorithms and other forms of software agents to perform tasks automatically, on behalf of human users. To achieve this vision, the semantic web relies on structured data and metadata about resources that can be passed between services.

Structured data is necessary to achieve the vision of the semantic web, but not sufficient. Not only must data

The vision of the semantic web is of a "web of data" that can be used by algorithms and other forms of software agents to perform tasks automatically, on behalf of human users.

be structured, but that structure must adhere to widely shared standards. If every web service developed its own schema for structuring its data, that would be the equivalent of every town and city developing its own type of fire hydrants: there could be no collaboration between fire departments because no department's hoses would fit any other department's hydrants. Only when everyone—or at least a significant portion of everyone—is using the same standards, is widespread collaboration possible.

The quote at the start of this chapter makes this point explicitly for linked data. Almost no matter what kind of resources need describing, a schema or a controlled vocabulary or a thesaurus has already been developed to describe it. Do you need to describe fire ecology? Railways? Offshore drilling? Astronomical objects? Web services? Someone out there has created a thesaurus for you. To be sure, many of these will not be free to use: a niche market exists for businesses developing taxonomies for niche markets. But even if you're using a proprietary standard, you can still share data with others who are using that proprietary standard, even if not with the rest of the world. And, of course, it's linked *open* data only if the standard being used is open—that is, free to implement. The quote at the start of this chapter is an argument for using shared standards, whether open or closed. Do not reinvent the wheel: almost guaranteed, a wheel has already been developed that will suit your needs.

THE FUTURE OF METADATA

Metadata, as we saw in chapter 1, is fundamental to the operation of libraries. This was true in the time of Callimachus, and it is no less true today. Many types of collections of resources exist, however, maintained by libraries as well as by organizations of all types. Metadata is fundamental to the operation of all of these types of collections. In the modern era of ubiquitous computing and structured data, metadata is perhaps more important than ever before. As the volume and variety of resources online increases, metadata will continue to be fundamental to the future.

Among the most interesting projects currently ongoing in the library world are Europeana and the Digital Public Library of America (DPLA). Both are collections of materials from cultural heritage institutions (libraries, archives, and museums), digitized and made available online. Neither host these digitized materials; all digital objects are hosted by the cultural heritage institutions themselves (what Europeana calls Partners, and the DPLA calls Hubs). The role of Europeana and the DPLA is that of a portal: to provide functionality to enable users to access these materials via searching, browsing, and application program interfaces (APIs).

Metadata is central to providing this functionality. Both Europeana and the DPLA have developed custom metadata schemas: the Europeana Data Model (EDM) and the DPLA Metadata Application Profile (MAP). Both of these articulate an abstract model as well as a set of properties specific to each entity (called a *class*) in the abstract model. For example, both metadata schemas differentiate between the cultural heritage object itself (what the DPLA refers to as the *SourceResource* class) and the web resource that is the digital representation of the source resource. Both further articulate other types of entities: aggregations or collections of the source or digital resources, places, and time spans. Both the EDM and the MAP then articulate a set of properties of these entities. For example, the properties of the SourceResource, in both the EDM and the MAP, include creator, description, subject, title, isPartOf, references, and replaces, and many of the other 15 Dublin Core elements and larger set of Dublin Core Terms. Several unique properties have also been developed for the EDM, and subsequently adopted by the MAP: for example, incorporates, isDerivativeOf, and isSimilarTo. The EDM (and by extension the MAP) also incorporates elements from other metadata schemas, including the Open Archives Initiative Object Reuse and Exchange (OAI-ORE), and the Creative Commons Rights Expression Language.

In short, Europeana and the DPLA have taken metadata schemas created for several different use cases, selected those elements that are relevant for describing the universe of cultural heritage, and built a custom data model and element set for that purpose. In doing this, Europeana and the DPLA are at the forefront of a growing movement to develop domain-specific metadata.

Domain-Specific Metadata

Pandora is a popular online music service that makes extensive use of metadata. The heart of Pandora is the Music Genome Project®, which consists of approximately 450 characteristics that may be used to describe a piece of music. These characteristics are the equivalent of elements in a metadata schema, and run the gamut from the relatively simple (for example, key, tempo, beats per minute, gender of the vocalist) to the highly subjective (for example, vocal characteristics, degree of distortion of instruments). Pandora employs a team of musicians whose job it is to listen to every song that Pandora licenses, and to describe each song according to as many of these hundreds of characteristics as are relevant. Characteristics are the equivalent of elements, to which the Pandora team assigns values. Some of the controlled vocabularies from which values may be selected are probably straightforward, like the set of values for key (A, B, C, etc., and major or minor), beats per minute (an integer), tempo (adagio, andante, allegro, etc.), and gender of the vocalist. Some values are probably unique to Pandora, are Pandora's value-add in the highly competitive music marketplace.

It is easy to apply descriptive metadata to digitized music files, but it is difficult to do it well. In part this is because music both evolves rapidly and is a highly subjective experience. On the one hand, some characteristics defined in the Music Genome Project are quite stable: for example, the set of values for key, tempo, and beats per minute. On the other hand, some vocabularies that provide values for certain characteristics change over time, as genres of music evolve, and the technology used to record and process music evolves. For example, the genre "house music" not only has a large number of subgenres; it is an active area of musical innovation, so new subgenres emerge frequently. As Pandora adds songs in the genres "Complextro," "Dutch house," "Moombahton," "Nu-disco," and whatever subgenre of house music will emerge next, those values are presumably added to the controlled vocabulary used for the characteristic "genre." Thus Pandora—and presumably all other music services—face the challenge of constantly having to update their metadata, both characteristics and the controlled vocabularies that provide values to them. Even classical music—a genre in which one might expect description to be well established—faces this challenge. Many performers record versions of the same pieces of music, for example, and the metadata for online music services does not always capture the distinction between the composer and the performer. For this and other reasons, descriptive metadata for classical music is an area of active development.

Music is, of course, not the only domain in which custom metadata exists. The field of education, for example, has a fairly long history with metadata. The Institute of Electrical and Electronics Engineers (IEEE) Standard for Learning Object Metadata was first developed in 2002 to describe "learning objects": usually (though not necessarily) digital resources that may be used to support teaching and learning around a single learning objective. The LOM consists of a set of categories, each of which contains a set of elements that describe it. For example, the *Educational* category contains elements such as *TypicalAgeRange* and *TypicalLearningTime*, while the *Rights* category contains the *Copyright* element. Many learning management systems (LMS) used in K–12 and higher education contain functionality to support LOM, so that a learning object, or collection of learning objects, can be imported into the LMS if associated LOM metadata is present.

Moreover the field of education is an area of active metadata development. One area that has traditionally resisted standardization in higher education is transcripts: while many institutions of higher education use the same enterprise systems, student transcripts are still most often printed and sent by mail. Recently, however, companies such as Parchment are developing schemas that represent entities such as students, courses, and programs, which enable institutions to export and import student transcripts and other credentials.

Publishing is another field that both has long history with metadata and is a current area of active development. Publishing metadata has traditionally consisted of simple descriptive metadata: publisher, date of publication, ISBN, etc. With the advent of ebooks, as well as the rise of self-publishing platforms such as Amazon's Kindle Direct Publishing, Lulu, and others, publishers (and self-publishers) are discovering that the richness and quality of one's metadata is critical to whether or not a title is discovered by readers.

APIs

Application programming interfaces (API) are one of the most interesting uses of metadata on the web, yet APIs are often not even recognized as an application of metadata. An API is a set of functions that may be used to interact with a piece of software, often a web service. Most web services (Twitter, YouTube, Flickr, Goodreads, Evernote, Dropbox, etc.) have APIs. Some web services have multiple APIs. Amazon, for example, has APIs for their products, payments, web services, Kindle, and several other parts of their business. Google has APIs for most of their products. APIs are often bidirectional: different functions let the user export data from or import data to a web service.

Web services such as Flickr, YouTube, and Amazon, of course, have well-developed user interfaces. These "front end" interfaces are generally rich with features that enable a user to interact with the resources hosted by the service (photos, videos, products, etc.). APIs, however, provide something of an end-run around this front end, enabling interaction both with the resources and metadata about the resources. APIs are not secret backdoors; they're deliberately created to provide an alternative method of interacting with the web service, often for algorithms such as software agents.

APIs are an area where what is *data* and what is *metadata* is largely in the eye of the beholder. From the point of view of the web service, everything provided via the API is data, since there may not be any distinction in how different pieces of data are stored, and the API may provide access to both resources and metadata. An entity-relationship model for a database may not differentiate between data that's a resource and data that's metadata: it's all just data. From another point of view, however, only the resource itself is data (the tweet, the video on YouTube, the digital object hosted on a museum website, etc.); everything else is metadata about it.

As web services have proliferated, APIs have proliferated right alongside them. Some APIs in fact get as much or even more traffic than the associated front end website for the service. This is why they are worth discussing in this chapter on the future of metadata: APIs are becoming an increasingly popular mechanism by which the metadata about resources (and yes, the resources themselves) may be accessed.

APIs, of course, allow individuals to create applications in the "ecosystem" of a web service: applications that create custom YouTube playlists, for example, or that "mash up" data from two or more services. The DPLA in particular encourages the development of apps that make use of data from the API, highlighting these in an App Library. Some of the more interesting of these apps include *DPLA Map*, an app that identifies resources in the DPLA near the user's current location, and *WikipeDPLA*, a browser plugin that inserts links into Wikipedia articles to relevant items in the DPLA's collections.

The service IFTTT (If This Then That) exists entirely thanks to the APIs provided by other services. IFTTT enables users to create "recipes" that export data from one service's API and import it into another service's API, conditional on some event: for example, one's Fitbit activity summaries can be added to a Google spreadsheet once per day, or one can receive a text message every time the International Space Station is overhead at one's location, or one's Nest Thermostat can be set to a specific temperature when one enters a particular geographic area. In this way IFTTT provides a mechanism for connecting the structured data from (as of this writing) well over 150 services together.

APIs allow algorithms access to the metadata stored by services. Recall from the example in chapter 7 of scheduling a medical appointment, that this is exactly Berners-Lee and colleagues' vision of the semantic web. As services make more data available via APIs, other services can be built that make use of that data. IFTTT is not currently sophisticated enough to schedule one's medical appointments, but it is certainly a step in that direction.

David Weinberger, in his excellent book *Small Pieces Loosely Joined*, articulates "a unified theory of the web": specifically, that it is composed of small pieces, loosely joined. Less tautologically, Weinberger's thesis is that the web has exploded large entities. He uses the example of documents: large texts no longer need to be bound together as a unitary entity called a book, instead a text can be composed of small entities loosely joined by links. What makes Weinberger's book prescient is that this also holds true for other sorts of entities: in particular, datasets and services.

What makes it possible for the web to be composed of small pieces loosely joined? Metadata. Passing structured data back and forth enables online services to be small and focused, yet rely on other services to provide needed data. Recall Bijan Parsia's "more is more" argument for the semantic web: when more data is freely available, more tools and services can be built that make use of that data. Tim Berners-Lee's vision of the semantic web is premised on the Web of Data being composed of small pieces that pass metadata back and forth. The Web of Data might in fact equally well be called the Web of Metadata.

eScience

One domain in which an increasing amount of data is becoming available, and in which there is a significant benefit to enabling small pieces to be loosely joined is in eScience. eScience is computation-intensive and data-intensive research methods and analysis, and includes, though is not limited to, what is commonly referred to as "big data" science.

There is, of course, much debate around what exactly constitutes "big data": the Human Genome Project, for example, may be considered to be big data science, though an entire human genome is only about 200 GB, while the Large Hadron Collider produces an equivalent amount of data in under 5 minutes. Regardless of the volume of data, most eScience projects also involve intensive use of

What makes it possible for the web to be composed of small pieces loosely joined? Metadata.

computation to conduct analysis—for example, in weather modeling, where increasingly powerful supercomputers have been employed to develop increasingly detailed and accurate forecasts.

The fact also remains that even a "mere" 200 GB is too large a dataset for any single person, or even team of people, to grasp in its entirety. This is where metadata comes in. A metadata record, as a surrogate for a dataset, is often more useful than the dataset itself as an access point for interested researchers—just as a library catalog card or an entry on Amazon may be more useful than a whole book as an access point for interested readers. First one has to identify a useful dataset (or book), and only after that does one actually make use of it.

Descriptive metadata for resource discovery enables eScience, but provenance metadata enables trust in the products of eScience. A dataset associated with a published journal article, and hosted by the journal publisher, inherits, so to speak, the imprimatur associated with peer reviewed scholarly literature. For a dataset self-hosted by a researcher, the authority behind that dataset may be less clear. Thus metadata about the provenance of datasets becomes critical, for any future reuse of that data.

The provenance of a dataset may be addressed at two levels: the dataset as a whole, and the individual values in it. Provenance metadata for a dataset might include statements such as the funding agency, names of researchers involved in the data collection, and methodologies employed in the research. Provenance metadata for the individual values in a dataset might include statements such as the methodology employed to collect a specific data point, and any analyses or transformations that produced a particular data point.

Some of the provenance metadata for individual values in a dataset is referred to as "paradata"—somewhat confusingly, as the term "paradata" (recall from chapter 5) also refers to use metadata about learning objects. In the context of provenance metadata, however, paradata is a term for data that's automatically captured about the process by which data is collected. For example, paradata about a dataset from a telephone survey might include the date and time of each call, which calls were to phone numbers where no one answered, and every keystroke and mouse movement made by the interviewer: in other words, data that can be automatically collected by the systems used by the telephone survey interviewers. Paradata is created at the time of data collection, and it provides data about the creation of a dataset. Another type of provenance metadata is "auxiliary data," an even less well-defined term. Auxiliary data is often considered to be any data beyond a dataset itself—in other words, any metadata about a dataset. More specifically, auxiliary data may include both paradata and variables imported from other datasets, such as Census or other demographic data from sources external to the organization that created a dataset. The proliferation of terms to describe different categories of provenance metadata is an indication of just how important provenance metadata is for eScience.

Increasingly, it is the default for applications to store the history of files, as a wiki stores every edit made to every page. This functionality of a wiki enables a user to view the history of a page, to identify the other users (or at least their IP addresses) who made each edit, and sometimes a user's comments concerning why they made an edit. Even more robust history-tracking functionality will be critical for eScience, since trust is even more important for a scientific dataset than it is for a Wikipedia entry. eScience may rise or fall with the availability of provenance metadata, to enable the identification of the relationships between a resource and entities that have influenced its history.

Politics of Metadata

While the data collected by scientific instrumentation and empirical research is critical to the progress of science, the data that more people are likely to be concerned with are data about themselves. Consumer products and services generate vast quantities of data about ourselves and our behaviors. We knowingly trade our personal privacy for the convenience of using such products and services: while hardly anyone ever reads Terms of Service agreements, these documents do specify that information about the user is collected and analyzed.

Many web services collect and analyze data about their users in order to provide a greater degree of customization and personalization in the user experience. Google Now, for example, is a service that proactively provides information to the user—such as notifications that based on current traffic one should leave for the airport now, and what the best route is to take. Microsoft's Cortana and Apple's Siri possess similar functionality. In order for these services to work, however, it is necessary for them to have access to a great deal of personal data: it is possible to provide a notification that one should leave for the airport now, only if the service has access to the user's calendar and current physical location.

Computing power is increasingly embedded in common everyday objects: not just smartphones and home electronics but vehicles, roads and bridges, medical devices, even the monitoring and control systems in buildings. This emerging "Internet of Things"—the expansion of the Internet to computing devices embedded in a wide range of physical objects—is entirely dependent on the collection and analysis of structured data. Some of this data is environmental and not associated with individuals, but much of it is individual and even quite personal. And, as in the example of scheduling a medical appointment, for the Internet of Things to work and to fulfill its potential, much of this data must be shared across services.

By and large, we trust that the services we use and subscribe to keep our personal data to themselves and their partners: the data that Amazon, for example, has collected about my purchasing habits gives Amazon a competitive edge in keeping my business. Of course, we know that companies share our data with their partners, though generally we have the option to opt in or out of such sharing. Perhaps we're fooling ourselves, but by and large we imagine that our data, while not private, is at least restricted.

So why did the news about the NSA's collection of phone metadata feel like such a violation of privacy? It wasn't that the phone company collected data about our phone calls. It was the revelation that this data was being handed over to another organization, without our consent, that violated this imagined trust.

Telephone companies and governments have collected metadata about phone calls since long before the term "metadata" was even invented. Perhaps one of the earliest technologies for systematically collecting this type of data exhaust is the *pen register*, a term that dates to the era of the telegraph. A pen register is defined in the US Code (Title 18, Part II, Chapter 206, §3127) as "a device or process which records or decodes dialing, routing, addressing, or signaling information transmitted by an instrument or facility from which a wire or electronic communication is transmitted." More narrowly focused data collection is performed by the *trap and trace device*, which collects only data to "identify the originating number" or other originating address of an electronic communication. In other words, pen registers, and trap and trace devices collect metadata about electronic communication, be it telegraph messages, phone calls, emails, text messages, or any other medium. Importantly, under the US Code, pen registers and trap and trace devices cannot collect "the contents of any communication": recording the contents of a phone call, for example, is considered wiretapping under the US Code. The contents of a text message or a tweet, however, are merely the value for one field in a very large record.

One of the early reactions to the Snowden revelations in 2013 was the position that since the NSA was not engaging in wiretapping, there was no cause for concern. This "it's only metadata" argument is a valid legal position, given that under US Code Title 18, a pen register or a trap and trace device may collect the metadata about electronic communications, while wiretapping has required a warrant since the 1967 US Supreme Court case *Katz v. United States*.

However, recall the MetaPhone study, discussed briefly in chapter 1. Researchers at the Stanford Law School Center for Internet and Society attempted to replicate the NSA's data collection of phone metadata: study participants installed the MetaPhone app on their smartphone, and this app collected data about the device. This data included, among other things, the phone numbers called by study participants' phones, and the time and duration of these calls. By querying public directories, the researchers could identify the owners of these called phone numbers, businesses and individuals.

The MetaPhone researchers write: "We found that phone metadata is unambiguously sensitive." The metadata is not the problem, however, where privacy is concerned, but the inferences that can be made from it. For example, recall the study participant who called "a home improvement store, locksmiths, a hydroponics dealer, and a head shop." Individually, each of these calls is relatively innocuous: if each of these calls had been made by different study participants, it would raise no eyebrows. It is the fact that these calls were all made by the *same* study participant that prompts us to make an inference about this individual's activities. Of course, an inference is circumstantial evidence, at best, and without more information, there is no way for us to know whether or not our inference is correct. But what makes phone metadata unambiguously sensitive is that it enables these kind of prejudicial inferences to be made.

The Fourth Amendment to the US Constitution states that:

> The right of the people to be secure in their persons, houses, papers, and effects, against unreasonable searches and seizures, shall not be violated …

An exception to this, however, is what is known as the third-party doctrine. This was summed up in the 1979 US Supreme Court case *Smith v. Maryland* as follows: one has "no legitimate expectation of privacy" for data voluntarily provided to a third party, such as a telephone company. This voluntarily provided data includes the sort of personal metadata that one must provide to the telephone company in order to set up an account. Of course, the "third party" here is not limited to a phone company; it may include Internet service providers, or indeed any commercial entity to whom one provides information. All this data can be collected by law enforcement without a warrant, with no violation of the Fourth Amendment.

In the current era of ubiquitous metadata, there has naturally been a great deal of discussion in the legal community about the third-party doctrine, whether or not it continues to be appropriate, and whether it needs to be changed. In particular, US Supreme Court Justice Sonia Sotomayor has stated that the third-party doctrine is "ill-suited to the digital age, in which people reveal a great deal of information about themselves to third parties in the course of carrying out mundane tasks." Justice Sotomayor was referring, at least in part, to data exhaust, and it is not

Metadata—voluntarily provided and data exhaust alike—will be a significant legal and political issue in coming years.

clear just how voluntary the revealing of such data can be said to be.

Metadata—voluntarily provided and data exhaust alike—will be a significant legal and political issue in coming years. Metadata for describing and administering web resources, metadata for APIs, metadata describing music, metadata about the provenance of art objects and scientific datasets: all of these and more will continue to evolve, and tools will be developed to manage this metadata. This metadata and tool development will give rise—is already giving rise—to an entire subsector of the technology industry. Still, the metadata that most people are likely to care more about is metadata about themselves, and who has access to it. This personal connection to metadata is likely to drive legal and political debates. Just as the Snowden revelations brought the word "metadata" into the public eye, so will metadata continue to be front and center in ongoing discussions around personal privacy.

GLOSSARY

Administrative metadata
Information to inform the management of an object. For example, this book is copyrighted by MIT Press.

Controlled vocabulary
A finite set of terms that may be used to provide a value for an element. Terms may be organized as a hierarchy or a simple list.

Descriptive metadata
Descriptive information about an object. For example, the author of this book is Jeffrey Pomerantz, and the date of publication is 2015.

Dublin Core
An element set developed to be the core set necessary to describe any online resource.

Element
One of a predefined set of statements that can be made about a resource, according to a schema. The predicate in a subject-predicate-object triple. *See also* Value.

Encoding scheme
A set of rules for how values for a specific type of data may be constructed or selected. *See also* Controlled vocabulary; Syntax encoding.

Linked Data
Data and datasets shared on the open web and containing links to other data using standard web technologies.

Object

A resource that has a relationship with another resource that is the subject of descriptive metadata; a resource that is used to describe another resource. For example, Leonardo da Vinci, as the creator of the *Mona Lisa*. *See also* Subject; Predicate.

Ontology

Like a thesaurus, a finite set of terms, organized as a hierarchy that can be used to provide a value for an element. Additionally this includes a set of rules for action, often in the form of software algorithms.

Paradata

In the context of education, this is metadata about educational resources. In the context of research methodology, this is metadata about the creation of a dataset, created at the time of data collection.

Predicate

A category of relationship between a resource (the subject) and some other thing (the object). For example, creator, or date of publication. *See also* Subject; Object.

Preservation metadata

Information necessary to support the process of preservation of an object. For example, this book should be stored in an environment with about 35 percent relative humidity.

Provenance metadata

Information about the entities and processes involved in the life cycle of a resource.

Resource Description Framework

A framework for describing resources using subject-predicate-object relationship triples.

Record
A set of subject-predicate-object statements about a single resource, usually created using a single schema.

Relevance
How well an information resource or resources fulfills an individual's information need: a subjective and contextual judgment call.

Resource
An information object; the subject of descriptive metadata. *See also* Subject.

Resource discovery
The process of identifying information resources that might be relevant to an individual to fulfill an information need.

Rights metadata
Information about the intellectual property rights for a resource.

Schema
A set of rules about what sorts of subject-predicate-object statements may be made about a resource.

Semantic web
A vision of the World Wide Web in which semantic data is embedded in webpages and links, to be parsed by software agents.

Structural metadata
Information about how a resource is organized. For example, this book is composed of 8 chapters, which are organized in numerical order.

Structured data
A dataset organized according to a data model.

Subject
A resource; the subject of descriptive metadata. For example, the *Mona Lisa*. *See also* Predicate; Object.

Subject analysis
Analysis of a resource to identify what its subject is, or what it is about.

Subject heading
A finite set of terms that may be used to describe the subject of a resource. The terms may be organized as a hierarchy or may be a simple list, for example, the Library of Congress Subject Headings.

Syntax encoding
A set of rules for how to represent a specific type of data. For example, ISO 8601 is a syntax encoding scheme for representing dates and times.

Technical metadata
Information about the functionality of a system. For example, a digital photograph was created using a camera of a particular make and model, with a particular X- and Y-resolution.

Thesaurus
A finite set of terms, organized as a hierarchy that may be used to provide a value for an element. The hierarchy is usually composed of *IS A*, *part of*, or *instance of* relationships, for example, the Art & Architecture Thesaurus.

Triple
A subject-predicate-object statement about a resource. *See also* Subject; Predicate; Object; Resource.

Uncontrolled vocabulary
An infinite set of terms that may be used to provide a value for an element. Any word or phrase may be used as a value, or a new term may be invented uniquely.

Unique identifier
A name or an address that identifies an entity uniquely, without any confusion with other entities. For example, a physical address uniquely identifies a location, or a Social Security number uniquely identifies a person.

Use metadata
Information about how an object is used, for example, how many downloads an electronic book has received, and on what dates.

Value
The data assigned to an element. The data may be selected from a controlled vocabulary, developed using an encoding scheme, or created uniquely. *See also* Element.

FURTHER READINGS

Chapter 1

About Metadata

Baca, M. 2008. *Introduction to Metadata,* 2nd ed. Los Angeles: Getty Research Institute.

Hillmann, D. I. 2004. *Metadata in Practice.* Chicago: American Library Association.

Zeng, M. L., and Qin, J. 2008. *Metadata.* New York: Neal-Schuman.

About Information Science

Bates, M. J. 2006. Fundamental forms of information. *Journal of the American Society for Information Science and Technology* 57 (8): 1033–45. doi:10.1002/asi.20369.

Bates, M. J. 2008. Hjørland's critique of bates' work on defining information. *Journal of the American Society for Information Science and Technology* 59 (5): 842–44. doi:10.1002/asi.20796.

Bates, M. J. 2011. Birger Hjørland's Manichean misconstruction of Marcia Bates' work. *Journal of the American Society for Information Science and Technology* 62(10): 2038–44. doi:10.1002/asi.21594.

Buckland, M. K. 1991. Information as thing. *Journal of the American Society for Information Science* 42(5): 351–60. doi:10.1002/(SICI)1097-4571 (199106)42:5<351::AID-ASI5>3.0.CO;2-3.

Glushko, R. J., ed. 2013. *The Discipline of Organizing.* Cambridge: MIT Press.

Hjørland, B. 2007. Information: Objective or subjective/situational? *Journal of the American Society for Information Science and Technology* 58 (10): 1448–56 . doi:10.1002/asi.20620.

Hjørland, B. 2009. The controversy over the concept of "information": A rejoinder to Professor Bates. *Journal of the American Society for Information Science and Technology* 60(3): 643–643. doi:10.1002/asi.20972.

Losee, R. M. 1997. A discipline independent definition of information. *Journal of the American Society for Information Science* 48(3): 254–69. doi:10.1002/(SICI)1097-4571(199703)48:3<254::AID-ASI6>3.0.CO;2-W.

Saracevic, T. 1975. Relevance: A review of and a framework for the thinking on the notion in information science. *Journal of the American Society for Information Science* 26(6): 321–43. doi:10.1002/asi.4630260604.

Saracevic, T. 2007. Relevance: A review of the literature and a framework for thinking on the notion in information science. Part III: Behavior and effects of relevance. *Journal of the American Society for Information Science and Technology* 58(13): 2126–44. doi:10.1002/asi.20681.

Saracevic, T. (nd). Relevance: A review of the literature and a framework for thinking on the notion in information science. Part II. In *Advances in Librarianship*, vol. 30, pp. 3–71. Emerald Group Publishing Limited. Retrieved from http://www.emeraldinsight.com.libproxy.lib.unc.edu/doi/abs/10.1016/S0065-2830%2806%2930001-3.

About Subject Analysis

Beghtol, C. 1986. Bibliographic classification theory and text linguistics: Aboutness analysis, intertextuality and the cognitive act of classifying documents. *Journal of Documentation* 42 (2), 84–113. doi:10.1108/eb026788.

Chandler, A. D., & Cortada, J. W., eds. 2003. *A Nation Transformed by Information: How Information Has Shaped the United States from Colonial Times to the Present.* Oxford: Oxford University Press.

Hjørland, B. 2001. Towards a theory of aboutness, subject, topicality, theme, domain, field, content ... and relevance. *Journal of the American Society for Information Science and Technology* 52(9): 774–78. doi:10.1002/asi.1131.

Hjørland, B. 1992. The concept of "subject" in information science. *Journal of Documentation* 48 (2): 172–200. doi:10.1108/eb026895.

Hjorland, B. 1997. *Information Seeking and Subject Representation: An Activity-Theoretical Approach to Information Science.* Westport, CT: Praeger.

Hutchins, W. J. 1978. The concept of "aboutness" in subject indexing. *Aslib Proceedings* 30 (5): 172–81. doi:10.1108/eb050629.

About the History of Library Catalogs

Hopkins, J. 1992. The 1791 French cataloging code and the origins of the card catalog. *Libraries and Culture* 27(4): 378–404.

Strout, R. F. 1956. The development of the catalog and cataloging codes. *Library Quarterly* 26 (4): 254–75.

Chapter 2

About Networks

Benkler, Y. 2007. *The Wealth of Networks: How Social Production Transforms Markets and Freedom*. New Haven: Yale University Press.

Castells, M. 2009. *The Rise of the Network Society*. Vol. 1: *The Information Age: Economy, Society, and Culture,* 2nd ed. Malden, MA: Wiley-Blackwell.

Easley, D., and Kleinberg, J. 2010. *Networks, Crowds, and Markets: Reasoning about a Highly Connected World*. New York: Cambridge University Press.

About Classification

Barlow, J. P. 1994 (March). The economy of ideas. *Wired, 2*(3). Retrieved from http://archive.wired.com/wired/archive/2.03/economy.ideas.html.

Shirky, C. 2005. *Making Digital Durable: What Time Does to Categories*. Retrieved from http://longnow.org/seminars/02005/nov/14/making-digital-durable-what-time-does-to-categories/.

Shirky, C. 2005. Ontology is overrated: Categories, links, and tags. Retrieved from http://www.shirky.com/writings/ontology_overrated.html.

VIAF: The Virtual International Authority File. (2014). OCLC. Retrieved from http://viaf.org/.

Chapter 4

METS

Metadata Encoding and Transmission Standard. http://www.loc.gov/standards/mets/.

MPEG-21

Cover, R. (nd). MPEG-21 Part 2: Digital Item Declaration Language (DIDL). Retrieved January 27, 2015, from http://xml.coverpages.org/mpeg21-didl.html.

Provenance

Luc Moreau, L., and Groth, P. 2013. Provenance: An Introduction to PROV. San Rafael, CA: Morgan Claypool Publishers. Retrieved from http://www.morgan claypool.com/doi/abs/10.2200/S00528ED1V01Y201308WBE007.

PREMIS http://www.loc.gov/standards/premis/.

PROV http://www.w3.org/2001/sw/wiki/PROV.

W3C. (2013). PROV-DM: The PROV Data Model. http://www.w3.org/TR/prov-dm/.

W3C. (2011). Provenance Interchange Working Group Charter. http://www.w3.org/2011/01/prov-wg-charter.

Rights

Creative Commons. http://creativecommons.org/.

Creative Commons. (nd). Describing copyright in RDF: Creative Commons rights expression language. http://creativecommons.org/ns.

Creative Commons. 2013. CC REL. CC Wiki. https://wiki.creativecommons.org/CC_REL.

W3C ODRL Community Group http://www.w3.org/community/odrl/.

WikiScanner

Griffith, V. (nd). Wikiscanner. http://virgil.gr/wikiscanner/.
Silverman, J. 2014. How the Wikipedia scanner works. HowStuffWorks. http://computer.howstuffworks.com/internet/basics/wikipedia-scanner.htm.

Projects That Use GPS Metadata

I Know Where Your Cat Lives. http://iknowwhereyourcatlives.com/.

Microsoft Photosynth. http://photosynth.net/.

Chapter 5

Data Exhaust and Surveillance

Brunk, B. 2001. Exoinformation and interface design. *Bulletin of the American Society for Information Science and Technology* 27(6). Retrieved from http://www.asis.org/Bulletin/Aug-01/brunk.html.

Guardian US interactive team. 2013 (June 12). A Guardian guide to metadata. *The Guardian*. Retrieved from http://www.theguardian.com/technology/interactive/2013/jun/12/what-is-metadata-nsa-surveillance.

Risen, J., and Poitras, L. 2013 (September 28). N.S.A. gathers data on social connections of U.S. citizens. *The New York Times*. Retrieved from http://www.nytimes.com/2013/09/29/us/nsa-examines-social-networks-of-us-citizens.html.

Paradata

Gundy, S. V. 2011 (November 9). Why connected online communities will drive the future of digital content: An introduction to learning resource paradata. Retrieved from http://connectededucators.org/why-connected-online-communities-will-drive-the-future-of-digital-content-an-introduction-to-learning-resource-paradata/.

US Department of Education. 2011. Paradata in 20 minutes or less. Retrieved from https://docs.google.com/document/d/1QG0lAmJ0ztHJq5DbiTGQj9DnQ8hP0Co0x0fB1QmoBco/.

Projects Mapping Social Networks

The Oracle of Bacon. http://oracleofbacon.org/.

The Erdös Number Project http://www.oakland.edu/enp/.

Chapter 6

Date, C. J. 2012. *Database Design and Relational Theory: Normal Forms and All That Jazz*. Sebastopol, CA: O'Reilly Media.

Halpin, T. 2001. *Information Modeling and Relational Databases: From Conceptual Analysis to Logical Design*. San Francisco: Morgan Kaufmann.

Musciano, C., and Kennedy, B. 2006. *HTML & XHTML: The Definitive Guide*, 6th ed. Sebastopol, CA: O'Reilly Media.

Pilgrim, M. 2010. *HTML5: Up and Running*. Sebastopol, CA: O'Reilly Media.

Powers, S. 2003. *Practical RDF*. Sebastopol: O'Reilly Media.

Van der Vlist, E. 2002. *XML Schema: The W3C's Object-Oriented Descriptions for XML*. Sebastopol, CA: O'Reilly Media.

Chapter 7

Linked Data
DBpedia. http://dbpedia.org/.

Heath, T. (nd). Linked data: Connect distributed data across the web. http://linkeddata.org/

schema.org http://schema.org/.

J. Paul Getty Trust. 2014. Getty vocabularies as linked open data. http://www.getty.edu/research/tools/vocabularies/lod/index.html.

New York Times Company. 2013. Times Topics. http://www.nytimes.com/pages/topics/index.html.

W3C. 2013. W3C DATA ACTIVITY building the web of data.

http://www.w3.org/2013/data/.

W3C. 2015. W3C linked data.

http://www.w3.org/standards/semanticweb/data.

Wikimedia Foundation. (nd). Wikidata. https://www.wikidata.org/.

Wikimedia Foundation. 2004. Wikidata/Archive/Wikidata/historical.

https://meta.wikimedia.org/wiki/Wikidata/Archive/Wikidata/historical.

Semantic Web
Berners-Lee, T. 1998. Semantic web road map. W3C. Retrieved from http://www.w3.org/DesignIssues/Semantic.html.

Shadbolt, N., Hall, W., and Berners-Lee, T. 2006. The semantic web revisited. *IEEE Intelligent Systems* 21(3), 96–101. doi:10.1109/MIS.2006.62.

Swartz, A. 2013. *Aaron Swartz's A Programmable Web: An Unfinished Work*. San Rafael, CA: Morgan Claypool Publishers. Retrieved from http://www.morgan-claypool.com/doi/abs/10.2200/S00481ED1V01Y201302WBE005.

Chapter 8

Services Mentioned in This Chapter
DPLA http://dp.la/.

Europeana. http://www.europeana.eu/.

Google Now. https://www.google.com/landing/now/.

IEEE International Conference on eScience. https://escience-conference.org/.

IFTTT. https://ifttt.com/.

Internet of Things Consortium. http://iofthings.org/.

Open Archives Initiative. (nd). Object Reuse and Exchange (OAI-ORE). http://www.openarchives.org/ore/.

Pandora Media, Inc. 2015. About the Music Genome Project®. http://www.pandora.com/about/mgp.

Parchment. http://www.parchment.com/.

Linked Data in Libraries

DuraSpace. 2014. Linked data for libraries (LD4L). https://wiki.duraspace.org/display/ld4l.

Flynn, E. A. 2013. Open access metadata, catalogers, and vendors: The future of cataloging records. *Journal of Academic Librarianship* 39(1): 29–31. doi:10.1016/j.acalib.2012.11.010.

Greenberg, J., and Garoufallou, E. 2013. Change and a future for metadata. In E. Garoufallou and J. Greenberg, eds., *Metadata and Semantics Research,* pp. 1–5. New York: Springer International. Retrieved from http://link.springer.com.libproxy.lib.unc.edu/chapter/10.1007/978-3-319-03437-9_1.

Kemperman, S. S., et al. 2014. *Success strategies for e-content.* OCLC Online Computer Library Center, Inc. Retrieved from http://www.oclc.org/go/en/econtent-access.html.

Schilling, V. (nd). Transforming library metadata into linked library data: Introduction and review of linked data for the library community, 2003–2011. Retrieved January 28, 2015, from http://www.ala.org/alcts/resources/org/cat/research/linked-data.

FIGURE CREDITS

BIBLIOGRAPHY

Abelson, Hal, Ben Adida, Mike Linksvayer, and Nathan Yergler. ccREL: The Creative Commons Rights Expression Language. (Creative Commons, 2008). http://www.w3.org/Submission/ccREL/.

Anonymous. Former CIA Director: "We kill people based on metadata." *RT* (May 12, 2014). http://rt.com/usa/158460-cia-director-metadata-kill-people/.

Apache Software Foundation. *Apache HTTP Server Version 2.4 Documentation.* (2015). http://httpd.apache.org/docs/current/.

Beckett, Dave. RDF/XML syntax specification (revised). W3C (February 10, 2004). http://www.w3.org/TR/REC-rdf-syntax/.

Berners-Lee, Tim, James Hendler, and Ora Lassila. The semantic web. *Scientific American* (May 2001): 29–37.

Berners-Lee, Tim. Linked data. W3C (July 27, 2006). http://www.w3.org/DesignIssues/LinkedData.html.

Biodiversity Information Standards (TDWG). Darwin Core. (accessed February 20, 2015). http://rs.tdwg.org/dwc/.

Broder, Andrei, Ravi Kumar, Farzin Maghoul, Prabhakar Raghavan, Sridhar Rajagopalan, Raymie Stata, Andrew Tomkins, and Janet Wiener. Graph structure in the web. Computer Networks 33 (no. 1–6, June 2000): 309–20. doi:10.1016/S1389-1286(00)00083-9.

Brown, Olivia. Classical music needs better metadata. Future of Music Coalition (March 5, 2013). https://futureofmusic.org/blog/2013/03/05/classical-music-needs-better-metadata.

Bryl, Volha. The DBpedia data set (2014). http://wiki.dbpedia.org/Datasets 2014.

Camera & Imagine Products Association. Exchangeable image file format for digital still cameras: Exif version 2.3. (2012). http://www.cipa.jp/std/documents/e/DC-008-2012_E.pdf.

Carmody, Tim. Why metadata matters for the future of e-Books. WIRED (August 3, 2010). http://www.wired.com/2010/08/why-metadata-matters-for-the-future-of-e-books/.

Cha, Bonnie. A beginner's guide to understanding the Internet of Things. Re/code (January 15, 2015). http://recode.net/2015/01/15/a-beginners-guide-to-understanding-the-internet-of-things/.

Cole, David. We kill people based on metadata. NYRblog (May 10, 2014). http://www.nybooks.com/blogs/nyrblog/2014/may/10/we-kill-people-based-metadata/.

Conley, Chris. Metadata: Piecing together a privacy solution. ACLU of Northern California (February 2014). https://www.aclunc.org/publications/metadata-piecing-together-privacy-solution.

Cook, Jean. Invisible genres & metadata: How digital services fail classical & jazz musicians, composers, and fans. Future of Music Coalition (October 16, 2013). https://futureofmusic.org/article/article/invisible-genres-metadata.

Couper, Mick, Frauke Kreuter, and Lars Lyberg. The use of paradata to monitor and manage survey data collection. In *Proceedings of the Survey Research Methods Section, American Statistical Association*, 282–96. American Statistical Association (2010). http://www.amstat.org/sections/srms/proceedings/y2010/Files/306107_55863.pdf.

Crimes and criminal procedure. US Code 18 (2008), §1–6005.

Cyganiak, Richard, David Wood, and Markus Lanthaler. RDF 1.1 concepts and abstract syntax. W3C (February 25, 2014). http://www.w3.org/TR/rdf11-concepts/.

Cyganiak, Richard. The linking open data cloud diagram (2014).

De Montjoye, Yves-Alexandre, César A. Hidalgo, Michel Verleysen, and Vincent D. Blondel. Unique in the crowd: The privacy bounds of human mobility. *Scientific Reports* 3 (March 25, 2013). doi:10.1038/srep01376.

Digital Library Federation. *Metadata Encoding and Transmission Standard: Primer and Reference Manual, Version 1.6* (2010). http://www.loc.gov/standards/mets/METSPrimerRevised.pdf.

Digital Public Library of America. Digital Public Library of America. (accessed February 20, 2015). http://dp.la/.

Digital Public Library of America. Metadata application profile, version 3.1. (accessed February 20, 2015). http://dp.la/info/map.

Dublin Core Metadata Initiative. Dublin Core Metadata Element Set, Version 1.1. (accessed February 20, 2015). http://dublincore.org/documents/dces/.

Dublin Core Metadata Initiative. Dublin Core Metadata Terms (accessed February 20, 2015). http://dublincore.org/documents/dcmi-terms/.

"Documentation," schema.org (accessed February 20, 2015). http://schema.org/docs/documents.html.

Duhigg, Charles. How companies learn your secrets. *New York Times* (February 16, 2012), sec. Magazine. http://www.nytimes.com/2012/02/19/magazine/shopping-habits.html.

Dunbar, R. I. M. Neocortex size as a constraint on group size in primates. *Journal of Human Evolution* 22 (no. 6, June 1992): 469–93. doi:10.1016/0047-2484(92)90081-J.

Enge, Eric, Spencer, Stephan, Fishkin, Rand, and Stricchiola, Jessie. The Art of SEO: Mastering Search Engine Optimization (Theory in Practice). Sebastopol, CA: O'Reilly Media, Inc. (2009).

European Union. Europeana data model: Mapping guidelines v2.2. (accessed February 20, 2015). http://pro.europeana.eu/documents/900548/5f8f7f4c-1af7-447d-b3f4-f3d91e39397c.

Europeana. Linked open data—What is it? (February 14, 2012). Video file retrieved from http://pro.europeana.eu/linked-open-data.

Europeana.eu. Europeana (accessed February 20, 2015). http://www.europeana.eu/.

Gartner, Inc. Gartner says the Internet of Things installed base will grow to 26 billion units by 2020. (December 12, 2013). http://www.gartner.com/newsroom/id/2636073.

Gellman, Barton, and Ashkan Soltani. NSA infiltrates links to Yahoo, Google data centers worldwide, Snowden documents say. *Washington Post* (October 30, 2013). http://www.washingtonpost.com/world/national-security/nsa-infiltrates-links-to-yahoo-google-data-centers-worldwide-snowden-documents-say/2013/10/30/e51d661e-4166-11e3-8b74-d89d714ca4dd_story.html.

Gil, Yolanda, James Cheney, Paul Groth, Olaf Hartig, Simon Miles, Luc Moreau, and Paulo Pinheiro da Silva. Provenance XG Final Report. W3C (2010). http://www.w3.org/2005/Incubator/prov/XGR-prov-20101214/.

Golbeck, Jennifer, Jes Koepfler, and Beth Emmerling. An experimental study of social tagging behavior and image content. *Journal of the American Society for Information Science and Technology* 62 (no. 9, 2011): 1750–60. doi:10.1002/asi.21522.

Golder, Scott A., and Bernardo A. Huberman. Usage patterns of collaborative tagging systems. *Journal of Information Science* 32 (April 1, 2006): 198–208. doi:10.1177/0165551506062337.

Google. Meta tags that Google understands (accessed February 20, 2015). https://support.google.com/webmasters/answer/79812.

Gorman, Siobhan, and Jennifer Valentino-DeVries. New details show broader NSA surveillance reach. *Wall Street Journal* (August 21, 2013), sec. US. http://www.wsj.com/articles/SB10001424127887324108204579022874091732470.

Gracenote, Inc. Gracenote (accessed February 20, 2015). http://www.gracenote.com/.

Grad, Burton, and Thomas J. Bergin. Guest Editors' Introduction: History of database management systems. *IEEE Annals of the History of Computing* 31 (no. 4, 2009): 3–5. doi:10.1109/MAHC.2009.99.

Greenberg, Jane, Kristina Spurgin, and Abe Crystal. Final Report for the AMeGA (Automatic Metadata Generation Applications) Project. Library of Congress (2005). http://www.loc.gov/catdir/bibcontrol/lc_amega_final_report.pdf.

Gregory, Lisa, and Stephanie Williams. On being a Hub: Some details behind providing metadata for the Digital Public Library of America. *D-Lib Magazine* 20 (no. 7/8, July 2014). doi:10.1045/july2014-gregory.

Hafner, Katie. Seeing corporate fingerprints in Wikipedia edits. *New York Times* (August 19, 2007), sec. Technology. http://www.nytimes.com/2007/08/19/technology/19wikipedia.html.

Heath, Tom, and Christian Bizer. Linked data: Evolving the web into a global data space. Synthesis Lectures on the Semantic Web: Theory and Technology. San Rafael, CA: Morgan Claypool. http://linkeddatabook.com/editions/1.0/.

http://lod-cloud.net/.

IEEE Computer Society. 1484.12.1-2002—*IEEE Standard for Learning Object Metadata*. (accessed February 20, 2015). http://standards.ieee.org/findstds/standard/1484.12.1-2002.html.

International DOI Foundation. (accessed February 20, 2015). http://www.doi .org/.

International Organization for Standardization. ISO 8601:2004. *Data Elements and Interchange Formats—Information Interchange—Representation of Dates and Times*. http://www.iso.org/iso/catalogue_detail?csnumber=40874.

Iverson, Vaughn, Young-Won Song, Rik Van de Walle, Mark Rowe, Doim Chang, Ernesto Santos, and Todd Schwartz. MPEG-21 Digital Item Declaration WD (v2.0). ISO/IEC (2001). http://xml.coverpages.org/MPEG21-WG-11-N3971-200103.pdf.

J. Paul Getty Trust. Getty vocabularies (accessed February 20, 2015). http:// www.getty.edu/research/tools/vocabularies/index.html.

J. Paul Getty Trust. Getty vocabularies. (accessed February 20, 2015). http:// www.getty.edu/research/tools/vocabularies/.

Karabell, Zachary. Americans' fickle stance on data mining and surveillance. *Atlantic* (June 14, 2013). http://www.theatlantic.com/national/archive/2013/06/americans-fickle-stance-on-data-mining-and-surveillance/276885/.

Katz v. United States, 389 US 347 (Supreme Court 35).

Kessler, Brett, Geoffrey Numberg, and Hinrich Schütze. Automatic detection of text genre. In *Proceedings of the 35th Annual Meeting of the Association for Computational Linguistics and Eighth Conference of the European Chapter of the Association for Computational Linguistics* 32–38. ACL '98. Stroudsburg, PA: Association for Computational Linguistics (1997). doi:10.3115/976909.979622.

Kleinberg, Jon, and Steve Lawrence. The structure of the web. *Science* 294 (no. 5548, November 30, 2001): 1849–50. doi:10.1126/science.1067014.

Kreuter, Frauke, ed. *Improving Surveys with Paradata: Analytic Uses of Process Information*. Hoboken, NJ: Wiley (2013).

Library of Congress. *Data Dictionary for Preservation Metadata: PREMIS Version 2.2*. (2012). http://www.loc.gov/standards/premis/v2/premis-2-2.pdf.

Library of Congress. Draft rights declaration schema is ready for review. (July 1, 2011). http://www.loc.gov/standards/mets/news080503.html.

Library of Congress. LC linked data service authorities and vocabularies. (accessed February 20, 2015). http://www.getty.edu/research/tools/vocabularies/.

Library of Congress. The Library of Congress linked data service. (accessed February 20, 2015). http://id.loc.gov/.

Lithwick, Dahlia, and Steve Vladeck. Taking the "Meh" out of metadata: How the government can discover your health problems, political beliefs, and religious practices using just your metadata. *Slate Magazine* (November 22, 2013). http://www.slate.com/articles/news_and_politics/jurisprudence/2013/11/nsa_and_metadata_how_the_government_can_spy_on_your_health_political_beliefs.html.

Masinter, Larry, Tim Berners-Lee, and Roy T. Fielding. Uniform resource identifier (URI): Generic syntax (January 2005). https://tools.ietf.org/html/rfc3986.

Mayer, Jonathan, and Patrick Mutchler. MetaPhone: The sensitivity of telephone metadata. *Web Policy* (2013). http://webpolicy.org/2014/03/12/metaphone-the-sensitivity-of-telephone-metadata/.

McIlvain, Eileen. STEM exchange and paradata concepts. University Corporation for Atmospheric Research (2014). https://wiki.ucar.edu/display/nsdldocs/STEM+Exchange+and+paradata+concepts.

Milgram, Stanley. The small-world problem. *Psychology Today* 1 (no. 1, May 1967): 61–67.

MLB Advanced Media, LP. Boston Red Sox 2015 Downloadable Schedule. (2015). http://boston.redsox.mlb.com/schedule/downloadable.jsp?c_id=bos&year=2015.

Mutchler, Patrick, and Jonathan Mayer. MetaPhone: The sensitivity of telephone metadata. *Web Policy* (March 12, 2014). http://webpolicy.org/2014/03/12/metaphone-the-sensitivity-of-telephone-metadata/.

New York Times Company. Linked open data. (accessed February 20, 2015). http://data.nytimes.com/

Olsen, Stefanie. Web browser offers incognito surfing—CNET News. CNET (October 18, 2000). http://news.cnet.com/2100-1017-247263.html.

ORCID, Inc. ORCID (accessed February 20, 2015). http://www.getty.edu/research/tools/vocabularies/.

Pandora Media, Inc. About the Music Genome Project (accessed February 20, 2015). http://www.pandora.com/about/mgp.

Parsia, Bijan. "A Simple, Prima Facie Argument in Favor of the Semantic Web." Monkeyfist.com, May 9, 2008. https://web.archive.org/web/20080509164720/http://monkeyfist.com/articles/815.

Powell, Andy, Mikael Nilsson, Ambjörn Naeve, Pete Johnston, and Thomas Baker. DCMI Abstract Model. Dublin Core Metadata Initiative (2007). http://dublincore.org/documents/abstract-model/.

Raggett, Dave, Arnaud Le Hors, and Ian Jacobs. HTML 4.01 specification. W3C (December 24, 1999). http://www.w3.org/TR/html401/.

Risen, James, and Laura Poitras. N.S.A. gathers data on social connections of U.S. citizens. *New York Times* (September 28, 2013), sec. US. http://www.nytimes.com/2013/09/29/us/nsa-examines-social-networks-of-us-citizens.html.

Rogers, Everett M. *Diffusion of Innovations*, 5th ed. New York: Free Press (2003).

Rosen, Jeffrey. Total information awareness. *New York Times* (December 15, 2002), sec. Magazine. http://www.nytimes.com/2002/12/15/magazine/15TOTA.html.

Rusbridger, Alan, and Ewen MacAskill. Edward Snowden interview: The edited transcript. *The Guardian* (accessed January 27, 2015). http://www.the-guardian.com/world/2014/jul/18/-sp-edward-snowden-nsa-whistleblower-interview-transcript.

Schmitt, Thomas, and Rocky Bernstein. CD text format (2012). http://www.gnu.org/software/libcdio/cd-text-format.html.

Smith v. Maryland, 442 US 735 (Supreme Court 1979).

Tanenbaum, Andrew S., and David J. Wetherall. *Computer Networks*, 5th ed. (2010) Boston: Prentice Hall.

The Open Graph protocol (accessed February 20, 2015). http://ogp.me/

University Corporation for Atmospheric Research. *ISKME to manage National Science Digital Library*. (December 16, 2014). https://www2.ucar.edu/atmosnews/news/13512/iskme-manage-national-science-digital-library.

Van Hooland, Seth, and Ruben Verborgh. Linked data for libraries, archives and museums: How to clean, link and publish your metadata. Chicago: American Library Association (2014).

W.S. *A Funeral Elegy for Master William Peter*, ed. by Donald W. Foster from W.S., *A Funerall Elegye in memory of the late vertuous Maister William Peeter.* London: G. Eld for T. Thorpe (1612).

W3C. Date and time formats (accessed February 20, 2015). http://www.w3.org/TR/NOTE-datetime.

W3C. HTML (accessed February 20, 2015). http://www.w3.org/html/.

Weibel, Stuart, Jean Godby, Eric Miller, and Ron Daniel. OCLC/NCSA Metadata Workshop Report. Dublin Core Metadata Initiative (nd). http://dublincore.org/workshops/dc1/report.shtml.

Weinberger, David. *Small Pieces Loosely Joined: A Unified Theory of the Web.* New York: Basic Books (reprinted 2003).

Witty, Francis J. The pínakes of Callimachus. *Library Quarterly* 28 (April 1, 1958): 132–36.

INDEX